First Russia, Then Tibet

Robert Byron was born of an old family on 26 February 1905. Wiltshire was the background to his strong sardonic patriotism. He was educated at Eton and Merton College, Oxford, where he was one of the earliest collectors of Victoriana as a light-hearted prelude to his challenge to Victorian aesthetic values and accepted classicism. Byron was only twenty-two when he wrote *The Station* from a visit to Mount Athos. This was followed by *The Byzantine Achievement* and *The Birth of Western Painting*, seminal works for the appreciation of the Byzantine contribution. In 1933 the publication of *First Russia, Then Tibet* assured his reputation as a traveller and connoisseur of civilizations. Journeys through Russia and Afghanistan inspired *The Road to Oxiana*, for which he received the Literary Award of the *Sunday Times* for 1937.

Byron was a combative personality with a gift for friendship; among his closest companions were Harold Acton, Evelyn Waugh, Henry Yorke (Greene), Alfred Duggan and, later, Nancy Mitford. He wrote frequently on architecture and was a great admirer of Lutyens and a founder of the Georgian Group. In the Second World War in 1941 Byron perished at sea on his way back to Meshed as an observer. This cut short a life of remarkable achievement and lasting vision.

ROBERT BYRON

FIRST RUSSIA, THEN TIBET

PENGUIN BOOKS

914.7

PENGUIN BOOKS

Published by the Penguin Group
Penguin Books Ltd, 27 Wrights Lane, London W8 5TZ, England
Penguin Books USA Inc., 375 Hudson Street, New York, New York 10014, USA
Penguin Books Australia Ltd, Ringwood, Victoria, Australia
Penguin Books Canada Ltd, 10 Alcorn Avenue, Toronto, Ontario, Canada M4V 3B2
Penguin Books (NZ) Ltd, 182–190 Wairau Road, Auckland 10, New Zealand

Penguin Books Ltd, Registered Offices: Harmondsworth, Middlesex, England

First published by Macmillan & Co. Ltd 1933
Published in Penguin Books 1985
5 7 9 10 8 6 4

Printed in England by Clays Ltd, St Ives plc
Filmset in Monophoto Ehrhardt

TO EMERALD CUNARD

CONTENTS

Thanks are due to *Country Life*, the *Daily Express*, the *Week-End Review*, *Harper's Bazaar* and the *Architectural Review* for permission to reproduce the substance of articles.

THE TRAVELLER'S CONFESSION

It has been the boast of some travel books to contain nothing that can either instruct or improve their readers. The boast is one I should like to make; for a book that entertains by its art alone will always be more welcome than one that forces attention upon its learning or righteousness. Of these qualities, it is true, the following pages are innocent enough. But the motives that prompted the journeys they describe were not so innocent. I have travelled, I must confess, in search of both instruction and improvement. As member of a community, and heir to a culture, whose joint worth is now in dispute, I would discover what ideas, if those of the West be inadequate, can with greater advantage be found to guide the world. And to this end I would also know, in the language of my own senses, in whom and what the world consists. These vast considerations, let me hasten to add, find small place in the present volume. But they are responsible for its general attitude, since it is only from the sum of isolated journeys that even the shadow of an answer to them can ever be expected.

A conception of the whole world in terms of personal knowledge is held by contemporary opinion to be not only impossible as an attainment, but contemptible as a goal. Real knowledge, according to this view, is the prerogative of the specialist, and is contained, as it were, in cells to which he alone has access. A specialist has been defined as 'one who grows to know more and more about less and less'; as the cells multiply, the scope of each diminishes and the truth contained in it shrinks correspondingly. To suggest that real knowledge must come from a study not of this or that particular cell, but of the relationship between them all, is to invite ridicule and hostility. For the bureaucracy of the mind, like that of the State, is jealous of those who would scrutinize the harmony of its departments. Yet for some persons there exists an organic harmony between all matter and all activity, whose discovery is the purpose of their lives and whose evidence, being inexhaustible, can only be selected by the good judgement and perpetual curiosity of the individual. From this process derives that most invaluable of human resources, an absolute standard of worth capable of unlimited extension.

These persons are the travelling species. The *pleasures* of travel need no reiteration. But when the impulse is so imperious that it amounts to a spiritual necessity, then travel must rank with the more serious forms of endeavour. Admittedly there are other ways of making the world's acquaintance. But the traveller is a slave to his senses; his grasp of a fact can only be complete when reinforced by sensory evidence; he can know the world, in fact, only when he sees, hears, and smells it. Hence that craving for personal reconnaissance which can only be lulled by acquaintance with the broad compartments of race, politics, and geography that comprise our earth. From the specialist's point of view such acquaintance must always be superficial. The traveller can only reply that at least he desires to know more and more about more and more.

This book presents two excursions whose very diversity is symbolic of those formidable contradictions which make it a privilege and a puzzle to be alive in the twentieth century. The first part is concerned with Russia, where the moral influence of the Industrial Revolution has found its grim apotheosis; the second with Tibet, the only country on earth where that influence is yet unknown, where even the cart is forbidden to traverse plains flatter than Daytona Beach, and the Dalai Lama himself rides in a man-borne palanquin. Prior to the Industrial Revolution each country had evolved a unique tradition of civilization. In Russia the tradition has succumbed completely to the virus of the machine. In Tibet it has remained as completely immune from it. Among nations which enjoy such traditions, the two countries represent the extremes of political, social, and mental difference from the accepted mean. These extremes are confirmed even by their appearance. Russia is lower and more colourless, Tibet

THE TRAVELLER'S CONFESSION

higher and more coloured, than any country on earth. Such confirmation is more than a coincidence. It is an explanation.

Extremes of this kind must provoke different reactions in the same traveller. The ideas of Russia are preached, and act, as a challenge to those of the West. The ideas of Tibet offer no challenge; they maintain, simply, a passive resistance towards those of the West. Thus in Russia one must think, argue, and defend. In Tibet one need only observe and sympathize. Russia, moreover, presents a sort of caricature of the West; art, politics, and thought alike have derived from Europe and can only be understood in terms of their European ancestry. Tibet has no relation to the West whatsoever; the historical faculty becomes superfluous; observation consists in the assimilation of pure novelty. These differences are reflected in the form of my book. The contrast between its two parts is more than one of subjects; it lies between different states of the traveller's mind. If the book has a unity, it must be looked for in this contrast. And also, perhaps, in one other thing. I have written throughout, I hope, with respect for the aspirations and convictions of my fellow-men, even when I cannot share them.

PART I
RUSSIA

'Tell me, sir, how shall the mind be elevated if the body be exhausted with material preoccupation? Consider the complex conditions under which a Northern family is obliged to live. Think of the labour expended upon that unceasing duel with the elements – the extra clothing and footwear and mufflers and mantles, the carpets, the rugs, the abundant and costly food required to keep the body in sound working condition, the plumbing, the gas, the woodwork, the paintings and repaintings, the tons of fuel, the lighting in winter, the contrivances against frost and rain, the never-ending repairs to houses, the daily polishings and dustings and scrubbings and those thousand other impediments to the life of the spirit! . . . At close of day, your Northerner is pleased with himself. He has survived; he has even prospered . . . He fancies he has obtained the aim and object of existence. He is too dazed with the struggle to perceive how incongruous his efforts have been. What has he done? He has sacrificed himself on the altar of a false ideal. He has not touched the fringe of a reasonable life. He has performed certain social and political duties – he knows nothing of duties towards himself. I am speaking of men from whom better things might have been expected. As for the majority, the crowd, the herd – they do not exist, neither here nor anywhere else. They leave a purely physiological mark upon posterity; they propagate the species and protect their offspring. So do foxes. It is not enough for us.'

NORMAN DOUGLAS

I

THE NEW JERUSALEM

The European visitor to Russia who values the inheritance of European humanism finds himself regarded as a baneful reactionary full of pontifical formulas which aim not only at the pursuit of 'objective truth', but at the immediate destruction of the Russian State. In compensation he will derive – unless already infected with prejudices of hate or enthusiasm – an exhilarating stimulus to rational thought from this attitude towards himself, a realization that his world's horizon has been suddenly extended beyond all preconceivable expectations. He will discover, possibly against his will, a preponderance of what he has been taught to call obscurantism and tyranny which must necessarily outweigh the best of social purposes. Nevertheless he will be obliged to admit that so great an intellectual stimulus must itself contain the seed of intrinsic good. The question is how to explain this contradiction.

Let no one concern himself with this essay whose hope is for information about Russia of a detached, scientific kind – a mere observation of phenomena such as naturalists conduct in tide-forsaken pools. The Bolsheviks are men, not animals. I meet them as a man, not as a social zoologist. Since their every word is spoken in defence of a dogma, so then let mine be. This must be a personal account, a mobilization of personal feelings in defence of the European tradition; an attempt to keep in view a more scientific truth than that embraced by the records of the field-naturalist, and to see Russia, not as reactionaries and enthusiasts both see her, in ethical relation to the present, but in cultural relation to the future. The forces at work are older than the Revolution, and will long survive it. They are inherent in the country and people, though hitherto partially concealed beneath a Western veneer. Hence the shock of their emergence and the universal curiosity as to their future part in history.

I cannot sufficiently emphasize the fact that the opinions here expressed are entirely confined to those which formed of their own volition in my own mind and which, in fact, did not take conscious shape till I had returned to England and settled down to consider the evidence I had collected. During a large part of my time in Russia I enjoyed the hospitality of Sir Esmond Ovey, H.M. Ambassador to the Soviet Government, and of Lady Ovey; I spent much of my time with other members of the Embassy; and I naturally sought the company of various Englishmen resident in Moscow. Of the kindness they all showed me, and of the pains they were at to promote my journeys and inquiries, I can only make this bare acknowledgement. But I must affirm categorically that the colour of the interpretation which I put on such facts as I gathered is entirely my own. So indefinite had this interpretation remained till the very end of my stay in Russia, that if one had asked me, as the ship sailed out of Odessa, what colour it was, I could not have answered him. This question was in fact put both in Constantinople and London. I had no answer to make, and was considered in consequence either a dullard or an equivocator.

The assurance of my address is the assurance of the ignorant. If I claim a good enough eye and a sufficient experience of other countries to have enabled me to appreciate the visual arts of Russia, and to judge them by general standards, it is only to admit my disadvantage in seeking to paint their present environment. For my concern with laboratories, feats of engineering, and isolated social experiments, is so faint as to be negative; and it is chiefly these particular branches of Bolshevist activity which arouse the enthusiasm of foreign visitors. In six weeks one must choose one's field; I chose to avoid conditioned reflexes, Ford lorries, and abortion clinics. Yet it needed no knowledge of engineering to feel the romance of 'construction' at Dnieperstroi – as I felt it before at Sukkur – nor the uplift of an Astor to pay credit to some hyperborean Demeter for the apple cheeks and fur-lined helmets of the children in the streets. If, sometimes, a note of rancour sounds, blame it on that immemorial

Russian bureaucracy, which chose to regard me, rather in spite of itself, as an undesirable character. This arose from my irresponsibility in visiting Russia neither with an avowed purpose nor as a conducted tourist. Nearly all foreigners buy their tours beforehand, and are therefore obliged to keep to set routes. This is not to say, as so many people infer, that the visitor is only shown what the authorities want him to see. On the contrary, free movement within Russia to-day – except in the Turcoman republics, which are reserved for American millionaires – entails fewer formalities than before the Revolution. The advantage of the conducted tours is simply their remarkable cheapness; and since they are, very conveniently, 'conducted', the tourist is naturally treated to the show-pieces of the existing regime. But as these seemed to me, even by anticipation, both extremely un-interesting and fundamentally insignificant, I trusted to my own arrangements, and may here take the opportunity of thanking those who helped me make them. Travelling was consequently more difficult, but equally more entertaining. Should any echo of the laughter provoked by my journeys reach the ears of my Russian friends, they will be able to ignore, or at the best pity, such irreverence. Levity is the music that accompanies the European's whoring after false gods, gods which, in fact – and all fact is Marxist – do not exist. The orthodox Marxist, like the orthodox Christian, need only give thanks that he is not as others, and leave them to stew in their own delusions. Doubt is unbecoming to him, and susceptibility to foreign opinion is tantamount to doubt.

The supreme moments of travel are born of beauty and strangeness in equal parts: the first panders to the senses, the second to the mind; and it is the rarity of this coincidence which makes the rarity of these moments. Such a moment was mine, when, at the age of three, I ventured on to a beach in Anglesey, and found a purple scabious; such again, when I stood on the Jelep La and surveyed the peaks of Tibet; and such once more, as I walked up the side of the River Moskva late in the afternoon of my second day in Russia. The Red Capital in winter is a silent place. Like black ghouls on the soundless snow the Muscovites went their way, hatted in fur, lamb, leather, and velvet, each with a great collar turned up against the wind that sweeps down the river from the east. With bent heads they hurried past, impervious to collision with one another, or myself, as though desensitized by a decade of mass-living. Farther on, at the corner by the bridge, stood a line of hackney sledges, whose owners, the rearguard of capitalism, sat huddled in their portentous blue coats. Other sledges of robuster build trailed by, bearing piles of hay and boxes. When they came to the slope by the bridge, they all began to go sideways, while their horses scrabbled at the ice.

This, at last, was Red Russia; this horde of sable ghosts the Bolshevists, the cynosure of an agitated world. It was more than Russia, it was the capital of the Union, the very pulse of proletarian dictatorship, the mission-house of Dialectical Materialism. I looked across the river. Before me stood the inmost sanctuary of all: the Kremlin.

A curious irony has dowered the creed of utilitarianism with this edifice as the symbol of outward power. While collective man sits within, the walls deny him and the domes laugh aloud. Fantastic one has always known it to be from photographs. But the reality embodies fantasy on an unearthly scale – a mile and a half of weathered, rose-coloured brick in the form of a triangle that rises uphill from its base along the river. These airy walls, which in places attain a height of forty feet, are hedged with deep crenellations, cloven and coped in white stone after the Venetian fashion. Their impalpable tint and texture might suggest rather the protection of some fabled kitchen-garden than the exigencies of medieval assault. But from their mellow escarpments bursts a succession of nineteen towers, arbitrarily placed, and exhibiting such an accumulation of architectural improbability as might have resulted had the Brobdingnagians, during a game of chess, suddenly built a castle for Gulliver with the pieces. As my eye moved westward, seven of these unbelievable structures marked the half-mile prospective, itself slightly askew, of the base-wall. At either end the angle-towers were taller than the rest, each a cylinder finished with a machicolated balcony and surmounted by an octagonal cone, a kind of dormered cracker-hat tapering skywards to a bronze pennant. Between these two marched five squatter towers – steep, rectangular cones of dark green tiles, broken by a middle storey of the same rosy brick, but varying in height and breadth. These five towers, though they vary in particular dimensions, reflect a pattern introduced by the Tartars. Thus the historian may distinguish a Sino-Byzantine fusion accomplished under the aegis of Italian architects. Be that as it may — my attention was elsewhere. For now, within the walls, rose a white hill, as it were a long table covered with a cloth of snow, lifting up to the winter sky the residences of those vanished potentates, Tsar and God: to the west the two palaces, nineteenth-century Russo-Venetian, cream-coloured against the presage of snow in the sky; the little Italian palace of the fifteenth century, whose grey stone façade of diamond rustications conceals the tiny apartments of the early Tsars; and then the Cathedrals: that of the Annunciation with nine onion-domes; that of the Dormition, where the coronations took place, with five helm-shaped domes; and that of the Archangel Michael, whose central bulb stands high above its four smaller companions; nineteen domes in all, each finished with a cross, most of them thinly gilt; and then, higher than all, the massive belfry, crowned with a flat onion; yet still overtopped by the ultimate cupola of the tower of Ivan Veliki, colossal in solitude, the climax of this Caesaropapist fantasia. I looked down to the river below me; I looked up to the sky; I looked to the right and I looked to the left: horizontally and vertically, towers and domes, spires, cones, onions, crenellations, filled the whole view. It might have been the invention of Dante, arrived in a Russian heaven.

And then as the lights came out and the snowflakes, long imminent, began to wander down in front of them, the scene became alive. As I reached the turn to the bridge, a company of soldiers came marching up the opposite street; the Red Army! visible agent of proletarian power and hardly less fantastic to my eyes than its fortress over the river. In their grey serge dressing-gowns swinging right down to the feet, and their grey serge helmets with pointed Tartar crowns, they looked like so many goblins on an infernal errand. Tramp! tramp! swung the grey serge skirts; but not a footfall sounded. From the shoulders of each goblin slanted a pair of skis, taller than the man himself, and ready to whisk him down upon some country churchyard to prod the dead. As they wheeled round to cross the bridge, they broke into a ringing chorus, taking those earnest, melancholy parts which are associated with all Russian singing. The theme of the words was doubt-less Revolutionary, and, if so, not ill-suited to the effect achieved — as though the troops of ancient Russia were sallying out to a Holy

War. It was quite dark now; the snow falling fast. Behind the chanting goblins the Kremlin rose aglow with electricity, like some ghostly back-cloth to the hurrying city, tower upon tower, dome upon dome, piling up from the rose-red ramparts and the snowy eminence within them, to the last gigantic onion of Ivan Veliki, 450 feet above the black river.

I followed the soldiers, and, climbing a steep road parallel with the east wall of the Kremlin, reached the Red Square. Half-way across the expanse of floodlit snow a queue had formed, ant-like in the distance, to see Lenin. The tomb was open.

I took my place next to a young Turcoman. His pale, aquiline features, properly moulded and furnished with bones, were those of an individual, and seemed companionable, despite the outlandish fleece that crowned them, among these casual-bred Slavs. But for a group of peasants clad in leather and shod with birch-bark, they presented the usual characterless appearance of all urban populations – the mass-man about to pay his Russian homage to his new and Russian Christ.

A halt preceded our entry while they swept out the snow left by the previous pilgrims. Then, two by two, the Turcoman with me, we entered the bronze wicket in the low balustrade. Two sentries, with fixed bayonets and sheepskin ruffs, stood on either side of the door. The vestibule was blank, but for the Soviet emblem – hammer and sickle on a globe supported by sheaves of wheat – in silver relief on the grey stone. Turning to the left, a flight of stairs and a sub-terranean corridor led us down to the vault.

In the midst of this tall, dim interior, sheeted with sombre, close-grained stones, the mummy lay on a tall pedestal sheltered by an inverted cradle of plate-glass, and brightly lit. Below, in pairs at either end, stood four sentries. We lengthened into single file. Mounting a flight of steps, I took my view and, in virtue of the atmosphere, paid my homage. Round the walls, I noticed, ran a frieze of vitreous scarlet lightning.

Lenin must have been a very small man. He rests on a bed of dun-coloured draperies, which engulf his legs with the tasteful negligence of a modiste's window. His upper part wears a khaki jacket buttoned at the neck. The finely modelled hands and features are of waxen texture, like the petals of a magnolia flower. The beard and moustache turn from straw-colour to brown, a fact which caused Bernard Shaw more surprise (so he told me) than anything else in his self-patented Russian Elysium. One might have said: A nice little man, fond of his grandchildren, and given to pruning his trees. I wondered whether a countenance so placid and benign was not really made of wax. For rumour insists that the sewers of the Kremlin recently overflowed into the shrine, to the detriment of its keepsake. But when I got outside, I had not walked a hundred yards before I met an old man with features, beard, and expression exactly similar to those I had just examined. So that there need be nothing inherently false about the present appearance of the relic.

The Red Square was so called long before the Revolution, since the Russian words for 'red' and 'beautiful' are the same. Still the snow falls, each flake softly sparkling in the electric haze. At the north end of the great white oblong rises the blood-coloured bulk of the Historical Museum, a building in Ye Olde Russian style, but now transformed into something fairy-like by the snow filigree on its twin steeples and twisting rooflets. Along the Kremlin side runs the same crenellated rose-red wall, interrupted by three towers. That near the Museum, which carries a slender, cold green spire, was blown up by Napoleon, but rebuilt according to the old design after his departure. At the other end of the square, to the south, stands the famous Spassky tower, a castle of brick surmounted by Gothic pinnacles and finials of white stone, which remind one of Wren's Tom Tower, and were actually built by an Englishman, Christopher Holloway, in 1625. This bears a rich octagonal steeple, decorated with a gilt clock-face. From the topmost apex shines the emblem of the Tsars, a golden eagle, whose glinting double heads act as a signpost to the stranger lost in the 'China Town' opposite.

These two towers, with one other on the west side, are the chief entrances to the Kremlin. Between them the wall is broken by a blind tower of the rectangular double-cone type, above which appears a flat dome of green copper, in the austere Greek style of the later Catherine period. From this dome floats a plain red flag, emblem no longer of the rowdy May Day farce in other capitals, but invested with the dignity of its architectural surroundings. Beneath the wall runs a series of low tribunes in grey-white granite. These are interrupted, immediately below the tower, by Lenin's tomb, which is backed by a screen of small black fir-trees.

The tomb is squat and powerful, instepped like a Ziggurat, and polished like a public-house. It is built of red Ukrainian granite and black and grey Ukrainian labrador, which contains flecks of iridescent blue like those on a butterfly's wing. The lantern is surmounted by a monolith of red Karelian porphyry, $26\frac{1}{4}$ feet in length and weighing 59 tons. The colour of the granite is not our anaemic pink, but a deep rhubarb-red, slightly tinged with ochre. This colour strikes a mean between the scarlet flag and the pink walls, and fits the monument harmoniously upon its ancient stage.

The architect of the mausoleum is Stchousev. His original design, which stood for five years, was of wood. The present, though similar in character, is stronger and more ruthless. It is constructed – or gives the illusion of being constructed – of superb blocks of stone, whose gigantic size is reminiscent of the Inca walls. The form is gained partly by the use of the three colours, black, grey, and red, as an instrument of proportion, and partly by the irregular succession of steps on which these colours are employed. But these steps, though irregular, are far from haphazard. Their ratios, both of height and width, are calculated with the utmost nicety, so as to increase the effect of power and strength. The base of the monument is slightly above the level of the Square, and is enclosed within a low parapet, whose front corners are rounded, and whose rear corners are finished with two small pavilions. This parapet, these pavilions, as well as the long rows of tribunes which run parallel with the Kremlin wall, are built of a greyish white granite, only semi-polished, and having a very close and hard texture. Within the parapet on either side of the entrance have been planted small fir-trees, which, it must be hoped, will not be allowed to grow too high.

Last of all, at the far end where the ground begins to slope down to the river, rises the famous church of Basil Blajenny – Basil the Blessed. Lying slightly below the general level of the square, yet with no other buildings behind it, it closes the panorama like some phantom ship ice-bound against the skyline. Or in circus mood one might compare it with a giant's coconut-shy, whose drab nuts have been replaced by sea-urchins, leeks, pineapples, and peeled pomegranates at different levels – multicoloured fruits, spiral, spiked and fluted, that tempt Lenin's ghost to warm itself on cold nights by potting snowballs at them. There are always a few nocturnal drunks about the Red Square. Perhaps some staggering mystic, or a frozen cabman, or a posse of GPU raiders, passing by in the small hours, have already seen that all-familiar figure clambering wraithlike up its mausoleum for one more shot at the embodied past. I can hardly be sure that I myself, after a certain party at the Metropole, did not discern one or two extra-human missiles hurtling through the air towards that green pine-apple with the red scales ... But the less of this the better. When I emerged from inspecting Lenin's more solid remains on this particular afternoon it was barely tea-time. Suddenly the Spassky clock rang out the hour on the last of the Moscow bells, whose deep melodious chimes never failed, so long as I stayed in the town, to give me a little start of melancholy and pleasure. And as the first clang echoed over the snow and along the red walls, a black smoke of crows shot up into the sky, cawing and croaking their contempt for that motionless anachronism, the Tsar's eagle.

The vision was over. I had exchanged the experience of a moment for a memory that will support me till I die. I shall never see Moscow again as I saw it on that afternoon.

But beside the Moscow of dreams waited a Moscow not less unique – that of men. I left the square by the side of the Historical Museum, where the Iberian gateway used to stand, and, crossing the Opera Square, came to the Hotel Metropole. Here I was to deliver three precious lemons for the use of Albert Coates, who was suffering from a carbuncle. I was also to meet a young English communist named Morgan.

I expected a hatchet-faced consumptive. I perceived a Nordic giant. Morgan was once a chauffeur, but having seen light in a Russian film, had made his way to the land of promise and creative outlet. As that land had seemed to him from a distance, so it had continued to seem, despite loneliness, language difficulty, and food shortage during the early months. I admired his courage in having overcome such obstacles. He now worked with a band of students drawn from thirty-seven nationalities, dividing his time between Materialistic philosophy and the Moscow film studios, and receiving a salary on which he lives.

I had brought him some parcels, which, being ignorant of their contents, I had persuaded the customs officials at Negoreloje not to open. He seemed to assume, therefore, that I, too, had found light. Our conversation was, consequently, at cross-purposes. It started with my asking the waiter for some vodka.

M.: We don't want any of that dope here.

R.B.: Sorry, but I can't live without alcohol.

M.: Oh, well, I suppose you'll grow up some time.

R.B.: I suppose so. But I'm beginning to doubt if I shall ever grow up into a communist. (Morgan looked surprised.) Anyhow, I'm not interested in politics. What I want to know is, not whether the Five-Year Plan is going to succeed, or how many million peasants will know the alphabet in ten years' time, but whether anything *really* important, any advance in human thought or happiness, is going to come of so much misery as the Russians have gone through. I feel it will; but I can't see how it can, when you substitute a banal ideology for the free exercise of the mind. Soviet culture, for example – what and where is it?

M.: You're full up with the old ideas; you don't understand. Our art must be a collective art, and we've got to produce an intelligentsia that will think and create collectively. It was different during the revolutionary period, when everyone was *inspired*. The construction period, which we're settling down to, is harder to express in art.

R.B.: You mean there isn't the same epic feeling of excitement?

M.: That's right. The struggle goes on though, just the same.

R.B. (*petulantly*): I wish to God you'd tell me what you mean by this struggle you all talk about. Struggle with what? I shouldn't have thought there was anyone left in Russia to struggle with by now.

M.: Don't you understand that *everything's* a struggle. If I put this glass of water on this table, the glass and the table are at war – their actual contact is a struggle. It's the same in social evolution. The workers can only build socialism by struggling, by continuing the class war right through.

R.B.: So that when you've done away with classes, all you do is to create new ones and make an aristocracy out of a few million factory workers, who rule the country by oppressing, i.e. struggling with, the remaining majority. How anything creative, or even interesting, can come from this obsession with class, I fail to see. It's worse than England.

M.: There's not much you do see. Now look at Beethoven. Of course we admit he was a genius. But you can see how the class-struggle of the time comes out in his symphonies. Or Wagner. When he had been exiled for revolutionary opinions, he wrote the *Ring*. Then he became a good bourgeois again, and the result was *Parsifal*.

R.B. (*soothingly*): *Parsifal* is dreadful, I admit. I suppose if I translate what you're trying to tell me into ordinary language, all it means is that genius is the product of environment. There's nothing very new in that. And may I ask whether you think Newton could ever have thought out the law of gravity in the environment of modern Russia?

M.: Of course he could have. Our laboratories here are better equipped than any in Europe.

R.B.: I'm talking about thought, not experiment – something that goes on in one person at a time. If you take all the great periods of human invention, scientific or otherwise, you'll find that people were free to think as they wished. There was an atmosphere of disinterested inquiry. The nineteenth century in England, for example – it produced Marx's *Capital among other things, and he says as much in the preface.** Or the Renascence ...

M. (*incredulously*): The Renascence!! Coo! there you are. The Renascence was simply a phase in the class-struggle, the beginning

---

* 'The social statistics of Germany and the rest of Continental Western Europe are, in comparison with those of England, wretchedly compiled ... We should be appalled at the state of things at home, if, as in England, our governments and parliaments appointed periodically commissions of inquiry into economic conditions; if these commissions were armed with the same plenary powers to get at the truth; if it was possible to find for this purpose men as competent, as free from partisanship and respect of persons, as are the English factory-inspectors, her medical reporters on public health, her commissioners of inquiry into the exploitation of women and children, into housing and food ... In England the progress of social disintegration is palpable. When it has reached a certain point, it must react on the Continent ... For this reason, as well as others, I have given so large a space in this volume to the history, the details, and the results of English factory legislation. One nation can and should learn from others.' – *Capital*, Preface to the first edition, 1867.

of the capitalist age, when the merchants and the bourgeoisie began to rise to power.

R.B. (*firmly*): My dear Morgan, you remind me of an evangelical preacher, who's right before God, when everyone else is wrong. I don't mind being wrong. But I haven't come all the way to Russia to argue with people like St Athanasius. It's too boring. I admire your enthusiasm, and I wish to understand what gives rise to it. It doesn't help me in the least to be told that everything that ever happened was a manifestation of the class-struggle. Do you think there were revolutions among the lung-fish? I dare say the Revolution was an excellent thing for Russia. I wouldn't put the clock back for a moment. But what I want to know is whether it holds the seed of hope for the rest of the world beneath this desiccated husk of class ideology.

M.: We're absolutely different. You can't be expected to have the right outlook. You're . . .

R.B.: I'm of a different class, you mean?

M.: That's it. Your voice – it sounds affected to me.

R.B.: Perhaps it is. But I don't see that that's any reason why we should start a class war over this table, or why the GPU should send old professors to the Urals for writing about Byzantine icons.

M.: They belong to the wrong class – they're our enemies. The intellectuals have let us down too often. We can't take any more risks, when the war may come at any moment.

R.B.: There you go again. *What* war?

M.: It's happened once. What about the Intervention?

R.B.: D'you think the whole of England is peopled with Churchills?

M.: I don't know about that, but war's coming all right. Why, it's beginning already in Manchuria. What's more, I tell you seriously that in two or three years' time I hope to be inviting my comrades from here to stay with me in Buckingham Palace.

R.B.: That's a very bourgeois ambition. (*Inconsequently*) Do you get on with Jews?

M.: I'm pretty used to them after living in the East End. I like them. Still, they're not quite the same as yourself. Let's go up and see Sylvia Chen.

R.B.: Why, is she a Jewess?

M.: No, she's a daughter of Eugene Chen and a French negress. Her brother's a commander in the Red Army, and she's a dancer.

We went upstairs to Miss Chen's apartment. Though her shelves groaned with the early fathers of Materialism, she was temporarily engrossed with the difficulty of obtaining new dance records, since Jazz is proscribed by the Russian customs as 'ideologically incorrect'. Even Morgan, now released from argument, admitted the hardship of this deprivation. They put on an old record, and Miss Chen hopped about, a pretty creature against the antiquated plush of her surroundings.

'What are you going to do in Russia?' she asked me.

I said I hoped of course to go to Leningrad, and also to Novgorod to see the old churches.

'Churches?' she answered. 'Whatever interests you about that kind of dead stuff?'

I felt I could hardly explain.

II

CREED AND OBSERVANCE

(1)

I have given the above conversation as one specimen out of many. I had come to a new world: Morgan was to me as the kangaroo to Captain Cook or as the Erewhonians to the Edwardians. Yet since he was neither beast nor fiction, I could not, and cannot, treat him and his like with the polite detachment of a zoologist.* This is the normal attitude of the visiting foreigner, than which, if the Russians only realized it, nothing is more insulting to them. Nevertheless, beneath the insane babble of Marxian clichés, I was conscious of forces whose reality was not to be denied, and whose significance aroused my avid curiosity. This curiosity, I knew, would go unrequited unless I could see beyond the fanatics and jargon that obscure every view in modern Russia.

The first condition of understanding for the stranger is to realize that the Revolution and all that followed it were the outcome of processes which began with Russian history and will end with it. The Byzantine Orthodox Church has always been distinguished from the Catholic in that its ideal is rather the attainment of heaven on earth by means of contemplation than the pursuit of a satisfactory after-life. From the domination of ideas which this Church exercised from the tenth century on, no Renascence ever delivered Russia. Nor were the serfs, as in other countries, liberated from their material slavery

---

* The original publication of this phrase in the *Architectural Review* has enriched the Russian vocabulary. On 8 April 1933, *Pravda* appeared with the headline: 'Diehards' Zoological Hatred of the Soviet Government'.

by an economic demand for fluid labour. Thus the Russian has always conceived of progress as a mass-advance towards an immediate millennium rather than as a succession of steps taken by gifted individuals towards objective truth. While no country has produced more theorists on the theme of human betterment, their concern has always been with the prompt delivery rather than with the quality of the perfection supplied. Only by this means could the mass of humanity, whose mystic elevation has always been the keynote of Russian speculation, be adequately embraced. The individual, wedded to objective thought for its own selfish sake, was ignored as a permanent factor in the social scheme, for the obvious reason that the Russians have no conception of the individual in this sense – a fact which emerges plainly enough from those travesties of humanity which form the individual heroes of Russian novels.

In the last century, the rise of an intellectual class gave mouth and power to this Russo–Messianic concept of collective uplift. At the same time there arrived from the West the new industrial idea of a purely physical universe ruled by a God who was nothing more than a chemist-engineer. Such an idea, reacting on the pervasive mysticism of Orthodoxy and the fantastic sects that had sprouted from so fertile a soil, produced a philosophic vacuum, a kind of mystic nothingness, which was elaborated into a system by Bakunin (1814–76) under the name of Nihilism. Then began the classic era of sacrificial plotters, whose dramatic assassinations attracted the attention of the outside world. It was complacently imagined by their liberal sympathizers in other countries that the murderers, if slightly misguided in their methods, were inspired by the desire to free their country from a brutal autocracy. Even to-day this idea is ingeniously fostered in the minds of foreign tourists by the transformation of the fortress of Peter and Paul, where the chief rebels were confined, into a museum for the display of Tsarist atrocity. The hatred of the anarchists for the Monarchy was doubtless genuine and disinterested. But if anyone wishes to disabuse himself of the illusion that they wished to substitute for it a regime of Anglo-Saxon liberty, let him read the appendix to René Fülöp-Miller's *Mind and Face of Bolshevism*, which contains quotations from *The Possessed* and *The Brothers Karamazov*, written by Dostoievsky in 1871 and 1879. Even these prophetic utterances are superfluous. For did not Lenin say that freedom was a bourgeois prejudice?

The European may stigmatize as merely destructive the Russian theorist's obsession with a joyless, unwilled mass-nirvana, and as impracticable his conception of the human mass as the one and only agent of human advance, obedient to the impulses of its Narcissistic mysticism. He may even be permitted a just indignation when these ideas threaten the structure of his own laboriously evolved tradition. But it serves no end to curse the Russians for thinking as they do, or to depreciate their ideal of enabling the mass to exchange its bestial sloth for an inspired self-immolation on the altar of industrial productivity. It is not our ideal. We aim at an increasing distribution of material benefits within a framework that preserves the prerogatives of the individual. But let us understand that Bolshevism, whether it prove economically feasible or not, derives directly and genuinely from the Russian view of the universe, which regards the passion of the mass-man for the sake of the mass-man as the highest form of human expression.

Meanwhile Nihilism and its like offered incentive to individual self-sacrifice, but no programme for co-ordinated action. This deficiency was to be filled in part by Karl Marx, who propounded a new philosophy of historical evolution, and in part by Lenin, who, with the usual Russian impatience to be in at the Second Coming, extracted from that philosophy a social doctrine capable of immediate application, and, since evolution was concerned, conceived himself to be the proper agent for speeding up that cumbrous process.

Karl Marx arrived in London in 1849, and there devoted himself to research among the voluminous materials that had already been collected anent the conditions of the English working classes. In his lighter moments he entertained a wholesome respect for class distinctions and established authority: 'he attended at the Society of Arts a soirée graced by the presence of royalty ... he liked his wife to sign herself "Jenny, née Baronne de Westphalen" ... finally, he accepted the office of constable of the vestry of St Pancras, taking the customary oath, and donning the regulation uniform on gala occasions.'* He retained his enthusiasm for Germany, 'sang the praises

* A. Loria, *Karl Marx* (London, 1920), p. 48.

of German music and literature', and regarded Germany's part in the war of 1870 as purely defensive.

His contribution to thought was his conception of society as something fluid, in a state of perpetual change and becoming, and his adumbration of a law governing this process. It is claimed that, as Darwin to biology, so he stands in relation to sociology. The claim is somewhat exaggerated, for whereas Darwin could base his deductions on the whole of the world's history, Marx was necessarily confined to that comparatively narrow field contained in the written records of a few thousand years. Starting with the premise that all 'value' is the outcome of labour, his law of evolution naturally developed a purely economic complexion: all societies are based on the exploitation of labour in some form or another, and since the exploiters cannot be expected to relinquish their privileged position of their own accord, it is only by explosions of violence that the changes rendered necessary by changing methods of economic production are brought about; these explosions are the outcome of a permanent, though generally latent, struggle – the class war; as for politics, morals, religion, art, and the rest, these are but the ideological expression of that struggle. In Marx's opinion, the moment was at last approaching when labour should free itself from the last of a succession of exploiting classes and assume the whole fruits of its own toil for itself. Thus his theory of social evolution dissolves, or is dissolved by those who would put it to practical use, in the mist of an imminent millennium. One is left in doubt as to whether, once the workers cease to be exploited, the Marxian law will continue to operate or not.

In putting forward his theory of the evolution of society according to economic laws, Marx added something to the general technique of historical inquiry. But in seeking to found, upon the basis of those laws, an all-embracing philosophy, he displayed a lack of scientific method which must be ascribed to the Jew's inability to apprehend the reality of emotions and ideals of which he himself has no personal experience.

It were redundant to indicate which particular points in the Marxian philosophy brought grist to the revolutionary mill. But it cannot be sufficiently stressed how easily these theories might have disappeared into the limbo enjoyed by most of their kind, but for their transformation into a militant creed of action at the hands of Lenin. For good or evil, Lenin was one of the most remarkable characters in history, not only by virtue of his influence on the fate of millions, but for his individual pertinacity and consistency in working towards an apparently impossible goal. In the Marxian theory he saw a practical instrument and he shaped it to that end. To read his works after those of Marx is like turning to the Athanasian Creed from the Sermon on the Mount. He found in Marx the raw material for both a politico-economic programme and a philosophy to uphold it. When the time came, the weapons were ready forged, and he brought them into play.

(2)

Into the exact nature of the political organism that to-day exists as the result of Lenin's activities, I do not propose to inquire; abler heads than mine have run themselves against this brick wall, and will continue to do so. But I wish to record a very definite impression on my part of the nervous insecurity and strain that prevails among all educated and semi-educated people in Russia, members of the Communist Party included. The incidents that contributed to form this impression were cumulative in their effect, and in any case too numerous to recount. Indeed, its origin was atmospheric as much as circumstantial. But if it was a correct impression, its importance is vital to the sifting of the ashes whence the phoenix of collective culture must eventually arise. The stranger must inquire what produces it.

In describing the system under which they live, the Russians themselves invariably make use of two terms, one political, the other economic. These are 'the dictatorship of the proletariat' and 'State capitalism'.

The 'proletariat' is a name for that hypothetical mass with whose aims Lenin, as a good Russian, necessarily identified his own. But the word, when used in the Marxian sense, denotes a fluid supply of labour, without anchorage or possessions, at the beck and call of economic, i.e. capitalistic, demand. Unfortunately, this particular kind of mass scarcely existed in Russia at the time of the Revolution. Thus the Bolsheviks, having established a government which has alienated the sympathies of the intellectual class by its tyranny and an economic system which, if judged by their own material standards, was, and is, a total failure from the point of view of the peasant, lack the chief support postulated by their creed, the very lynch-pin of the whole theoretical structure. Until this support is created – that is to say, until at least a bare majority of the Russian population has been recruited into the ranks of the true proletarian nucleus already centred in the large towns – the present rulers of Russia must continue in their present state of nervous insecurity, particularly when they consider the volume of existing discontent, passive though it be. Hence the frantic efforts that have been, and are being, made to create a fluid rural proletariat by impressing peasants into the collective farms – by, in fact, the artificial stimulation of that very process which the whole of *Capital* was meant to damn for ever and ever.

Says Marx, after lauding the independence of the English peasant before our great enclosures took place: 'What the capitalist system demanded was, on the other hand, a degraded and almost servile condition of the mass of the people, the transformation of them into mercenaries, and of their means of labour into capital.' Says Lenin, in his article on Marx written for a Russian encyclopaedia: 'If, finally, we wish to understand the attitude of Marxian socialism towards the smaller peasantry ... we must turn to a declaration by Engels expressing Marx's views: *"When we are in possession of the powers of the State, we shall not even dream of forcibly expropriating the poorer peasants.... Our task as regards the smallholders will first of all consist in transforming their individual production and individual ownership into co-operative production and co-operative ownership, not forcibly, but by way of example, and by offering social aid for this purpose."*'* Well might Marx cause an earthquake in the Highgate cemetery and Lenin burst his mausoleum to fragments, could they have witnessed the treatment of the Russian peasant carried out in their names during the last five years.

So bitter and so widespread has been the resentment aroused by this treatment that Stalin, temporarily at least, has had a stop put to it. It is the result, not of socialism, but of State capitalism, as the Russians admit. Marx was at pains to point out that capitalists always tend to absorb one another. 'Along with the constantly diminishing number of the magnates of capital ... grows the mass of misery,

* Lenin, *Collected Works*, Authorized English Edition, vol. xviii, p. 42.

oppression, slavery, degradation, exploitation.' Is this true of Russia, where the number of capitalists has been diminished to one? If so, what will be the result?

Either the peasants, incensed beyond all reason, will resist all attempts to proletarianize them; in which case they will be permanently at odds with the communist aristocracy of the towns, and the class war will go on, thus vindicating Marx's theory of evolution. Or they will surrender themselves to a joyless impersonal exploitation by the State, redeemed by elementary education and broadcast culture; and Marx's theory will either die of classless inanition or receive its most terrific vindication in a subsequent revolt on the part of the expropriated against the one grand expropriator – the State. Both alternatives hold possibilities well calculated to disturb the present rulers. They have staked everything on the Five-Year Plan. This, if it succeeds, should create a purely industrial proletariat of sufficient size to support them and recruited without the ill-feeling produced by compulsory measures. Meanwhile the tension, as of a man fighting for his life, pervades the whole country. It may not conduce to the pursuit of objective truth or the creation of great art, but it results in a great activity and exercise of the mind.

(3)

It was recognized from the beginning by Lenin and his coadjutors that allegiance to their politico-economic system must depend, in the long run, on a general acceptance of its concomitant philosophy by those capable of even the most rudimentary mental activity. In attempting to secure this allegiance they were at once face to face with the weakest link in their carefully forged chain for the bondage of the individual – with, in fact, a link so weak as to constitute a gap. To remedy this deficiency they have exercised an ingenuity which deserves the success it is receiving. But the very contrivances to which they are obliged to resort, reveal more clearly than anything else the totally unscientific character of the philosophy to which they are committed.

The exponents of Dialectical Materialism, as the creed enunciated by Lenin is called, regard the universe as composed solely of phenomena whose reality can be subjected to the empirical test of their own senses. Religion is their bane. It diverts man's attention and effort from the society in which he lives; its priesthood is invariably the agent of political and social stagnation. This view is rational enough, and, though one may take occasional exception to it, not difficult to acquiesce in or at last to understand. But the Materialists are also the victims of a frenzied and irrational hate for those ancient beliefs and institutions which symbolize, possibly in its crudest form, the search of mankind for a central Reality and, consequently, the prime obstacle to the spread of the New Gospel. This hate, amounting almost to dementia, has prevented them from conducting any detached inquiry into the reason why religion exists and always has existed. Ostrich-like they have failed to recognize that religion fulfils some fundamental human need.

After the Revolution, religion in Russia fell, or was thrust, into very general desuetude. No sooner did this happen than the needs which, however superficially or improperly, it had hitherto satisfied, made themselves apparent in an atmosphere of licence, restlessness, and disillusionment. Village life had lost its keystone; the peasant his theatre; among the educated or semi-educated classes was felt an equal lack of that faith or code without which life cannot be regulated. In addition, the new rulers were not slow to discover that they, too, had lost something, and that this was hardly the moment to dispense with the traditional ally of all government. 'Religion,' they had thundered, 'is the opium of the people.' The practical value of this maxim now became fully apparent to them. Since all pre-existing religions were proscribed by the new philosophy, there was only one course open to them in their need for a popular soporific. This was to erect the philosophy itself into a religion. And this they have done. They have preserved the jealousy of the God of Israel while dispensing with the God himself, and the external ceremony of the Orthodox Church while dispensing with the Church. In place of the single God enthroned in heaven, they have substituted the Mass enthroned on earth; in place of the Church, a hierarchy no less intolerant – YOUTH. It is a different kind of opium; its dreams are less reposeful. But it works.

The Italian Professor Achille Loria closes his monograph on Karl Marx with words which might almost be supposed, by one ignorant

35

of their context, to emanate from a newly discovered papyrus of St John the Divine:

For the day is coming. And in that day, when remorseless time shall have destroyed the statues of the saints and of the warriors, renascent humanity will raise in honour of the author of this work of destruction, upon the shores of his native stream, a huge mausoleum representing the proletarian breaking his chains and entering upon an era of conscious and glorious freedom. Thither will come the regenerated peoples bearing garlands of remembrance and of gratitude to lay upon the shrine of the great thinker, who, amid sufferings, humiliations, and numberless privations, fought unceasingly for the ransom of mankind. And the mothers, as they show to their children the suffering and suggestive figure, will say, their voices trembling with emotion and joy: See from what darkness our light has come forth; see how many tears have watered the seeds of our joy; look, and pay reverence to him who struggled, who suffered, who died for the Supreme Redemption.

True, the Rhine still waits its promised monument. But I could not help thinking, as I walked about Moscow on 22 January, what a graceful and at the same time inexpensive gesture the British Government might make by unearthing the bones of Marx and his Jenny in Highgate* and presenting them to Russia. Lenin, after all, is only second best. Still, he makes a very decent pilgrimage, and the patriot type of saint is certainly the more fashionable at the moment.

Lenin died on 21 January. For some inscrutable Russian reason his death is mourned, or was this year, on 22 January. The Red Good Friday proved the occasion for elaborate manifestations of dolour, such as mark the same season in Rome. To all shops and offices of any pretension, red banners, bearing the hammer and sickle in gold, and bound in black, had been distributed, and now hung motionless in the cold fog with which nature was participating in the national grief. The grandiose front of the Bolshoy Theatre, the Opera, was draped on either side with an immense arras of the same character; while across the portico the name LENIN was blazoned in scarlet light, like a gigantic IHS. In addition to this Latin ostentation, something of the English Sabbath had crept in. The sale of alcohol was forbidden,

---

*They share God's acre with those of Thomas Hood the poet, and Lillywhite the cricketer. Coleridge is round the corner in a coke-house. I am indebted for this information to Mr John Betjeman, the father of necropolitan research.

lest the dignity of the occasion should be marred by the usual inebriate holiday-makers. Even food was difficult to obtain. At the same time hotels and restaurants were crowded with congresses and delegations assembled to observe the sacred day. In the Red Square, a queue had formed such as one sees in London when a dead king lies in state, twisting and turning over the great expanse of snow, like one of those wire puzzles that have neither end nor beginning. From morning till night it shuffled convulsively along, a foot at a time. There might have been ten or a hundred thousand people; I could find no means of computing. But it struck me that none of them would have been there, to stand for an hour in a temperature of several degrees below zero, unless actuated by genuine emotion and a personal conviction of the solemnity of the occasion.

The instances of resemblance between the outward manifestations of the Materialist faith and those of the older religions could be multiplied indefinitely; they astonish the visitor at every turn. In factories and clubs, the icon corner has been replaced by the Lenin or the Marx corner: hideous busts of pseudo-bronze stand on pyramidical pedestals draped in red, bowered in red, and backed with red. In the separate rooms, less expensive coloured prints replace the erstwhile less expensive icons, forerunners of a new and monotonous hagiography depicting Stalin, Kalinin, Krupskaya, and Budenny. In the large towns, every third shop window teems with these frightful representations, of all sizes to suit all purses, and exhibiting a lack of artistry sickening to behold. On being told the sum formerly derived by the Pechersky Lavra in Kiev from the sale of holy pictures, I was anxious to learn what profit accrued to the present government from the same source. The answer to my inquiry was, that far from there being any profit, the State actually incurred a considerable loss in promoting the distribution of its blessed effigies.

In addition to dead saints, there are the living Early Fathers, the Jeromes, Clements, Origens, and Athanasiuses, who thunder out their daily commentaries on the central creed and its application to the daily emergency with the prolific inconsequence induced by modern printing facilities. In Kremlin, commissariat, club, factory, institute, and school, these Early Fathers reside and multiply, seeking heresies and definitions with the appetite of Byzantine Christologists.

Fortunately for their happiness, there is no end to either, since their dogma is based on the most uncertain of all sciences and the details of its proper practice are as elusive as quicksilver.

These Christian similes may sound far-fetched; but though individual definitions of what does and does not constitute a religion may differ, they do in fact convey better than any other the mental atmosphere of Bolshevist Russia. It is as easy for us — for me — to laugh at the ideological hair-splitting and Salvation Army jargon that have grown up round the Materialist creed as it was for Gibbon to ridicule the Monophysites and the Monothelites. Yet the purpose of these ideological and Christological controversies is the same, and an eminently comprehensible one: namely, to expand the provisions of a central creed so as to cover every possible contingency by a formula that shall be intelligible to the illiterate or the semi-literate mass. Where the parallel may possibly lose its force is in the nature of the spiritual force or faith behind the two religions.

The faith that inspired the earlier Russian revolutionaries was, as I have tried to explain, a conviction that the redemption of humanity must and could be attained through the mental and material advance of humanity in the mass. This was Lenin's faith. It may incorporate a kind of devil-worship. But judged by the measure of his devotion to his faith, Lenin was a great and noble man. I could not help asking myself, when in Russia, whether, now, this same faith was not giving place to external boastfulness and megalomania, a kind of hollow, inverted Fascism. One hears too much about the enthusiasm of YOUTH, in Russia as everywhere else. The very phrase is suspicious; it cloaks an emptiness; great movements cannot draw their force from supporters in a state of petrified immaturity. Russian YOUTH may feel itself predestined to dominate the globe. Drunk with titanic visions, it may hurl itself down mines and into factories. For the moment, the Five-Year Plan provides a psychological safety-valve to this bursting intoxication, this class-chauvinism. But where is the original faith? What will sustain the young shock-brigaders and komsomols of to-day twenty years hence, if the reward should not prove equal to their hope?

To these questions, to the question whether Materialism is destined to endure for centuries as a vital force, or to crumble away like a nerveless tooth, I can put no answer. Meanwhile, it seeks to reinforce its dominion with every device of jealous obscurantism and personal oppression known to the medieval Church or the Spanish Inquisition. The faith may survive the longer for such conditions, the social structure gain in strength. But art and culture must either die, as they died with Julian the Apostate, or assume a form as yet unknown, as they assumed in the Gothic cathedrals. So far, only darkness is descending, while the new light has not begun to shine. But the Dark Ages lasted four centuries. Must Russia wait as long, plunged in her scientific night?

At a certain stage of their development [wrote Marx*] the material productive forces of society come into conflict with the existing production relationships, or, what is but a legal expression for the same thing, with the property relationships within which they have hitherto moved ... A period of social revolution then begins. With the change in the economic foundation, the whole gigantic superstructure is more or less rapidly transformed. In considering such transformations, we must always distinguish between the material changes in the economic conditions of production ... and the legal, political, religious, aesthetic, or philosophic, in short, ideological forms, *in which human beings become conscious of this conflict and fight it out to an issue.*

The italics are mine. They enshrine the kernel of Bolshevist truth: thought, creative power, can have but one beginning and one end, one incentive and one purpose – the furtherance of the class-struggle.

Education thus becomes a question of instilling into children (from the ages of six to sixty) the belief that the continuance of this struggle is the proper aim of all human beings and the particular aim of all good Russians. As far as general principles are concerned, a specious amorality is inculcated by the most elementary copybooks. Spy on your neighbour and cherish the machine! is the motto of Russian childhood. In the towns, the principal churches are occupied by a litter of posters and photographs which remind one of a dismantled coffee-stall. Closer examination reveals a pictorial exposure of the iniquities and class bias of all religions – Orthodox, Catholic, and Protestant Christianity, the Sects, Judaism, Mohammedanism, and Buddhism. The Calvinistic fury of Materialism can tolerate no rivals. Crowds of children trail round behind their teachers, as we see them at the Burlington House exhibitions, imbibing knowledge of the hard and fast line between the

---

* *A Contribution to the Critique of Political Economy* (Chicago, 1904).

new Right and the new Wrong as laid down in these Anti-God Museums. The same line is apparent in the Press and in public entertainments. At the Press it becomes no Englishman to throw stones; I can only blush in guilty silence. But on the Moscow wireless, during the English programme, I heard one thing that might have shocked even Mr Maxton. The speaker was describing the industrial activity of Sverdlovsk, a town in the Urals once known as Ekaterinbourg. In their spare time, he said, smiling children and workers might be seen going in and out of the house of Ipatiev – now a museum – 'where the family of Romanov met the fate it justly deserved'. The man's voice, I thought, faltered as he spoke his silly text. And well it might. If this is how the Bolsheviks conduct their propaganda abroad, the world is safe from revolution for a long time. I should like to go to Sverdlovsk and see the children smiling in the death-cellar of those other children. The sight would bear noble witness to the power of the new faith, and also to that cowardly, hypocritical pretence of infallibility, mark of all religions, which must needs brazen out the most repulsive accidents.

The atmospheric oppression of a land where the only truths are the class war and the machine, and where all culture must be subservient to those ends, is alleviated by the novelty – one might even say eccentricity – that results. The air is mixed with laughing-gas. But it is a stifling air – how stifling I only realized on reaching Kiev, which preserves in some indefinable way its old university tradition of the humanities and allows one to breathe normally again. Not that I was unhappy in Russia. I can truthfully say that in no foreign country have I ever enjoyed myself so positively, been so sheltered from boredom, or felt such regret at departure. But this was partly due, I must confess, to the pleasant feeling of pugnacity that woke in my bosom. The system is intended for the world – that is clear from the start. Try your damned religion on me, I felt, and you'll get as good as you give! And so they did, now and then. Yet I could not but respect persons so deeply engaged in a definite purpose and so homogeneously subscribing, with heart or lip, to a definite belief. Such fixity was hardly to be despised by a member of that nation whose chosen patriots are Noel Coward and Winston Churchill. It was rather to be envied.

My first real consciousness of the Great Untruth was brought to the surface by a Beethoven concert conducted by Oscar Fried in the Moscow Conservatorium. They were playing the Pastoral Symphony. It was not a bad performance, though the instruments lacked tone. When it was at an end, I looked up and remembered where I was. And then, suddenly, it came to me that here – not in capitalism, nor in Christianity, but here on the concert platform in these tattered scores – was the enemy that Materialism can never conquer and that must ultimately and inevitably conquer Materialism. It seemed to me that to allow such a performance to take place in public was simply an act of quixotic folly on the part of the authorities. In theory, no doubt, the Pastoral Symphony provides exemplary illustration of the class war in rural Austria. In practice . . . I turned my attention to the audience and read, or thought I read, my own thoughts in their faces. Only a group of shock-brigaders, young hierarchs in tall boots, looked sullen, as indeed it was their duty to do. They would have explained to me, had I reproached them for their attendance, that music, above all arts, conduces to the socialization of emotion. This means, in ordinary language, that it moves a lot of people at once. But if I had asked them how it is that certain compositions wield this invaluable power in a greater degree than others, or whether the emotion produced by them is not the outcome of a highly incorrect revelation of abstract beauty, I do not know what they would have replied. The functions of art are one thing. Its creation and effect are another. Either art must be proscribed in its entirety, as St Clement of Alexandria recommended; or, if its effect is considered beneficial to the general mass, then the individual must be allowed free play with abstractions in order to create it. The learned doctors of Materialism argue that a class war for the redemption of humanity should be abstraction enough for any artist. This may be so. A spontaneous culture may spring from the soil of mass-betterment. But I could see no signs of it. When I asked for any, they could only answer with Christ: 'A wicked and adulterous generation seeketh a sign; and there shall no sign be given unto it.' This was disappointing. Still, I persisted in my search.

At Morgan's instance, I went to see the two most recent sound-films made in the Russian studios. Russian films of the revolutionary or epic period have aroused great hopes. These, depicting the present period of construction, proved by contrast somewhat disappointing.

The first was called *Sniper*. It opened with a regiment of British troops in kilts made of duster-cloth being cheered off to the front to the strains of 'Tipperrarr-ee', which tune, I afterwards learnt, they had been taught to sing by Morgan. A confusing succession of incidents on various fronts followed, during which No-man's-land was suddenly transformed into a maize-field, in order that harvesting women, whom the German Army was gallantly assisting in their labours, might be shot down by the Allied guns. Finally, the scene changed to the new Russia, in which all the workers but one of a certain factory devoted their leisure hours to rifle-practice. This one, a feckless youth, maundered about with a tennis racquet; until one day the capitalist invasion began, and the tennis racquet proved of little service in defending either its owner's person or his fatherland. I was reminded of those ridiculous British productions sponsored by the Empire Marketing Board to promote imperial fellowship. And I must say, in all justice, that even the Moscow Press was loud in its denunciations of such crudity.

The other film, on the other hand, had been acclaimed as a national triumph, and has presumably obtained popularity abroad, since I afterwards found it showing in Constantinople and it has since been seen in London. The photography was generally good and in parts excellent. Its title may be rendered as *The Way into Life*.

The theme was the redemption of those homeless children that have grown up like animals and have infested Russia since the great famine. They are shown at first as thieves and thugs. Then, while sleeping in a cellar, they are rounded up and transported to a deserted church in the country which they turn into a workshop. Their gradual transformation into useful members of society is effected by a kind of scoutmaster who seeks to inculcate into them the public school sense of honour, and is materially assisted in this admirable work by the hero of the film, a worthy Tartar boy named Mustafa. But evil influences persist. While the scoutmaster is away, a disaffected section of the boys, despite the opposition of those led by Mustafa, breaks all the machines. The scoutmaster, on return, cannot conceal his pain, but instead of reproaches he produces a toy train from a brown-paper parcel. This he sets going on toy rails; and, inspired by its example, they start to build a real railway. Meanwhile the disaffected section has discovered a log-hut in the woods where prostitutes congregate and vodka circulates freely. To this horrible resort they lure Mustafa and his disciples, now clad in smart lounge suits. But when the orgy is at its height, the latter, at a sign from their leader, draw revolvers, shoot up a number of strange but repulsive men, and bind the evil women, who are now in a state of blubbering dishevelment. By now the line is finished. The night before the opening Mustafa goes down it on a trolley, singing a Tartar song as the dawn breaks, the birds begin to chirp, and the bull-frogs to croak. But an enemy lies in wait; the trolley is upset and Mustafa stabbed to death. After some delay the ceremonial first train, manned by the now fully reclaimed boys, starts its opening journey without him. Then they find his body, and placing it reverently on the front of the engine, steam into the terminus of a small town, where rejoicing at once gives way to grief. In real life, I am glad to say, Mustafa is still with us. Moscow now realizes that he is human after all, and that he is more broad-minded in his pleasures than the film would have us believe.

There were moments in this film of real emotional solemnity, such as that of the Tartar song at dawn. But for me these were entirely overshadowed by the didactic unreality of the whole story, and by the catechism in Right and Wrong which the audience was obliged to answer in order to keep abreast of the plot. It was the atmosphere of *Eric, or Little by Little* and *The Fairchild Family* over again, with the same fascination of the contemporary social document. I would have given half my time in Russia to have read into the hearts of my fellow-spectators, and to have discovered whether this crude antithesis of Materialist values had inspired them with real emotional piety, or had rendered their entertainment, as it had mine, just a little tedious.

It would be possible to continue indefinitely the list of experiences which went to prove how utterly impossible, and, from the Materialist point of view, undesirable, it is that any form of disinterested, non-political, or non-economic culture should ever flourish on the soil of modern Russia. But there came to my notice one final instance which revealed, more plainly and more grotesquely than anything else, the mendacious and futile obscurantism to which the new religion finds it necessary to resort in its own self-defence. There hangs in Moscow one of the finest and most representative collections of modern French pictures that has ever been assembled. Over the entrances of each room are printed notices, which are designed to assist the appreciation of less sophisticated visitors. In appending a selection from these notices, I withhold comment that would be impertinent to the intelligence of the English reader and offensive to my Russian friends:

MONET: Age of transition from capitalism to imperialism. Taste of the industrial bourgeoisie.

CÉZANNE: Age of the preliminary period of imperialism. Taste of the industrial bourgeoisie.

PISSARRO and SISELEY: Age of the preliminary period of imperialism. Taste of the industrial bourgeoisie.

GAUGUIN: Taste of the rentier.

CROSS and SIGNAC: Taste of the lower and middle bourgeoisie under the influence of the lower industrial bourgeoisie.

VAN GOGH: Taste of the small bourgeoisie.

MATISSE: Age of distorted imperialism. Taste of the rentier.

(4)

While the doctrine of Materialism ascribes all artistic creation to the genius of the mass and epoch rather than to that of the individual, it must perforce admit that the concrete fruits of such creation do owe their shape to some effort on the part of the individual, even though his proper function is only to interpret and organize the taste and emotions of the mass and epoch; and that the successful fulfilment of this function, impersonal though it be, requires of the individual a degree of concentration and thought which distinguishes him from the common herd and thus postulates the existence of an intelligentsia. 'We workers,' say the good partymen, 'will create our own intelligentsia.' So they may do – though how, neither they nor I can explain. But whatever its origins, this intelligentsia will constitute a different class from that of the 'workers and peasants', and as such a suspect class. All disinterested thought, such as we regard as the first condition of cultural development, is rendered impossible in Russia by the jealousy of the prevailing religion. But even those of the intelligentsia who sincerely subscribe to that religion – 'one must believe in it, or one cannot live here', said the son of a former landowner, now an engineer, to me – even they are subject to a system of bewildering impediments which makes the foreign observer wonder how their task can be adequately performed and whether anything truly inventive can ever result from their efforts. I would emphasize the fact that I am writing here, not of the disgruntled dispossessed, but of those who are honestly desirous of working for and with the new system, but whose vocations necessarily place them in the intellectual class.

Sixty years ago one of Dostoievsky's characters spoke as follows concerning the social system adumbrated by another:

One thing in his book is good, the idea of espionage. In his idea every member of the society spies on the others, and is bound to inform against them when necessary. All are slaves and equal in their slavery ... First of all, the level of education, science, and innate natural talent falls. A high intellectual level is possible only to superior talents; but we have no need of superior talents. Superior talents have always seized power for themselves and led to despotism. Men of talent cannot help becoming despots, they have always done more harm than good; therefore they are driven out or put to death.*

This prophecy is somewhat exaggerated, since Materialism has great need of superior talents and its exponents admit the fact. But it contains much that the visitor to Russia can recognize.

Those less fortunate observers, who are obliged to commit themselves entirely to the excellent facilities offered by the Russian tourist agency, remain completely oblivious to that unique state of affairs which most clearly distinguishes the lives of Russian humanity from those led by humanity in any other part of the globe. This state of affairs consists in the universal, all-pervasive practice of espionage and suspicion conducted among all grades of the Materialist society. I heard it said that one in every fourteen persons in the whole of Russia is in some way or other an agent of the secret police. Whether this is true, I do not know. But my own short experience revealed to me that even the boldest flights of fiction conceived by the late Mr Edgar Wallace had visualized nothing to compare with the reality of those excitements which the Russian people are daily privileged to enjoy. Now that I am back in England, no report circulated by the die-hard Press seems too preposterous to believe, even though, in nine cases out of ten, I do not believe it. At times, during my visit, I began to doubt my own sanity; but never for long; some conversation with those who had actually experienced the ordeals of Russian citizenship or residence always intervened to restore it. Plotters, saboteurs, informers, kulaks,

* From *The Possessed*, quoted by René Fülöp-Miller in *The Mind and Face of Bolshevism*.

assassins, counter-revolutionaries, and the ever-renascent bourgeoisie, native or foreign, lurk behind every window, playing their assigned rôles with the ineradicable malignancy of the Vauriens in Elmer Rice's *Purilia*. Against these vile creatures, the Communist Paragonians, members of that unspotted élite, the party proper,* are engaged in ceaseless warfare. It is a kind of film-land, where all the types are prearranged and Goodness shines with perpetual brightness in its everlasting victory over Sin. Even prostitutes, being forbidden a trade-union, cannot flourish.

The secret police are known as the GPU. This is pronounced Gaypayooh – but only by foreigners. By Russians the term is never uttered. They may sometimes talk in whispers of the 'three-letter men'. But generally they prefer not to mention them at all. It became one of my favourite amusements to enunciate the fatal syllables in public places, in order to watch the tremor of surprise and apprehension elicited from everyone within hearing. On one occasion, it happened that my companion and I had inadvertently settled ourselves in a railway compartment reserved for the State couriers. The first of them to arrive naturally expostulated, and on seeing that we did not under-stand, pointed to the red tabs on his collar. 'Oh!' I said, compre-hending, 'you're a GPU man, are you?' At which even he, who was, started as though I had stuck a pin into his behind. He proved afterwards a Crichton of courtesy and assistance, even getting out of his bed at three in the morning to see us comfortably off the train.

But there is another and repulsive side to the picture. It must be remembered that the majority of those who enjoy the real power in Russia to-day are men who spent their early lives hunted from pillar to post by the Tsarist Okhrana; they were imprisoned; they were sent to Siberia; and the old spirit of suspicion and *revanche* still lives in them. Lenin and Trotsky were different. They too may have harboured these feelings. But their constructive energy outweighed them. To-day Russia is ruled by men of meaner mould, men whose twisted outlook infects the whole Soviet Union with a spirit of malice and suspicion. The whole air is poisoned by this evil. Every man lives in fear of his neighbour. Even the school-children are admonished, in the books from which they learn to read, to train themselves as spies in their own

* This body numbers only about two millions.

46

villages. I do not exaggerate. I talked with persons who had been recently summoned to cross-examination by the GPU and with persons who had recently been the victims of their midnight raids. I learned from first-hand of their cold chamber. I found that distinguished scholars whom I had wished to meet had 'disappeared'. I experienced personally their postal inquisition. Yet such information was acquired purely by chance in the most casual fashion. I was far too interested in the permanent Russia as it was and ever shall be, and was enjoying myself far too much there, to go nosing about in search of evil. Finally, after the Foreign Office had begged me to extend my stay, some unknown authority thought it better not to extend my visa. But then, I thought, in a country that celebrates its October Revolution in November, one should not be surprised that the Foreign Office cannot grant its own visas.

It is none of my purpose or business to censure the government of Russia and the priesthood of Materialism for maintaining a body of agents and police such as have always been found necessary to uphold the government and religion of that country. It may reasonably be assumed, from the historical evidence, that the Russian people and those who comprise the rest of the Union can only be governed by a despotism based on espionage, and that some such body must always be inherent in the Russian State. I am simply concerned to note the mental effect of such a system, whose rigour has been steadily increasing during the last five years, and whose brunt is borne mainly by the intellectual class, not necessarily on account of subversive activity, but simply because it is the intellectual class. It is they who are pilloried as the public enemies in theatrical trials; it is they whose every word and action is circumscribed by terror of the 'ideologically incorrect', whose avocations are supervised by semi-literate youths chosen from the party ranks, whose numbers are continually depleted to swell the Ural camps, and whose families suffer from cruel uncertainty. Such measures *may* be necessary; there may be enemies lurking in their midst; considering the difficulties under which they work, I should be surprised if there were not; these things again are not for me to affirm. But what I will affirm, and what I would beg the reader to share with me, is my contempt for those foreign intellectuals, and particularly those English ones, who, while finding in Russia the exemplar of social and economic planning, the climax of constructive politics, the paradise of YOUTH – in short, the model towards which all truly progressive persons must look for world redemption – are so intoxicated with admiration that they can spare no word of sympathy for their fellow-intellectuals, the men in Russia likest to themselves, for whom there is no place or hope under the system they so ardently covet. That this system would immediately, on attaining power, annihilate these miserable hypocrites, these hypnotees of every windblown theory, these bastards by uplift out of comfortable income, is the one satisfaction I could derive from its introduction into England. These Fabian ghosts, these liberal politicians, socialist editors and female peace-promoters, are the very people who anathematize without cease the tyranny of Hitler and his treatment of the German intellectual. But in Russia, where they are building not only socialism but Fordson tractors, the treatment of the intellectual does not matter: what counts freedom of thought or scholarship or individual creation beside the regeneration of the Great Unwashed? Very little, I dare say. And as little as these things count in that new world, just so little in this old one count those men whose inheritance they are and who renounce them for a mess of Bolshevist pottage. Let us rather have amongst us the red revolutionary who tries to seduce the troops and goes to prison for it, than these Russophil enthusiasts who acclaim the downfall of their own kind as the ultimate triumph of civilization.

Despite its cruelty, it is possible to argue that the old intellectual has deserved his fate, on account of his procrastination of soul and his slowness to ally himself with the new movement when it rose to power. But it is not only the old intellectual that falls under the ban of prevalent suspicion. The new – the inventors, planners, engineers, specialists, editors, architects, film-producers, and their like, all the prophets of the modern age – suffer from the same intolerable lack of freedom. In 1930 the campaign waged against them by the GPU reached such a pitch of fury that the authorities began to count the cost. Rykov produced figures to show how the Five-Year Plan was being hampered by this insensate policy. Until at last Stalin, who is a realist when the truth penetrates to him, called off the terror. The GPU, it was felt, was getting too big for its boots, with the result that administrative measures were taken to diminish its power. At the same time the salaries of the specialists were increased. These measures, it is evident, have since been reversed, and the terror re-started, in order to throw the blame for the failure of industrial projects on to specialists and foreigners. In any case the evil has been done, and it will take more than temporary half-measures and periods of leniency to undo it. Maurice Hindus asks: 'Can Russia make man as inventive, as creative, as constructive as a capitalist regime which lays at the feet of a Ford, a Rosenwald, a Woolworth, a Rockefeller, all the rewards that this earth can afford? This is the crux of the Communist challenge to Capitalism.'* In my opinion, this is not the crux; the national enthusiasm for the work in hand seemed, among nearly all those I met – even among such minor actors in the drama as archaeologists and museum curators – to provide its own reward. Where the crux lies now (Hindus wrote at the beginning of 1929) and where the whole system is threatened with breakdown, is in the terror of responsibility which has resulted from the preposterous campaign against the intellectual of the last five years. One of the foreign specialists in the country assured me that no sooner did he leave his office on one of those frequent trips to which his business called him, than his whole department absolutely ceased to function owing to the positive physical fear that now accompanies the taking of any decision whatsoever. Certainly, he said, there were other difficulties in the way of the Five-Year Plan; these difficulties, however, could be overcome. But in this doctrinal and actual proscription of the intellectual class he saw an insuperable obstacle to the Plan's success. And he prophesied that unless the psychological effects of the last three years were removed – unless, in fact, the class war should cease – the immense factories now in construction would either have to be placed under the management of foreigners or bankrupt the State by their total failure.

In concluding this very incomplete account of the psychological atmosphere in which the Russian intellectual moves and attempts to have his being, I would mention two last factors whose significance is by no means negligible and which serve, in some degree, to counterbalance the disabilities enumerated above. These are Russian nationalism and the paradox involved in the Russian worship of the machine.

* *Humanity Uprooted*, p. 82.

The Allied intervention in Russia after the war was over was the most futile, most stupidly conducted, and most subsequently harmful adventure that modern history can show. The Materialist philosophy had postulated at least a brand of internationalism, even if that brand meant only loyalty to international socialism. Owing to the intervention and the attitude that the greater part of the foreign Press has inherited from it, there has resulted in Russia a mental isolation from the rest of the world which was at first merely negative, but which is now crystallizing into a positive national egotism of the most pronounced kind. Owing to the general impossibility of travel, of corresponding with foreigners, or of obtaining foreign books, both the educated and the semi-educated Russian honestly believe that in themselves alone is concentrated all the really progressive thought of the whole world; in which belief they are confirmed by the agreement of the foreign enthusiasts. This state of affairs, though it hardly conduces to a profitable use of the world's intellectual resources, sustains the Russian intellectual in his present difficulties by placing him, at least in his own estimate, in the van of human affairs. His vanity, moreover, is flattered by the enormous curiosity which his country continues to arouse. It is not unpleasant to be regarded either as a bogy or as a saviour, but never as a nonentity, by virtue of one's very nationality. In addition, this mental chauvinism is reinforced by continual war scares. The reader may find it hard to believe, but I can assure him that I emerged into the streets of Moscow one morning to discover the hitherto sober trams adorned with posters calling on the wise citizen to buy his gas-mask before it was too late. Malicious rumour said that the army stocks having been found to be defective, it was now sought to unload these essential household requisites on the civil population at seven roubles apiece. Be this as it may, no Russian seemed to think the admonition absurd. 'What about the Intervention?' came the inevitable retort. But the real explanation is, that deep down in the hearts of the population endures an older patriotism than that inculcated by Materialism – a patriotism which must always be associated with 'Holy Russia'. I was told of a certain evening at the opera about a year before, when it happened that the principal singer had ended his part, the climax of the piece, with the words: 'GOD SHALL SAVE RUSSIA'. Whereupon the audience rose to its feet in the stress of its collective emotion and cheered away its feelings till the roof shook. It was not the voice of the old Christians that cheered, but the voice of Russia, of the Russia that has stood and shall stand till the world's end.

The paradox involved in the prevailing adoration of the machine lies in the fact that this cult should find its most devoted adherents in the most unmechanical country in the world. In the early days of this century, when Russian literature and Russian ballet swept over Western Europe, an idea grew up that the average Russian lived in a romantic Slav twilight, a cherry orchard of his own incapacity, where everything was excused by wringing of hands and a reference to temperament. Whether this ever was so, I doubt; it certainly is no longer. Russian incompetence of to-day is something cosmic, almost brutal, scorning excuse and seeking none. Should circumstances happen to obtrude it on the foreigner, and he happens to remark on it, this is considered an exhibition of bad form on both sides. During one week in the Ukraine, my companion and I experienced no less than five railway mishaps, in one of which – though fortunately it happened to the train in front – nineteen people were killed and over forty injured. Our eyebrows rose; finally, when the memory of this tragic accident had evaporated, we broke into uncontrollable laughter, and teased our guide till the poor man almost lost his faith in Progress. Was this the country of the Five-Year Plan, we asked, rejoicing in our ribald scepticism. But our inquiry lacked generosity. For those five mishaps explained precisely why Russia *is* the country of the Five-Year Plan.

On another occasion, when there was no boat waiting at the end of the journey, I discussed the question more calmly with an intelligent young Jew, who fully understood my detestation for the machine cult. He replied that to appreciate its meaning, I must realize what the Russians had gone through during the period of Civil War, the Intervention, and the great famine. When the first party of foreign tourists reached Leningrad in 1926, forty cars were needed to transport them to Tsarskoe-Selo. Forty pre-war cars were collected, and twenty-five more to act as a reserve. Even so, that party failed to arrive at Tsarskoe-Selo, which is about twenty miles away. He said that when, some time later, the first new cars that had been seen since the Revolution arrived from America, crowds followed them in the streets in order to touch them, as though a Cardinal were in progress with his ring outstretched.

He himself had been among them. And though he smiled at the memory, he still treasured the rapture he had experienced on seeing the first Russian-made lorry actually in movement. Then he went on to speak of his father, a poor nep-man, who had been taken away and never seen again after the reversal of the New Economic Policy. What a restricted life he had led, immersed in his family and his little business. Now here was his son, my friend, partaking in great events, mover in a great world force – though only a tourist guide. He was happy; I have never known anyone more content. Yet this youth, who had placed a sacramental finger on the first Ford car, was as impatient and active as myself in climbing about rickety scaffoldings in the biting cold to study the fourteenth-century frescoes of the Novgorod churches.

Those who see fit, like I did and still do, to loose their gibes at the Russian cult of the machine, should recall England of the 'forties and 'fifties. Let them read Macaulay's panegyric on his country's factories and railroads, couched in the language of an artist before the Parthenon; and having read, let them envy rather than despise a country that can still enjoy, in the twentieth century, that blend of assurance, novelty, and excitement which produced our own greatness in the nineteenth. We have had time to profit by the mistakes of our native materialists, our Victorian rationalists and economists. So perhaps will the Russians also profit when the time comes. Meanwhile the air is fresh and stimulating. The intelligentsia of Russia, both the survivors of the old and the children of the new ages, are victims of every disadvantage that dogmatism and jealousy can invent. But they escape, notwithstanding, the one supreme disadvantage that can afflict an intelligentsia – that of lethargy and complacence.

Last, and most precious of possessions, they have still their own country. They have escaped the desperate fate of the *émigrés*. I met one lady in Moscow, the avowed survivor of an old Russian family, who had recently married a foreigner, and, having obtained his nationality, was able to leave Russia and visit her friends of the old days in Paris and Riga. This lady has suffered much from the Bolsheviks – particularly during the last two or three years. But she assured me that after experience of the mental Bourbonism by which her old friends sustain their lingering hopes of a restoration, she was glad to think she still lived amid the fears and discomforts of Red Moscow. Because she was still a patriot, they ended by regarding her as a traitor. It is this patriotism which, above all else, makes the lives of educated men and women in Russia to-day still worth living.

III

THE RUSSIAN AESTHETIC

It has already been explained that the antagonism between Russia and the West is more than a conflict between principles of ownership and industrial morality. The word 'Bolshevism', divested of those flesh-creeping associations so gallantly propagated by the Tory imagination, represents not merely an economic system, but a fundamental way of thought inherent in the Russian species. To this way of thought has been added an abstract and all-embracing philosophy, which was consciously and sensibly elaborated by Lenin as an instrument of revolution and which bears the name of Dialectical Materialism.

The basic proposition of this creed is that everything perceptible to the senses is real and that everything real holds in itself the germ of organic change. Such a doctrine is in essence mystical, in that it opposes the physical or chemical explanations of change, and therefore of life, put forward by mechanistic thinkers. It thus contains a great and practical truth and is well adapted to its present function – that of a religion whose outward manifestations have already been shortly described. But behind it, and more important to the understanding of Bolshevism's uneasy relations with the outer world, is that immemorial Russian sentiment of a cosmic national egoism which demands the regeneration of the mass rather than of the individual and produces introspection on a sacrificial scale. At the end of the last century, when Russian literature began to receive the fulsome appreciation of Western Europe, the implications of this sentiment were hardly realized. As a theme for Dostoievsky it was superb. As a theme for translation into practical politics it was not taken seriously, save in the sphere of Central

Asia, where the fears of Anglo-Indian strategists were finally set at rest by the Anglo-Russian Convention of 1907. Our affinity with Russia was with Russian artists, not with the visionaries whom those artists portrayed. Now the visionaries have become men of affairs. Their kingdom is of this passing, empirical moment, and they would like to include us in it. To this desire we do not agree.

Meanwhile the aesthetic genius of the race, which once inspired us with admiration, still persists, and will flower again – though whether in the immediate or the distant future is hard to prophesy. The reader in search of observations on this genius may feel by now that to have been lured, as he has been, into a maze of political and economic considerations, is nothing less than an abuse of this confidence. If he feels thus, I must ask him to remember that modern Russian culture is still in its embryonic stage – if indeed it has yet been conceived at all; that the main interest it presents is rather as a field for prophecy than as one of completed achievement; that even the embryo is still obscured by the shell of a still mortifying past on which has fastened the inevitable mushroom-crop of contemporary plagiarisms; and that if the foreign observer is to discern any sign of original life, he must seek it primarily in a study of the individual educated Russian and of the evolution he is now undergoing. Of that evolution, of its attendant pains and mental voltage, I have attempted some slight account.

To the traveller whose first stay in a new country is limited to a month and a half, and whose view of it can therefore be only cursory, the most easily apprehensible clue to the cultural genius of its people is their native architecture. In the golden helmets and onions of the churches, in the towered Kremlins, baroque palaces, Empire streets, Revivalist museums, and ferrocrete tenements, the history and character of the Russian people stand revealed. I ask myself what future can come of so incongruous a past and present as this diverse architecture symbolizes. And I find answer in a permanent and impersonal factor, separable from time and politics, which, for architecture in particular, must play a decisive part in the eventual development of Bolshevist taste, and on which all prophecy in that respect must be based. This is the consistently unique tradition of colour and form displayed by all the visual arts in Russia from the eleventh century onward. Architecture, being the most functional of the arts, is essentially the art of the mass. And it is in architecture that this tradition must find life again or prove itself sterile and the culture of the Revolution sterile with it.

The Russian aesthetic is often called, by the glib classifiers of Western Europe, an Oriental one. Certainly it may have borrowed a motive here and there from the Moslems and Chinese. But its essential spirit is a purely Russian one. And such superficial resemblances as its architecture or painting may display to those of the East, derive from the fact that each has had the same aesthetic problems to overcome. These lie, as always, in the landscape. The Russian scene provides neither form, nor colour, nor shadows of rich texture. Apprehensible form, gay colour, and rich magnificence, must therefore be supplied by art. But the Russian landscape is not merely negative. Its illimitable spaces and skies, its limpid summer clouds, and its precise outline of detail against the winter snow, all determine the manner in which its deficiencies shall be filled by artifice. It holds a latent power which likes to speak in terms of the grandiose and monumental. No difficulty is too great, no scheme too vast, for this power to overcome. It plans cities on a scale commensurate with the huge rolling rivers by whose banks they stand. At the same time it employs the poetry of field and village and the peasant love of fantasy. Somehow, by some genius of the people, aesthetic order results: buildings are grouped as though on a perpetual backcloth; paintings are composed; the domestic arts are sane. The lyrical note is absent; there is none of that intimate perfection which reaches to the hidden places of the mind. All is open, fully apparent on a glance, blatant even; there is no hidden measure, no economy of means; yet all is within bounds and betrays a love of well-being which is not dissimilar from that of our own prosaic isle.

For his means of architectural expression the Russian has always borrowed the grammar of some foreign tongue and made it the basis of a language entirely his own. The earliest was Byzantine, which he enlarged, as he has enlarged everything, heightening the churches out of all recognition and replacing the neat lead vaults and saucer-domes of the Greeks with helmets and onions. These in time he gilded, coloured, and patterned; he grouped them at different levels; he multiplied them into forests or inflated them singly to overwhelming dimensions. At length came the Tartar invasion. Round these churches grew walls and towers of Tartar pattern, to form the local Kremlins and fortified monasteries.

Then the Italians arrived, only to become more Russian than the Russians themselves. Venetian Gothic, classical pillarettes and arcades, machicolated balconies, elaborate rustications, and a wealth of faience, all came to swell the Russian harmony, brought by foreigners whose privileged position and adoption of Russian aims made them the counterpart of the specialists employed under the Five-Year Plan to-day. Released from the severe canons of their own countries, they threw themselves headlong into the Russian love of fantasy; they planned and they built with an emphatic eccentricity which is rendered none the less coherent by virtue of its very size. Far from being stifled by this foreign invasion the native motives, the gay colours and ubiquitous bulbosities, flowered anew like plants in a freshly manured garden. The eleventh-century cathedral of St Sophia at Veliki Novgorod, built under the direct influence of the Greeks, has less of a specifically Russian character than the riotous and variegated churches of the sixteenth century, built after two centuries of Italian predominance, such as those of Yaroslavl or the Moscow suburbs.

With the reign of Peter the Great, whom Lenin acclaimed as a spiritual ancestor, a new and more systematic process of Westernization began. Churches and the dwellings of the nobility became baroque. Rastrelli, the architect of the Winter Palace and Tsarskoe-Selo, covered Russia with stupendous belfries, towering accretions of arches and pillars, but as intrinsically Russian as the monasteries in which they stand. At length followed the Empire style which the Russians, though still depending on Italians for their original designs, made particularly their own. The ruthless interminability of their official buildings grew till the eye cannot grasp them. A Government colour-wash was invented, a flat tawny yellow, against which pillars and ornament stand out in white. Towers persisted, great spikes such as that of the Leningrad Admiralty. At the same time a charming domestic architecture grew up, massive and low-storeyed, as though the domestic architects were still building with beams and tree-trunks for their pediments and pillars. The ornament is bold but never florid in the German way; the space is always so filled as to create either a pattern or an almost exaggeratedly individual piece of design; there is always meaning.

As the last century progressed the Russians, like ourselves, fell victims to the prevalent revivalism. The most grotesque and extraordinary structures resulted from the inspiration of so varied a past; the palaces of the Wittelsbachs or the inventions of Sir Gilbert Scott seem Palladian in their simplicity when compared with these neo-Slav town-halls and Kremlinesque museums. Yet the innate feeling of the Russian race for the monumental, its long practice in the ordering of fantasy, its general lack of aesthetic inhibitions and love of aesthetic plain-speaking, have invested even these buildings with a virtue unknown to their contemporaries in other countries, and one which, under the magic of snow, attains almost to charm. This, of course, was the 'preliminary period of imperialism'. Finally, as the Boer War broke, a blast of *art nouveau* swept in from the West, to destroy the last vestiges of sanity and taste; though in Russia even this style assumed a form so freakish and preposterous as to rescue it from the smug suburbanism of its manifestations elsewhere. Follows an interval of ten years. When the curtain lifts there appear Lenin's tomb and the graceless, but still monumental, concrete structures of the new industrial era.

In the provision of colour, the Russians have always relied for their effects on flat, cleanly outlined fields. The tints are emphatic, almost elementary; but the natural taste of the people, their skill in harmonizing and interweaving the various colour-fields into a balanced rhythm, together with the gigantic areas over which – in architecture at least – colour is employed, prevent the dominance of that shallow folkiness which so often strikes a false note in pictorial and photographic reproductions. In this province more than any, the Russians have retained their Byzantine inheritance, as the icons show; but here again they have added their own principle of frank appeal to the eye rather than the mind. How that principle, applied to architectural colour, survived into the nineteenth century, may be seen to-day in the streets of Leningrad, where the present authorities have not only preserved and renovated the old Government yellow (said to have been introduced by an Italian to remind him of the sun), but are also engaged in restoring the palaces of the nobility to their original gay state.

But colour in architecture must display something more than gaiety alone. Without richness of texture and material it becomes as tedious as an eternal pantomime. No people has understood this precept better than the Russians, and no country has ever been more naturally favoured with the means of acting on it. Gold leaf for their domes they have always been able to afford. In the eighteenth and nineteenth centuries they lavished bronze and brass upon their interiors and exteriors with the profusion that, in other countries, attaches to stucco. But the glory of Russia, from the builder's point of view, is her native quarries. The variety of her marbles and glistering labradors, her close-grained porphyries and granites, her stones of even finer texture – so fine that their appearance when polished is almost metallic – and her semi-precious varieties such as lapis and malachite, is inexhaustible, and even yet has scarcely been exploited. No shade, no texture that an architect can want, is lacking.

From conversations with various eminent architects in Moscow, I gathered that an official architectural policy was now in process of inception which will eventually withhold its approval from the drab functionalism of the present era, and allow free play once more to the native genius of the country. The outstanding example of this genius, as it can and will be translated into the language of Materialism, is the Lenin mausoleum by the architect Stchousev. It achieves its success, as I have already mentioned, not by any compromise with the past – for a more ruthless, more uncompromising monument has scarcely been erected since the Pyramids – but by the harmony of its colour with the old surroundings. Before visiting the chief architects of Moscow, I had inspected the plans submitted from all over the world for the new People's Palace, which is to occupy the site of the Cathedral 'of the late Redeemer' recently demolished by explosion. This site is in the very heart of Moscow, and closely adjoins the Kremlin. Apart from the utter poverty of inventive ability displayed throughout the competition, I was concerned to notice that the designs were one and all of that gasometer or packing-case type which may be suitable to factories and even to tenements, but must inevitably have disfigured the centre of Moscow beyond redemption if erected on this site – as, indeed, the Tsik skyscraper on the other side of the river has succeeded in doing already. On my stating my apprehensions to the architects

Stchousev and Grinberg, they both replied that, though the prizes would be allotted as promised, it had been decided to use none of the designs on account of those very reasons I had put forward; that the authorities were now casting about for ideas of a different character, being convinced that the ferrocrete style of the present was entirely unsuited to the dignity of a great capital or to the Russian scene; and that one of the chief considerations in the choice of a new design would be the use of colour and of the fine Ural stones, by which means alone could a specifically modern building – which the People's Palace must and ought to be – avoid discord with its incomparable setting. There are those Russians, and plenty of them, who are sufficiently antiquated in their modes of thought to regard such discord as the very purpose of their artistic efforts. These victims of Materialist novelty fail to distinguish between 'discord' and 'difference'. The first is mean. The second may be mean. But it can also imply a contrast between equals in artistic merit which provides the highest form of intellectual stimulus and contains in itself a ground of harmony between the opposing monuments. Let the new architecture be different by all means. But first let it solve the problem of differing like a man instead of like a naughty child. When, some years hence, the People's Palace is at last erected, it will be possible to see how far Bolshevist taste has progressed towards this solution, and how far the aesthetic genius of the country has begun to recover from the shocks of the last fifteen years.

IV
MOSCOW

Upon the intellectual and aesthetic background which presented itself to me, and which I have here tried to describe, I can now impose the incidents of a personal journey and the treasures it discovered.

The tourist goes to Spain to see Spain, or to Italy to see Italy; but to Russia he goes to see Bolshevism. I went to Russia to see Russia. When I say this, people find it obscure and want to know whether the Five-Year Plan will succeed, as though I were an engineer or an economist to tell them. The true intellectual, I know, is equal to such questions. Having never so much as glanced at a factory in his life, he commits himself to the Intourist Travel Agency, spends three weeks gaping at belt-conveyors invented in Detroit, and returns to proclaim the dawn of human happiness. Meanwhile his opposite, the die-hard, sits at home brooding madly over bugs in the butter. Behind this fog of enthusiasm and prejudice, the Russia that was, is, and shall be has disappeared from the world's view. Landscape, people, habits of mind and behaviour, buildings, works of art, the new with the old, but seen always in relation to one another – it is these, rather than the arid spectacle of Socialist construction, that should provide the traveller's entertainment.

But the average traveller does not want entertainment. He is out for heaven or hell, Right or Wrong, and determined to find one or the other. Personally, I found Bolshevism even less attractive than the political systems of other countries, chiefly because it is more obtrusive and more chauvinistic, and because it regards the foreign visitor either as a subject for propaganda of the most tedious kind, or, if that does not evoke serious respose, as a heretic to be regarded with profound suspicion. Nevertheless, taken all in all, Russia can give much to the traveller who wishes to enlarge his experience and knows how to do so by seeing things not as he wishes them to be, but as they are. Past, present, and future exhibit a continuous inter-action, rapid and conscious as a film, whose novelty and scale are equalled in no other part of the contemporary world. I found little time for dislikes. I could only observe and be thankful that such a spectacle had not been denied me.

The proverbial traveller's tale has owed its greatest marvels to the pomps of outlandish potentates, to rituals of ceremony and manners employed to express the power of the one over the many. To-day, the most fabulous of all tales relates the power of the many over the one, and the absence, equally visible, not merely of pomps and cere-monies, but of the amenities hitherto enjoyed throughout the world by those born to wealth or rewarded with it. Elsewhere, the social structure rises in pyramid form. In Russia the pyramid has been inverted: the apex, now reduced to the intelligentsia, has its nose in the ground; while on it balances precariously a crushing horde of manual workers, invested with the austere but not always undecorative symbols of their new sovereignty. This gigantic base, now turned uppermost in mid-air while the technicians below are seeking to build it a stable foundation, itself rises in two steps. The topmost is that of the politically conscious, the urban proletariat; the lower, that of the politically angry, the peasants. But the topmost, though a minority, has control. It provided the initial force that made the great experiment possible; from its ranks is recruited the Communist Party proper, which numbers about two millions and forms an aristocracy of faith. This faith, in the ultimate success of the experiment, inspires and then accomplishes the decisions of the executives, central, federated, and provincial. The organism that was born in the faith of one man – the faith of Lenin – lives by faith; for material success is not yet established. At present the faith is strong, and its fount is the city of Moscow.

Thither, as to a new Jerusalem, come pilgrims from all quarters of the earth – pilgrims to worship and pilgrims to inquire. It needs only a first walk in solitude through the streets to realize that here is a society whose like the world has never seen. Enter the Kitai Gorod, the business and administrative quarter of the town, at five o'clock on a winter afternoon, when the offices are emptying. Streets are crowded; trams packed, and hung outside with festoons of humanity. Everyone wears snow-boots; the feet move with quick, short steps over the slippery hummocks of frozen snow. Only when two groups start to cross the road from opposite sides and collide in the middle beneath the nose of an oncoming tram does general confusion result.

This busy throng is too busy. Impervious to human contact, it jostles along in silence and with eyes fixed on the pavement, as though each molecule were seeking to be at some destination before its fellow. The sauntering foreigner is aware of a strange isolation, a kind of negative hostility, emanating not from the individual, who is generally pleasant when addressed, but from the impersonal mass claiming power over him, the individual. Thus must the Christian have felt in Constantinople during the sixteenth century, when Islam was in the flush of arrogance. And this is the first thing in Russia that the foreigner must realize, if he is to see Russia truly: that unless he can subscribe not merely to a reasoned belief in its aims, but to an inspired faith in the doctrine and practice of Marxism as the one and only means of human redemption: unless he can find within himself not only an admiration for the courage of the Russian experiment and the hardships endured in the testing of it, but a conviction that he himself would willingly assist in the adoption of it by the rest of the world: then, be he never so filled with a love of humanity in general and of Russians in particular, he is nevertheless an enemy of Russia and, while in Russia, is among enemies of himself. Intellectuals of other countries have deceived themselves into believing that there can be a meeting-ground half-way. This there can never be. Sport, intellectual interests, humour, or the remarkable amiability induced by vodka may provide a sort of No-man's-land on to which both sides sally out to bury their tenets and discover themselves to be members of the same species. But the armistice must always be temporary. The countless books on Russia issued during the last two or three years give a contrary impression. But it is precisely because the tours on which their authors embarked are simply a prolongation of this kind of armistice over a given number of weeks that the impressions conveyed by this literature are so radically misleading.

Before visiting Russia I had no preconception of this state of affairs; in fact, the crazy propaganda circulated by Conservative politicians had disposed me to think that personal contact would soon overcome barriers which, I imagined, existed only in the Conservative imagination. To find that those barriers existed also in the form of a religious fanaticism which demands unquestioning allegiance, and that the jargon of the Revolution, so grotesque from a distance, was actually the rubric of a vital creed, came as something of a shock, and compelled a certain admiration – for who in these days can afford to despise those who know their own purpose and follow it? Furthermore, it exercised, mentally, a tonic effect. To me, an Englishman born to every advantage of inheritance and opportunity that the modern world can offer, it seemed highly refreshing to be regarded, suddenly, as the offspring of a poisonous fungus. This is the joy of Bolshevism, from the traveller's point of view: it washes away the layers of complacence that accumulate through residence in the civilized – perhaps too civilized – capitals of the West. At the same time it stirs a new and combative faith in the ultimate future of Western civilization and a resolution never to sacrifice individual integrity of thought in face of a hierarchy of Slav ideologues who, having found a Saviour in the West as we found one in the East, would plunge the world into a second Dark Ages that his gospel may be put to the test.

Though stimulating to the mind, it might, you would think, prove drab and depressing to the eye, this working-class state where all property, amenity, quality, and reward have been reduced to the level of the lowest common need. So it might, but for the permanent, historic Russia which bears the new organism like a puling infant at her breast. Mother and child are each other's foil. Beyond all this crying and spilling of industrial milk lies a grand country, loving things on a grand scale and adorned, first and foremost, with a grand capital. Not Rome nor Paris can rival the Red Square of Moscow in the beauty of its shape, colour, and proportions. While as for the Kremlin itself, whose triangle of crenellated rose-red walls forms a circuit of a mile and a half, whose nineteen various but all unprecedented towers guard the palaces, churches, and barracks that shelter both the treasures of the past and the Government of the present – the Kremlin, as a visible symbol of Russian history, lies altogether outside previous visual experience, so magnificent is the scale on which colour and fantasy are presented.

Away from the famous monuments, the shopping streets are at first sight somewhat depressing. But what they lack in ostentation they make up for by lacking also that semi-erotic, semi-snobbish vulgarity which is essential to the advertisement and sale of goods in the West. Those who knew the town twenty years ago recall with regret the dashing troikas, the trays of flashing jewels, and the shop-keepers bowing their clients to the threshold. To-day only the most important thoroughfares are even properly paved and asphalted. These have been scheduled as 'shock-streets', whose avowed purpose is to impress foreigners with an illusion of prosperity; for the Russians, despite their chauvinism, suffer from the vanity of a débutante on the international stage. The window displays, miraculously achieved out of the most utilitarian objects, are fairly cheerful; and the crowds of purchasers in the big stores certainly give no impression of positive indigence, though their faces wear a harassed look. The Torgsin shops are the great lure. These were formerly reserved for foreigners, but have now been opened to such Russians as can pay in foreign currency; while those who cannot, gape enviously outside the window. Since Russians have been permitted to receive money from friends or relations abroad, millions have poured into this organization to help the Government pay its foreign bills. These are the sole luxury shops, though the luxuries are only such as an English working-man would consider his due at the week-end holiday.

Except when I wanted a new pair of snow-boots or a tin of biscuits for a journey, my interest in the Torgsin establishments was confined to their antique departments. Fine icons, of course, were to be expected. But the domestic taste of the eighteenth and nineteenth centuries proved a complete surprise. Instead of the florid plagiarisms of French elegance produced by Germany and Central Europe in those periods, Russian furniture and objects of virtue display a person-ality and a sense of quality as distinct as those of contemporary England. There is a great love of splendour, of colour and gilt, and a great use of ormolu and bronze in conjunction with rare and unfamiliar woods, such as Karelian birch, and with those superb close-textured Ural stones of which malachite is at once the best known and least decorative. But a natural instinct for good design prevents this richness from degenerating into mere pretentiousness. Unfortunately, the management of Torgsin have the strangest idea of current market values, and are so determined that no one shall purchase a bargain that it is impossible to purchase anything at all. On the other hand, the second-hand bookshops, which abound, provide an inexhaustible hunting ground, where the lavish pre-war publications of the St Petersburg presses on Russian, Byzantine, and Central Asian art – unobtainable elsewhere – may be had for about a quarter of their market value. Rare English editions are sometimes found, and in one shop I came on a series of magnificent aquatints of St Petersburg by Patterson which were worth £20 to £30 each before the war and were now for sale at £1 : 10s.

Though it is impossible to meet Russians except on specific business, the Moscow day is pleasantly varied. The first difficulty is to determine what day it is, since the names of our seven-day week have fallen into abeyance. You use the date, and when it happens to be divisible by six, you realize that the day is a holiday and all business is suspended. If, however, you succeed in remembering when the Christian Sunday falls, you can visit the private markets. The larger of these is the Sukharevsky, generally known as the fleamarket – for obvious reasons. I went with the daughter of the Norwegian Minister, who displayed the prowess of a prize-fighter as we clawed our way through the mob. It was literally a question of clawing; for as the ground was of frozen snow, very uneven and covered with an inch of water, the upright position was made possible only by the absence of space in which to fall down. If, after one had hit two or three obstructionists sharply in the ribs, the crowd happened to part, one either lurched forward on to one's enemy's neck or fell grovelling at his feet. Half the crowd were vendors; the other half, purchasers. The vendors just stand, gazing into eternity, and holding their wares at shoulder level. And what wares! Torn camisoles, threadbare goloshes, soiled shirt collars were the subject of protracted negotiation. One man, as we passed, thrust a single spat at us. My companion told me she had heard – though she could not absolutely vouch for it – that on one occasion a vendor had been seen whose only commodity was the ace of spades. Eventually we reached a row of photographers' booths. Though we shrank, in the interests of hygiene, from the scarlet-and-gold Cossack uniforms which sitters were in the habit of donning, the backcloth of an Italian garden, with a Zeppelin hovering above the cypresses, was not to be resisted. We posed ourselves before an apparatus like a Heath Robinson incubator, and the result was one which those who have been privileged to see it will not forget.

From the Sukharevsky we proceeded to the Arbat market, a smaller enclosure, where the dispossessed classes sell such treasures, icons, lace, and jewellery, as they have still retained. Here we met the director of the Antique department of Torgsin, who was also, like us, in search of bargains. Thence we took a tram. This statement may seem uninteresting. But the action itself resembled the Eton wall-game. After several sorties had been repulsed with severe casualties, we boarded the driver's platform, where only pregnant women are allowed. A little old man then slammed the door on my companion's arm, who was thus pinned like Jane Douglas defending her king. 'Damn you,' I said in English, very angry, 'what do you want to do that to a woman for?' 'Now, now,' replied the offender, also in English, 'you mustn't talk like that, because I understand everything you say. Please forgive me. I am blind.' At this I was filled with remorse, and to make amends we saw the poor old man off the tram at his destination, and put him on his right road.

That evening I went to the Metropole, in bachelor company, to 'see life'. Unlike India, where one cannot appear outside one's bedroom after dark except in evening dress, this entailed changing back out of a bourgeois dinner-jacket into a proletarian lounge-suit. On arrival at the hotel, we proceeded into an apartment like the Crystal Palace. At intervals over this gigantic hall stood enormous lamp-posts bearing each a basket of two or three hundred naked electric-light bulbs. On a dais thirty Gipsies were exhibiting voice and leg with that artificial verve peculiar to the modern cabaret. In the middle of the floor a fountain was plashing monotonously into a piscine tenanted by gyrating carp, whose movements were obscured by a sudden movement of coloured lights. This coincided with the arrival of the dance band. In company with a few others I took the floor with a girl from the Leningrad ballet. Later we moved to the bar, a stupendous perspective of bottles (and cyclamens in bows) which even Shanghai might envy. Behind this the barmaids of Renoir and Toulouse-Lautrec had come to life, so perfect of their type, so bewitchingly plump and peachlike, so masterfully coy, that they might have been trained for the part by Mr Cochran, made up by Mr Clarkson, and posed by Professor Reinhardt.

It was half-past three before we emerged into the silence of the snow-covered streets and the biting cold air. Across the Opera square we descried an *izvostchik* asleep on his sledge. He sat huddled in his great blue coat, with icicles twinkling on his beard. We woke him, settled ourselves under the rug, turned the corner by the Historical Museum, and galloped on to the Red Square. Above Lenin's tomb the red flag floated from a green dome over the rose-red Kremlin walls, symbol of the sleeping Muscovites' dominion. But they were not all asleep. As we reached the river a party of five came swaying up a side-street, playing a balalaika and singing softly to the night as though it were June and they nightingales.

My weeks in Moscow passed like a single day, so great was their variety. The resident foreigners proved a source of unfailing hospitality and entertainment – journalists rushing out to get their despatches censored by the Foreign Office, diplomats engaged in a civilized existence of their own, disciples of Marx ploughing their way through Lenin's commentaries on the Master, together with such isolated phenomena as Mr Chattopadaya, brother to Mrs Sarojini Naidu, complaining of the leniency displayed by the secret police towards its, and his, political enemies, or Albert Coates in his suite at the Metropole, lying in bed beneath a rubber-tree and offering all comers a glass of Caucasian wine. Plays, operas, concerts, and ballets filled the evenings; I came to know the subterranean labyrinths of the Bolshoy Theatre, with their refreshment counters for tea and cakes, as well as those of the Queen's Hall. In the audiences, the women wore homemade frocks of a pattern two years old, over which, if pretending to elegance, they draped silk shawls. Among the men, the high boots and blouses that were the rule three years ago had been displaced by nondescript lounge-suits of dungaree cut and hue and by collar and tie.

The proletariat is becoming bourgeois – but how bourgeois I realized only on learning that the sole industrial undertaking of the Five-Year Plan whose output is so far up to schedule is the Leningrad spat factory.

One Saturday night we drove to the Dragomilovsky Church in the suburbs, where a crowd of two thousand had assembled to hear the singing. As an antidote, next day I sought the Anti-God Museum, where photographs of Sir Henri Deterding, the Pope, and an Oxford friend cranking up a lorry during the General Strike, typified the forces of reaction. I visited the Kremlin, saw the superb collection of Elizabethan and Jacobean silver, and an English coach of 1625 covered with velvet, the vestments brought from Constantinople by the Metropolitan Photios in 1414, the ivory throne that came from Italy with Sophia Palaeologina when she espoused the Tsar Ivan III in 1467, the countless copes of Persian and Broussa velvets, and such masterpieces of Royal taste in the twentieth century as a platinum train in an Easter egg to commemorate the opening of the Trans-Siberian Railway, or a female leg in a high-heeled shoe carved out of agate and encircled with a diamond garter. I made my way through the churches and palaces, was shown the tiny apartments, already familiar from their enlarged version on the stage, where Boris Godunov played with his children, and at length, as I passed between the sentries on my way out, all but collided with Kalinin, the President of the whole Union of Soviet Socialist Republics.

Finally, on my last morning in Moscow, a party assembled at the State Bank to see the Crown Jewels. Elaborate precautions were taken as we marched through the vaults. Our coats were left behind. An armed guard tramped before and behind. Eventually we reached a small room where the whole of the imperial regalia lay flashing in glass wall-cases or set out, for personal touch, on a table covered with a green cloth. Fine jewels have always excited me. But to see the crown of Catherine, a trellised bulb set with five thousand matched diamonds, supported by buttresses of matched pearls as big in diameter as a cigarette, and surmounted by a ruby the size of a pigeon's egg – to see this object, which cost £10,400,000, within an inch of my nose, almost deprived me of speech. On recovering, I turned to the table and began fingering the insignia of the Order of St Andrew, of which the collar, composed of platinum and small diamonds and made in Genoa in 1776, was of exquisite design and workmanship. The guide was droning monotonously in a corner; the guard outside continued to stroke its revolvers; when suddenly the lights fused and I found myself standing in total darkness with the Andreyev collar in my hand. I dropped it like a hot cinder. Angry voices sounded outside, the officials from the Foreign Office set up a clucking of disturbed hens, and a roar of laughter went up from the visitors. After a quarter of an hour, during which I was much tempted to slip an ear-ring or two into somebody else's pocket, the lights went on again. So demoralized by this time were the nerves of our guards and guides that, when I left before the others, to keep another appointment, I was allowed to wander alone and at will through vaults filled with sacks of money, till at last, unchallenged and unnoticed, I found my way out into the street.

V

LENINGRAD

The difference between Moscow and Leningrad is the difference in visible terms between the historic alternatives that have always confronted the Russian State: sufficiency from within or attraction from without. At present the balance is in favour of the former, and Moscow is again the capital. Leningrad stands as a memorial to the dominion of Western ideas in Russia during the eighteenth and nineteenth centuries and to a last efflorescence of Anglophil liberalism, whose hope centred in the Duma and which failed, when the autocracy evaporated in 1917, to establish democracy in its stead. This failure resulted in the establishment of a new autocracy, sustained by a new orthodoxy and a new phase of mental isolation. While the Kremlin at Moscow exhales a paradoxical sympathy with this renewal of old tradition, Leningrad seems out of joint with Bolshevism and wears a sad air, as though mourning for an interlude which is past. Yet the town remains the most perfectly planned and most impressively classical city in Europe, and its beauty is a supreme monument to the individual genius of the Russian aesthetic.

It is customary to imagine the 'Palmyra of the North' as a purely Western city, planned in straight lines and executed in a variety of classical styles. Certainly the streets are mostly straight and the architectural styles borrowed from those of contemporary Europe. But the Kremlin of Moscow was built largely by Italians, and is yet the very essence of Russian imagination. Nor is Leningrad any less so. Since Russians demand of architecture colour, ornament, and, above all, a prodigious scale, Western forms are made to serve these ends, heightened by a kind of emphatic eccentricity which is often fantastic in the manner of John Martin or Rex Whistler, but never quaint in the manner of Nuremberg. Thus Leningrad is a city not of architectural units but of architectural landscapes, and landscapes which, if so hackneyed a distinction may be applied to so unusual a subject, are romantic rather than formal, despite their groves of pillars and boscage of applied trophies. The merit of this immense ostentation is its patent honesty. The national megalomania, combined with a sure instinct for bold, frank design, leaves no room for pretty vulgarity. Its expression may be conscious, and have become, in latter years, allusive. But it is never inhibited, like the Milan railway station. To walk about the streets of Leningrad is to enjoy more good building, more general and more immediately apprehensible, than is provided by any of the world's large capitals.

I cannot claim that my walks were more than casual, or that I devoted any particular attention to any particular building. Tired of sight-seeing in Moscow, I looked forward to a few days' coma. Actually, the interlude proved too interesting to be comatose. It began with the most unpredictable event: the train arrived, not of course on time, but before it. Consequently, the car from the Consulate had not yet reached the station. We had recourse to an antique vehicle which, though petrol-driven, stank like a growler and moved more slowly than any horse. Neither of us knew the address of the Consulate; but the driver thought he did, and dumped us on the threshold of a decayed hostelry called the Hotel d'Angleterre. A passer-by then said our destination was opposite the Kazan Cathedral in the Nevsky Prospect. So thither we returned, and had the pleasure of paying £4 for this circuitous adventure. The block where His Majesty's representative lives is owned by the Finnish Government – a tolerable landlord, he said. The windows look on to the cathedral, built in 1801, whose curving colonnades produce a miniature imitation of St Peter's piazza.

A little way below the Consulate, where the River Moika crosses the Nevsky Prospect – or Prospect of the 25th of October, as it is now called, in celebration of the 'November' Revolution – stands the Stroganov Palace, designed by Rastrelli in 1752, whose baroque façade displays white pillars on a lilac background. At the opposite corner, across the river, I noticed another building of a rich delphinium blue, also picked out in white. These colours have lately been restored by the present municipal authorities. The commonest of them, and not the least attractive, is the rich matt tawny yellow formerly employed on all the Government buildings and lately renovated to its original freshness. The Kremlin, I had thought, must always be the climax of Russian invention. But in Sakharov's Admiralty the voice of the Kremlin spoke again, in 1823. This interminable building is more than a quarter of a mile in length, and diversified with six porticoes, two of twelve pillars each upholding highly decorated pediments, and four of six. In the middle is a massive archway, almost horseshoe in appearance, flanked by two groups on pedestals of women upholding globes, and surmounted by a tower 229 feet high. This fantastic projection takes the form of a slender gilt spike, supported on a dome and upholding a ship of appreciable size in full sail. The dome rises from a square Empire colonnade, on top of which stand a row of statues. All the pillars, the panels of ornament and friezes, the rustications of the base, the keystones of the windows, and the triglyphs of the cornices stand forth in white against this gorgeous autumn yellow. No less enormous, and in the same colour, are the buildings of the General Staff, placed in a shallow curve opposite the Winter Palace; these have no tower, but are broken by a triumphal arch on which the ornament is in bronze. Across the huge Uritzky Square, where the massacre of 1905 took place, the Winter Palace itself appears as though on a distant horizon. This, again, was built by Rastrelli, but is now a drab brown. I suspect he intended it to be pink.

With the exception of the cathedral of Esztergom in Hungary, that of St Isaac in Leningrad affords the sole example of the Empire style used for ecclesiastical purposes on the grandest scale. Designed by Montferrand in 1817, its form is that of a cube whose four sides have each a portico. The pillars of these porticoes are monoliths of pink Olonetz granite, rising from bronze bases and terminating in bronze Corinthian capitals. The stone is grey, but a plain course of granite runs round the base on a level with the bottom of the pillars. At each corner of the parapet massive groups of bronze angels uphold stupendous torches, while gilt cupolas, supported on clusters of pink pillars, rise in pairs behind the east and west pediments. Above all towers the central dome, 330 feet high, resting on a tall drum encircled by a colonnade and topped by a ring of statues. Though the detail is of the most rigid classical kind, severe to the point of soullessness, the whole effect is one of extreme magnificence, which only Russia could have produced.

Sated with these overpowering monuments, we sought refuge in the Hermitage, which must contain more square miles, worse hung, of Domenichino and his like, than any gallery in the world. The Van Eyck 'Annunciation', the Botticelli 'Adoration', the Rembrandt of a 'Polish Nobleman', the Velazquez of 'Innocent III', and the 'Wharton' Van Dyck are all gone, and have not yet, so far as I know, reappeared on Mr Mellon's walls. But there are still forty Rembrandts left, which is enough for anyone, and was more than enough for me by the time I had tottered through a league or two of Dutch interiors and turned with loathing from two false Grecos. Tucked away in a corner I found a curious little English gallery, where mediocre pictures by Morland, Wright of Derby, Lawrence, Raeburn, and Romney are interspersed with decaying sideboards and broken chairs. These give a poor idea of our culture in the early imperialist period. But I must say, in all justice, that here were none of those absurd notices which disfigure the French collection in Moscow.

Later in the day, accompanied by Professor Waldhauer and an armed guard, we saw the famous collection of early gold ornaments, which has no rival in any museum. Part are Scythian, huge lobsterish beasts a foot long, whose design resembles nothing produced by any other race and whose material is almost butterlike in its glowing softness. Part have an Iranian look, typified in bicephalous bracelets and familiar from our own Oxus treasure. And part are Greek, from the Chersonese, of most exquisite workmanship and design. From these we proceeded to the collection of antique statuary, which has been much enriched from former private collections. Professor Waldhauer begged us to notice a life-like portrait bust of a Roman Jewess.

The following day we forsook art for history, starting with the Square of the Victims of the Revolution, a former parade ground known as the Champ de Mars, in whose midst a granite quadrilateral surrounds the common grave of 180 Red heroes. On the granite is carved an inscription written by Lunacharsky in ballad Russian and said to be very moving. Hence we drove to the old British Embassy, now 'the Institute of Political and Communistic Education in the name of Krupskaya'.

Here, among the tattered brocades, I caused consternation by mistaking a picture of Kalinin, the President of the Union, for one of Trotsky, and asking, in a voice of assumed indignation, how they dared expose such an object to their pupils. Crossing the Neva, we reached a small wooden church, built by Peter the Great, where a service was in progress attended by some fifty persons. Adjoining, our attention was pointed to the most hideous yellow brick structure, in a garden, the palace of the ballerina Kzeczinska, mistress to the Tsar. This house aroused popular fury at the time of the Revolution, and it was here that Lenin was conducted from the station after his famous journey in the sealed train, and took up his headquarters. After passing a mosque with a fluted dome of blue tiles in the style of Samarcand, and looking in at the mansion of a former rubber merchant, now a rest-house, where a multitude of deserving workers were playing chess beneath a somewhat fortuitous bust of the Saviour, we came to the fortress of Peter and Paul.

This renowned symbol of Tsarist tyranny, so glibly coupled with the adjective grim, has externally the mellow appearance of an old colonial fort, while, inside, it resembles the courtyard of a country brewery. An old-fashioned, rather dilapidated building, which it is forbidden to approach with a camera, is the Mint of the Soviet Union. Inside the cathedral, whose gilt spire, 390 feet high, is one of the most remarkable objects in Russia, are the imperial tombs; outside, a blue pavilion houses a carved boat known as the grandfather of the Russian fleet – a thing of sorry posterity in this generation. Behind the Mint, a sort of rambling farmhouse contains the famous prisons, now inhabited by realistic wax models in attitudes of profound despair. I could not help inquiring when it would be possible to visit the 'cold chambers' of the present GPU under similar conditions. Not that I supposed that Russia could, can, or ever will be governed without institutions of this kind. But the hypocrisy of thus rigging out the evils of the past because they were committed in the name of a crown instead of a hammer was too irritating to be borne in silence. Thereafter our guide, a man of intelligence, ceased his futile rote of moral tales.

My companion had had a cousin attached to the old Embassy, who died in 1916 and lies buried in the Lutheran cemetery on the Vassily Island. Since he was anxious to identify the grave and see what condition it was in, we drove to this desolate necropolis lying in a semi-built district of tenement houses. While the others sought information, I wandered alone through a forest of graves covered with snow and overhung with dank trees. Now and then some old lady in black would trudge slowly past, carrying a wreath of mauve flowers. Amid the lavish mausoleums of the past, with all their urns and pillars and funerary vulgarity, the new graves told of a simpler, harder age. A heap of fresh cut fir branches, or a wooden stele painted scarlet and marked with the Soviet star – these were the memorials of the present, and told also of the virtues of their age. They reminded me of soldiers' graves and of the fact, too easily forgotten, that every Russian to-day is engaged in a battle for soul and body whose like we in Western Europe can hardly conceive.

The streets and squares of Leningrad have not only good architecture, but poignant associations. In them were achieved the twin Revolutions of March and October. The ideas which produced that upheaval germinated in the previous century. But the history of its actual events dates from the night of 16 December by the Old Style, 1916, when the deputy Purishkevitch, drunk with his own heroism, proclaimed to a bewildered policeman that Rasputin was dead and Russia saved.

Fifteen years and a fortnight later I was walking by the side of the narrow, frozen River Moika, through the Mayfair of old St Petersburg. 'Our house on the Moika,' writes Prince Yusupov in his account of the affair, 'was chosen as the place where our project was to be carried out.' And unchanged the house on the Moika still stands, a long perspective of yellow stucco with the ornament picked out in white. Above the entrance a coat-of-arms on the attic storey recalls the magnificence of the family of Yusupov-Sumarokov-Elston. But below this, two placards, bearing white letters on a red ground, inform the passer-by that here may now be found the Club for Scientific Workers and the Club for the Trade Union of Educationalists. The afternoon was sad and dark. Nevertheless, I experienced, as always in Russia, that incommunicable exhilaration associated with a first sight of scenes often and untruthfully imagined.

It happened that my guide was a member of one of the clubs now contained in the palace, and he thought that, though foreigners were not usually admitted, an exception would be made in my case. A fat comrade, golden-haired and rubicund, greeted us with effusion, then galloped up the main staircase to switch on the several hundred lights of the central chandelier. Dazzled by the blaze, we proceeded to the state rooms on the first floor, through double doors of mahogany set with ormolu rosettes, through room after room, each richer than the last, furnished in the manner of palaces with silk hangings and gilt cupids, with tables of agate and porphyry, aubusson settees and chairs of Spanish leather, and mantelpieces of porcelain and malachite. Through the small and the big ballrooms we went, through the picture gallery, and down into the miniature theatre, a rococo auditorium about fifty feet long, lined with three tiers of boxes. Prince Yusupov himself could not have exhibited more pride in his surroundings than did our guide, who begged us to note how the precious chairs were kept in dust-sheets. On reaching the theatre he jumped on the stage and let down a drop-curtain depicting the Yusupov country house as though it were his own.

Only two or three of the state rooms were occupied. In one of them we found an artist who had just returned from a scientific expedition to Kamchatka and was hanging a series of landscapes illustrating the behaviour of volcanoes in those parts. Since he looked under-fed, I asked if he hoped to sell many. 'Certainly not,' he replied. 'The workers must not be deprived of culture.' Half of the pictures would go to the institute that had financed the expedition; the other half would remain his. Then his dream was to hold an exhibition abroad.

On returning to the ground floor, a series of passages led us to the winter garden, where the Scientific Workers and the Trade Union of Educationalists were eating soup. Beyond this was a billiard-room copied from the Alhambra, and beyond that the apartments of old Prince Yusupov, where they had recently discovered a safe under the floor. I asked about the great hoard of treasure that had been found walled up in the palace three or four years ago, and our guide replied that the whole place was honeycombed with secret passages. In fact, only the other day a workman had lurched into the building drunk and said he could show them some new ones, which he himself had built.

But next day, when he returned sober, he had been unable to find them after all.

The way now led through a series of locked doors and empty rooms, till suddenly we found ourselves in a small octagon about ten feet across and eight feet high. Each of the eight sides consisted of a wooden door painted white and inset with a broad panel of plate glass, behind which was a curtain of frilled blue silk. One door led into a still smaller bathroom, beyond which was a no less diminutive bedroom. The walls of both these sinister little apartments were thickly padded. A second door revealed a plain square room with two windows looking out on the Moika. This was now used as a military class-room; there were posters on the walls of tactical exercises, first-aid, and how to affix your gas-mask; a rifle on a stand was pointing into the street. A third door opened on to a cavern of darkness. But the other doors gave access to blank walls only, so that, once in the octagon, it was a matter of some minutes to find which door provided a way out of it. In addition, I had noticed that one of the previous doors leading to the octagon had had to be carefully propped open, as it was self-locking.

These were Prince Yusupov's private apartments, and here came, on the night of 16 December, 1916, the Grand Duke Dmitri Pavlovitch, Purishkevitch, and Dr Lazovert. The headquarters of the conspiracy, so to speak, were in the room looking out on to the Moika. Here Dr Lazovert placed crystals of cyanide of potassium in the chocolate cakes and the wine-glasses. But the scene of action was across the octagon in that black void. Peering in, I saw a tiny spiral staircase, barely two feet wide. The guide asked me not to descend, as it was slippery and dangerous. But I persisted, and found a cellar divided by an arch and covered in six inches of water; for a thaw had set in. From high up in the wall came a glimmer of daylight. According to Prince Yusupov, this dank apartment 'had originally formed part of the wine cellar. In day time it was a rather dark and gloomy chamber, with a granite floor, walls faced with grey stone, and a low vaulted ceiling ... I ordered some antique furniture to be brought down from the storeroom.' A large fire was lit. From the roof hung lanterns with coloured glass panes. Purishkevitch has also left an account of the proceedings. 'La chambre était méconnaissable. Je l'ai vue pendant les travaux et je fus frappé par cette transformation complète d'une cave qui en un si bref délai était devenue une élégante bonbonnière.'

Prince Yusupov, borrowing the Grand Duke's car, went to fetch Rasputin and arrived back with his guest about one o'clock. 'The prospect of inviting a man to my house with the intention of killing him horrified me,' observes the Prince in his book. 'I could not contemplate without a shudder the part which I should be called upon to play – that of a host encompassing the death of his guest.' A nasty complacency lurks beneath these protestations. But the conspirators had worked on one another's emotions till they had reached the state of Messianic exaltation which accounts for most things in Russian history. All Russians are saviours by vocation. These three, thinking to deliver the imperial throne of an unholy counsellor, merely precipitated the extinction of all they hoped to rescue.

On entering the house, host and guest crossed the octagon and descended by the spiral staircase to the cellar. There Rasputin ate the cakes and drank out of the poisoned glasses, while his host played the guitar and sang. Upstairs, in 'the study', Grand Duke and deputy waited. At length the Prince rushed in with the news that the poison would not work. After some discussion, he took a revolver and returned to the cellar. The others followed and stood listening at the top of the stair. A report was heard and a thud. The Prince emerged; the deed was done.

After an interval he returned to look at the body. As he did so the face began to twitch and the eyes opened. Suddenly Rasputin jumped to his feet and seized the youth by the throat. Yusupov struggled, got away, and fled up the stairs, while the monk could be heard crawling up them too on all-fours. But instead of making for the octagon, Rasputin escaped by a door off the staircase into the courtyard of the palace. Purishkevitch ran out after him, to see the enormous figure lurching across the snow. 'Felix, Felix,' Rasputin was shouting, 'I shall tell the Tsarina.'* Purishkevitch shot twice and the figure collapsed. Meanwhile the Prince was being sick in the bathroom. On learning that Purishkevitch had succeeded after all, he seized a loaded stick and fell

---

* The authenticity of this exclamation, as recorded by Purishkevitch, is doubted by those familiar with Russian parlance. Rasputin, or anyone else for that matter, would normally have referred to the Empress as 'Elizaveta Feodorovna'.

to battering the corpse in a savage frenzy. Purishkevitch was much moved by this spectacle. Then the police arrived, and they shot one of the best dogs to give colour to the bloodstains and the other shots. The dog's grave, said the guide, was still in the garden. We looked out. But the garden had been flooded, to make a skating-rink for the leisure of Scientific Workers and the Trade Union of Educationalists.

VI

VELIKI NOVGOROD

Beneath the organized frenzy of Bolshevist Russia to be up and doing, the hospitable, easy-going country described by pre-war travellers is no longer recognizable. Yet here and there, in places which have escaped the industrial and political tornado of the last fifteen years, the romance of 'Holy Russia' lingers on. Such a place, it seemed to me, was Novgorod. And its romance, even to one engrossed with the tradition of Constantinople, was not wholly archaic or irrelevant to the present. For Russian civilization was originally Byzantine; and from that source, given the conditions of the modern world, Bolshevism is the legitimate descendant.

It was still dark at seven o'clock in the morning, and the air biting cold, as the train steamed out on its way to Pskov, leaving me behind on Novgorod platform. When the sledge was found, we drove at a gallop through the sleeping streets, bounding over holes and ditches, till a black line of crenellations cut across the dimly paling sky and marked the Kremlin wall. An arch gave us entrance. Still at a gallop, we swerved to the right, clattered through a narrow tunnel, and drew up at the old Archbishop's Palace, now a rest-home for scientists. Opposite, I recognized the silhouette of St Sophia. Inside, a lamp-lit room awaited us, furnished magnificently with a late Empire suite of Karelian birch mounted in ormolu and upholstered in silk brocade of white floral pattern on a crimson ground. The lavatory was clean; there was hot water to shave with; I found a female comrade cleaning her teeth over the wash-basin. For breakfast came coffee boiled with milk and sugar, brown bread of the Hovis type, fresh butter, and cold cabbage-pie. As the dawn crept in at the windows we could see the leaden onions and golden helmet of St Sophia, static and impervious behind a curtain of gently falling snowflakes. Against the creamy walls of the cathedral, a line of low bare trees stood out from the dead white snow with feathery precision, like the skeletons of pressed ferns. As in the twentieth century, so it must have looked in the eleventh. I was reminded of the white paint and formal architectural backgrounds that appear in icons of the Novgorod school; and was saying so to my guide when the proprietress came in with registration forms. My passport? I had left it behind. She pretended consternation, and, foreseeing an argument, I gave her my English driver's licence and went out for a walk, leaving the matter to resolve itself, which it did.

Veliki Novgorod is so called to distinguish it from the *parvenu* Nijni Novgorod. In the old days, so revered was this capital of one of the first Russian city-states that schoolboys were taught to say 'Gaspadeen Veliki Novgorod – Sir Great Novgorod'. Towns in Russia that date from before the Tartar invasion of the thirteenth century and retain anything of their original character are comparatively few. Novgorod is the chief of them and resembles in size and charm an English cathedral city such as Salisbury, the centre of a large agricultural district and built round a Kremlin instead of a close. As a respite from the nervous tension of Moscow and Leningrad, from that scarifying political excursion on which the whole nation is embarked and whose whither no passenger can foresee, the memory of those two days spent in climbing about the oldest churches in Russia stand out like a month's holiday in a year of worry. When I asked our boy sledge-driver which of the two Communist youth organizations he belonged to, the Komsomols (scouts) or the Pioneers, and he replied with a contemptuous 'Neither!' my content overflowed. I had found a being indifferent to his own regeneration, and the world seemed real again. The officials responsible for the preservation of the monuments and paintings were evidently delighted that a foreigner should witness the scholarly care bestowed on them. So few bothered to come – only about two or three a year. Let me only say what I wanted to see and facilities would be granted. It was a pleasant change from the endless restrictions and formalities that harass the traveller elsewhere.

My first visit was to St Sophia, built between 1045 and 1052 in a style derived from Constantinople, but greatly heightened, and strengthened with massive piers in place of the slender pillars habitually used by the Greeks. The frescoes of the interior were the work of a century later, but have been twice restored, in 1838 and 1893, so that nothing remains in its original state but a dull fragment of Constantine and Helena. The most famous ornaments of the church are its bronze doors, presumably dating from the twelfth century. One pair, damascened and much polished, resemble the Byzantine doors of this date; though the double crosses rising from floriated bases seem to show Armenian influence. The other pair, said to have been brought from Kherson, display a series of reliefs whose iconography and style are of German inspiration. These have Latin inscriptions. My attention was also pointed to the walls of the bema, which are decorated with patterns of coloured stone and glass faience arranged in the fashion of *opus alexandrinum*. Built into the walls have been discovered a number of large clay jars, which were placed there to give resonance to the chanting.

A dark winding staircase and a succession of seven locked doors, each of which necessitated a great deal of fumbling, argument, and lighting of tapers, led to the Treasury, whose chief objects were brought out of their glass cases for me to examine. The first was a domed tabernacle of silver-gilt, eighteen inches high without its cross, which was added in the seventeenth century. The dome is supported on six nielloed pillars. Each of the six arches thus formed is closed by double doors, which bear reliefs of the twelve apostles. The fine workmanship of these reliefs displays a close Byzantine influence; likewise that of the six medallions on the dome. But the inscriptions, though Greek, are illiterate; and the filigree panels above the doors have an Oriental character, seemingly Armenian or Caucasian. Next followed a couple of massive silver-gilt vases, about ten inches high, and decorated with figures and vine arabesques in coarser relief. These, according to the curator, are the earliest examples of purely Russian metalwork in existence, and were made at Novgorod in the twelfth century under Greek influence. Round the rim of each runs a Biblical quotation; round the base, a legend ascribing the ownership of one vase to 'Petrov and his wife Barbara', and of the other to 'Petrov and his wife Mary'. The lettering is Slavonic. A fine Byzantine cross, about two feet high

and plated with silver-gilt worked in chevron pattern, was also produced. The medallions on the three arms and at their junction were
added in the seventeenth century and probably replaced others of
enamel. Finally came an ivory casket of the same date and style, and
exhibiting the same borders of rosettes and panels of dancing cupids
as the Veroli casket in the South Kensington Museum. I had begun to
speculate as to whether this might not have influenced the design of
the vases just described, when my notice was drawn to a huge gold lock,
bearing the cipher of a certain Grand Duke of Holstein. This Grand
Duke owed his throne to the Empress Elizabeth; and it is supposed that
at a meeting that took place between them in Finland he presented it
to her, and that she left it at Novgorod on her way back to the capital.
Thus it did not find its place among the other Byzantine treasures of
the cathedral till the middle of the eighteenth century.

Scattered about the villages outside Novgorod are a series of small
churches of the twelfth to the fourteenth centuries. These are humbler
in style and decoration than their contemporaries in the Kiev and
Vladimir districts – for Novgorod was only a merchant republic. But
their box-like severity, the preponderance of height over their other
dimensions, and their massive wall surfaces pierced by the fewest and
smallest of windows, express their function as outposts of culture and
civilization in the hostile north and give them an individual charm and
interest. The best known of them is that of the Saviour at Nereditsa,
built in 1198 and preserving unrestored its frescoes of the same date.

To Nereditsa, therefore, which is five versts from Novgorod, I said
I must go. The sledge was waiting; but where Nereditsa was our
youthful driver could not say. A map was found, and with its aid we
made our way through the town, skidded down a steep bank, and found
ourselves on the ice of the great River Volhov, among a colony of
stranded paddle steamers. A wind cold as cutting steel stung the grey
horse to a fresh gallop. We skimmed along the ice as though it had been
the track at Brooklands, crouching sideways under the rug with our
backs to the driving snow. In the opposite direction came other sledges,
of heavier build, trailing in from the surrounding villages a-heap with
cabbages and straw. At one point a line of stone piers forty feet high
crossed the river, gaunt and threatening in the snowscape. This was
the new railway bridge – though as yet there was neither railway nor

bridge. On the farther bank, a cluster of monastery domes broke the verge of a distant forest which had once, said the driver, been the estate of the Duchess Orlova. At length the church itself came in view, perched on a knoll and overtopped by an immense bulbosity. By its side stood a little bell-tower with conical roof. We struck uphill from the river, over the fields, and came to a village whose wooden houses were hung with fishing-nets and lobster-pots. Here we found the keeper of the church, an old fellow in a grey beard, who said that he and the other inhabitants of Nereditsa lived on an island like the English. Inside the church, scaffolding led right up into the cupola. If this failed to improve the architectural effect, it did at least enable the visitor to examine this most famous of the old Russian fresco-cycles at close quarters and in such comfort as the cold permitted. This was a pleasant change from the neck-breaking, hour-long scrutinies to which I have grown accustomed in the monasteries of Mount Athos. The character of the paintings resembled that of the 'popular' school which obtained in the Levant and South Italy up till the thirteenth century. It was curious to think that these frescoes, and I who was regarding them, so to speak, through Levantine eyes, were now little more than a hundred miles from the Gulf of Finland.

That evening my guide and I went to an entertainment. There was a dance between a peasant girl and her beau from the town, a flautist, and an ideological dialogue during which a professor of comic aspect raised a general laugh by saying that science had nothing to do with politics. For the next day we had planned a longer expedition; and when morning came, instead of the old grey, a dark brown mare stood harnessed to the sledge. This was a new purchase of the proprietress, who was in a great fuss, crooning 'Princessa! Princessa!' as she stroked the creature's nose, and admonishing the driver, this time a fully grown man, to take care of her. But indeed she was worthy of the fuss; we trotted down the street as fast as the grey had galloped, threading our way in and out of the other sledges, while the passers-by stopped to look. Our first stop was the Antoniev monastery, where a service was in progress, conducted by a very old priest in a gold cope. The candles were lit; the congregation numbered about a dozen. The old priest tottered behind the iconostasis to find the keys of an older church, in which a few fragments of uninteresting painting were still visible.

Thence we cantered along an embanked road, swept by polar blasts, till we came to the village of Volotovo.

I was still in search of frescoes, and our first business was to find the keeper of the church. The end house, we had been told. But we drove to the wrong end, and then back again, along the broad space between the double rows of wooden houses, each of which was banked with hay on one side to keep out the prevailing wind. In every garden stood tall poles, to whose tops nesting-boxes were fixed. On reaching the right house, we found only two women at home, who, though busy with household duties and gaping at the foreigner's apparition, begged us to enter. This we did, through the wood-shed, and sat in the kitchen-parlour. In one corner, by the window, a lamp was burning before a group of icons. A row of heavy coats hung on pegs near the stove, at which one of the women continued her making of meat pies. I examined an apparatus, painted with roses and steadied by the foot, for spinning yarn, while the other woman searched for the keys. When ready, she seated herself on my knee in the sledge, and we drove up to the church, whose little pathway, graveyard, and surrounding trees reminded me of England. Inside was another scaffolding, which I rather regretted, since, unlike Nereditsa, services are still held here. On making use of it, I regretted it still more; for as I stood perched in the drum of the cupola, seventy feet from the stone floor and chattering with cold, the whole structure began to rock. I made hurriedly for earth, but was not half way down when a weird, unaccountable rumble began to sound, distant at first, then growing nearer and louder, till, as I reached the ground, a deafening roar was heard right overhead. I rushed from the door and looked up. Out of the leaden sky swooped four aeroplanes, painted dark military grey with the red star beneath each wing, and so low that I could see their pilots. In a flash they were away, sailing over the shallow valley beyond the village and up into the sky again. I turned to the country church, built 580 years ago, to the dark firs shivering in the wind, and to the rows of crosses that might have moved some Russian Gray to write another elegy. I watched the armed power of the Soviet Union resolve into four specks and disappear. The old and the new Russia, changing yet unchanged . . . Snow was falling again, through the silent trees, piling the graves a little higher.

In the town of Novgorod itself are several small churches dating from the fourteenth century, of which those named after St Theodore Stratilates and the Transfiguration particularly attracted my curiosity. The architecture of these two represents a strange fusion of Greek and German influences. While both are square in plan and develop a Byzantine apse to the east, each wall of each square finishes in a triangle supporting the eaves of a double-sloped roof in the Western manner. From the midst of the roof, on the other hand, at the intersection of its four ridges, rises a Byzantine cupola. Inside, the vaults and arches of the Greek tradition persist unaltered.

To the church of St Theodore Stratilates I gained access with no difficulty and was able to study its paintings at my leisure. That of the Transfiguration offered an unexpected rebuff. The door proving unlocked, I pushed it open, and was about to enter the nave, when like a tigress from her lair sprang a female comrade in a scarlet beret and banged it in my face. After a minute or two, I tried again. Again the maenad sprang; but this time I had implanted knee and boot on the threshold, and she could only remain there, chattering and snarling, while I examined her bulbous unlovable visage and wondered, not that abortion had been legalized in Russia, but that the occasion for it should ever arise. At length, seeing that my strength was greater than hers and that I was gradually edging my way in, she called for help and was joined by a bearded Magog, whose added weight nearly broke my thigh and forced me to retire. By now I too was in a rage; for it happened that I wished to see the frescoes in this church above all others. Jumping into the sledge, I galloped to the office of the Museum Committee to protest. With genuine regret they told me that this church, alone of all those in the district, was not under their control, but was being restored by orders direct from Moscow. They were therefore powerless to help me. Despite their courtesy, it was some time before the nausea engendered by contact with so frightful a variant of the human species had altogether evaporated.

I learned afterwards, by a devious means and under pledge not to reveal the teller, that the work of 'restoration' then being pursued by the maenad and her companion consisted in stripping the gold off the iconostasis or altar-screen. Hence their reluctance to allow a foreigner inside. How well this reluctance was justified only appeared six months later. Nothing of course could have been more sensible than to dismantle the iconostasis, if the church was eventually to be restored and maintained primarily on account of its frescoes – as was in fact the case; for the Orthodox altar-screen, being very high, necessarily obscures many of the most important compositions in Orthodox iconography. I happened, however, to relate the story of my adventure and its cause to various compatriots, more by way of making conversation about my journey than with any other purpose. Consider my surprise therefore, when in the following autumn I met a friend in the hunting-field who had lately returned from diplomatic service in Cairo, and who told me the last news he had had of me was my 'report that the desecration of churches was still continuing in the Novgorod district'. I then understood what the maenad had been instructed to understand, and why every foreigner of independent movement in Russia is regarded as a potential agent of capitalist propaganda.

The bill at the Archbishop's Palace was 225 roubles for two of us for two days, of which food accounted for eighty, horses for seventy, and 'organization' for twenty-five. We had just repudiated the last item, and the proprietress had just opened some tinned sturgeon as a peace-offering, when a man rushed in to say that the train was leaving in twenty minutes, an hour earlier than he had expected. Two sledges were waiting. Behind Princessa we galloped once more through the dark streets, while the luggage followed with the grey and the populace scattered as though the Apocalypse were upon them. As the train puffed out of the station, it came to me, as it comes to me now, that of all the places in Russia I shall most wish to revisit, the chief is Veliki Novgorod.

VII

EARLY RUSSIAN PAINTING

One result of my visit to Novgorod was that, on returning to Moscow, I read a paper to an assembly of professors at the offices of VOKS, the organization which corresponds in Russia to the Society for Cultural Relations in London. My temerity in so doing was only excused by the fact that in no other way could I meet those of my audience, such as Professor Grabar, whom I particularly wanted to meet. Each sentence of my paper had to be translated into Russian by a lady interpreter with a headache, whose knowledge of English was largely confined to engineering technicalities. When I had finished, the chairman of the meeting expressed a polite interest in all I had said, but regretted I had told the company nothing of the social effects of El Greco's art. To this I replied, with some asperity, that I was perfectly certain the company were very glad, for once in their lives, to have had a respite from social effects. The lady with the headache thought it inadvisable to translate this remark. But those who understood English betrayed a cynical pleasure in their laughter.

My paper dealt not only with El Greco but also with Russian art as a parallel offshoot of the Byzantine tradition. The adverse circumstances attending its delivery deprived my arguments of what little force they might have had in English. But enough of their meaning was apparent for several authorities on Russian art to express their dissent during the discussion that followed. It is therefore with some diffidence that I present the following remarks on such examples of early Russian painting as time enabled me to see, both in Novgorod and Moscow. In doing so, I may be forgiven for two reasons; first, because a previous acquaintance with contemporary styles in Greece revealed that the development of those styles was paralleled in Russia with a closeness hitherto unsuspected by historians of Russian art; and secondly, because the whole subject of Russian painting has now been rendered so remote by political barriers that any light on it, however myopic, must be welcome to some people.

The difference between Byzantine and Russian painting is noticeable enough from reproductions and from such icons as are or have been available for study in Western Europe. I had always imagined it to be a difference between a parent art of intellectual and emotional significance and a bastard craft of shallow peasant decoration. But the error of this view was soon apparent. And so also were the causes that had given rise to it. For Russian art is in truth less profound, and concerned with a less abstruse intellectual goal, than that of Constantinople. Its compositions therefore wear a shallow air in reproduction and in its lesser paintings, which is not only foreign but inferior to the Greek manner; they appear, under these circumstances, to be preoccupied with mere patterns of colour or light and shade, patterns conceived in two dimensions only, whose artistic meaning is scarcely deeper than a patchwork quilt. To credit this second-hand effect is to misjudge a great tradition. Early Russian painting is extrinsic in character because its appeal is to the eye and fancy before the mind. But the appeal is made by means whose independent virtues deserve comparison on equal terms with those of the parent art. These means are the infusion of Byzantine formalism with a native poetry which is alien to the logical Mediterranean; a capacity for placing exquisite and elaborate detail against positive, unfussed backgrounds; superb courage in the use of brilliant colours, of which a glowing white is not the least remarkable; unerring taste in the juxtaposition of colours, whether in separate fields or closely interwoven; and finally, an impalpable translucency, born of snowscape and birch-tree and the broad sky of the plains. These qualities are subtle and elusive, and are easily mistaken, in the hands of second-rate masters or in photographs, for a folk-ridden travesty of the original Greek models.

Russian art began with the formation of the city-states and the adoption of Christianity by Vladimir, Prince of Kiev in 988. The chief monument of this early period is the cycle of mosaics in the cathedral at Kiev, which dates from the middle of the eleventh century. This is purely Greek. But the mosaics in the monastery of St Michael, also at Kiev, and dating from the twelfth century, are thought to be the work of Russian artists. These are remarkable mainly for their ineptitude, and beyond a white background display no specifically Russian characteristics. The frescoes which adorn the staircase of the cathedral at Kiev and date from the eleventh century have been so restored that their interest is entirely historical. Those which have survived in the church of St Cyril at Kiev are scarcely more than line drawings in red and white, and incompetent at that. In the Cathedral at Novgorod, decorated in the eleventh century, only a single fragment depicting Constantine and Helena has escaped restoration. This exhibits a crude incapacity which repudiates any tradition whatsoever and lacks even the primitive force of the untutored savage.

It is with the frescoes of Starya Ladoga and of St Demetrius at Vladimir (*c.* 1200) that the study of Russian painting should begin. These, unfortunately, I could not see. My survey must start in the Novgorod district in 1198. In that year was initiated the cycle of frescoes that still adorns the church of the Transfiguration in the village of Nereditsa, near Novgorod.

Six years later Constantinople fell to the Fourth Crusade. But the Latin Empire proved only an interlude, and the vitality of Byzantine culture persisted, and even gained new strength, as the Greek Empire shrank to its final end through the fourteenth and fifteenth centuries. To this vitality the mosaics of the Kahrieh and the frescoes of Mistra and Mount Athos are a sufficient witness. From it sprang the prime inspiration of the Novgorod artists in the fourteenth century.

The child had thus reached manhood ere the parent fell into dotage, and from the twelfth to the fifteenth centuries Russian and Byzantine painting followed two separate roads of artisitic discovery, gradually diverging, yet subject to the same changes of style, and permitting, therefore, classification into the same schools. At length, about 1410, Russia produced a great individual painter in the person of Roublev, who, though deriving immediately from the contemporary Greek source, crystallized the hitherto fluid idiosyncrasies peculiar to Russian painting into an authoritative national school. The divergence from Constantinople was completed, and by 1453, when that city was taken by the Turks, the tutelary function of Greek art in Russia had become superfluous. The full-fledged Cretan school, which followed, has no important counterpart in the main stream of Russian art. It produced El Greco. And he went West instead.

It was not until after the Iconoclast controversy of the ninth century that Byzantine art developed its official character of stereotyped iconography and gorgeous colour. The calculated splendour thus produced was symbolic of the abundant wealth and high civilization pertaining to a great capital. At the same time, during the Macedonian and Comnenan dynasties, other influences were at work in the provinces, which were destined to infuse the impersonal magnificence of the official art with qualities more human and sympathetic. These influences, particularly in Asia Minor, found expression in a school of illustrators descended from the Syrian miniaturists of pre-Iconoclastic times, whose chief concern was a lively realism adapted to the instruction of the illiterate through the medium of sacred pictures. Thus the figures are short and stumpy, but active, the heads are large, the mouths frown, and the faces in general retain that Hellenistic look of perpetual surprise which results from the raised eyebrows, staring pupils and white eyeballs of the Fayum portraits. The style produced by this tradition in the tenth and eleventh centuries has been called the Cappadocian, from the fact that its frescoes have chiefly survived in rock-cut churches to the south-west of the Euphrates.

In the twelfth century the influence of this style, while unwelcome in Constantinople, spread to Italy; and it also spread to Russia, as the frescoes of Nereditsa clearly show. Both in iconography and in the vigorous action of the persons depicted, these paintings closely resemble the mosaics in the monastery church of St Luke of Stiris, near Delphi, which were done in the eleventh and twelfth century and which in themselves betray a marked affinity with the work of the popular illustrators. In some scenes, particularly that of the Crucifixion, the Nereditsa frescoes seem even more directly connected with those discovered by Père de Jerphanion in Cappadocia itself. Their colour is sombre, emphatic, and opaque; there is no prophecy of the luminosity to come. Cold blues, ochre, red, and pink are the outstanding tints. The portrait of the founder, who holds the church in his hand, shows a bearded countenance of scowling melancholy in ochre and brown, surmounted by a fur-edged cap and finished with a long red robe of Byzantine patterned silk, which contrasts with a dark blue background. The general effect of the whole decoration is one of gloomy tensity and earnestness belonging to the North. Beyond this, there is little sign yet of native invention. Nevertheless, the inscriptions, though mainly in Greek, are interspersed with Slavonic letters, from which it is possible to infer that the artist was a Russian.

At the beginning of the thirteenth century Russia was overwhelmed by the Mongols; and it is not until the last half of the fourteenth that further cycles of frescoes are available to gauge the growth of a cultural tradition. In Greece, meanwhile, the influence of the popular illustrators had invaded the capital and had there joined forces with the wave of mysticism and insistence on the beauty of suffering that submerged the thought of the Empire in its last days and was the precursor, in Italy, of St Francis, Giotto, and the Renascence. The result was not, as at St Luke's of Stiris, the introduction of a crude dramatic convention; it now took the form of refining, elaborating and humanizing the various iconographic formulas in the light of new emotions. With emphasis on pain came also a new joy: the details of nature were better observed and utilized; colour grows brighter and more luminous. Two schools developed. The earlier, known as the Macedonian, worked on Mount Athos at the beginning of the fourteenth century, where its cycles may still be seen, not seriously restored, in the monastery of Vatopedi and the church of the Protaton at Caryes. The later and more joyous, dating from the last half of the fourteenth century and first decades of the fifteenth, flourished at Mistra in the Peloponnese, where its works survive chiefly in the churches of the Peribleptos and the Pantanassa.

The Macedonian school is represented in Russia by the paintings in the church of the Dormition at Volotovo, near Novgorod, which date from the year 1363. These paintings make it equally clear that a native tradition of inquiring mind and free invention was by now already established.

The most immediately noticeable resemblance between the Volotovo cycle and those of the Macedonian school on Mount Athos lies in the marked facial types which are common to both and which most particularly distinguish the Macedonian school from those that came after and before it. Prophets and Patriarchs, such as the David and Job at Volotovo, have tight woolly curls and beards, both white; they frown furiously; their heads project beyond their bodies, while their fore-heads overhang and their jaws are tightly compressed, so that the lower part of the face is small in comparison with the upper. Christ too remains unaltered: in the *Double Communion* at Volotovo, his equally frowning face, fringed by a longer but still compact black beard, is almost identical with that of his appearances in the Protaton at Caryes (*c.* 1310). The beardless faces are also similar, particularly those of the women, with their well-rounded, highly modelled chins and air of melancholy resignation – features which indicate, in the Byzantine sphere, a reversion to the forms of Antiquity. These faces are boldly constructed with broad impressionistic sweeps. But in the Russian church, impressionism has extended its field; even the faces of the hieratic Early Fathers such as St Clement, though singularly reminis-cent of their fellows in the Protaton, have exchanged the ancient convention for one less rigid and angular. In general, however, the sympathy these frescoes exhale is due to Greek inspiration and grows most poignant, as at Vatopedi on Mount Athos, in the *Crucifixion*, a scene of vivid humanity and sorrow. The choice of scenes and their arrangement also tallies with those of contemporary Greece. If the actual method of coloration is Russian, in its broad zones, light touch, and lack of all save essential interruptions, the colours themselves are seen to be mainly Greek. From the Macedonian school have come the prevailing flat mauve, dirty russet pink, and cold blue. Yet here and there are signs of a new spring, as in the beryl-green draperies of the women in the *Raising of Lazarus*. This derives, not from native sources, but from Mistra.

The native genius has none the less found its own means of expres-sion. Though the scheme of the whole Volotovo cycle is traditional, the iconography of many individual scenes shows a new departure and a first realization, in art, of Russian poetry and fancy. The figures are ethereal and elongated beyond even the Athonite canon. In movement, an airy grace has succeeded to hieratic pose and crude gesture. Indeed, something of the ballet has come to reawaken these ancient, sacred persons. In the scene of the *Annunciation*, a bending willowy angel, whose voluminous drapery and still poised wings bespeak the imminence of flight, beckons with tiny hand to a Virgin who shrinks within herself as a Danilova before the advances of a Lifar. The Virgin, moreover, has been recostumed; her mantle forms a kind of shepherd's hat with corners on each temple. In the theme of the *Maries of the Tomb*, the iconography has been radically altered; for though the usual angel is seated on the open lid, Christ is seen escaping, and the Maries, instead of standing upright, are prostrated before him, while agitated soldiers appear in the background. The *Ascension*, to a Byzantinist of conservative taste, is frankly extraordinary. There is no attempt at symmetry. Apostles and Virgin dart hither and thither in choreographic riot, while tongues of lightning escape from whirling clouds in a corner of the sky.

In addition to the subjects prescribed by Orthodox usage, the church at Volotovo contains four sketches of partly historical and partly artistic, but intrinsically Russian, interest. The first depicts the church itself, in process of dedication, and shows that from the time it was built until now not a stone of it has changed. The second portrays a banquet offered to a company of fantastically dressed notables in a contemporary monastery, one of whose white-robed monks serves the dishes from a side-table. The other two are portraits of Moses and Alexis, archbishops of Novgorod in the fourteenth century. These are rendered almost wholly in line and bear no relation to existing formulas, Greek or otherwise. Moses, it appears, died in 1359. But Alexis was archbishop when the church was built. His portrait is freer than the other; we see a true Slav face with sparse beard, high cheek-bones, and the contour of a peasant doll. This is an example of genuine characterization, evidently done from life with the purpose of creating a likeness rather than the symbol of a likeness. It is the first example of its kind in Russian art, and one which Greek painting, even in its post-Conquest phase, never attained to.

In 1910 and 1912 two events of great archaeological importance occurred in Novgorod. Frescoes were found under whitewash, first in the church of St Theodore Stratilates, then in that of the Transfiguration. The former were wholly uncovered. Of the latter, only the paintings in the cupola are as yet visible. But it is hoped that eventually the whole series will be revealed intact.

The significance of these discoveries lies in the recorded fact that the frescoes in the church of the Transfiguration were painted in 1379 by a Greek name Theophanes, who is known in Russia as 'the Greek', just as Domenicos Theotocopoulos is known in Spain. The lives of these two artists, Greeks in exile both, offer curious parallels. Both were known as philosophers. Both enjoyed the fame which attaches to persons of strong character and artistic audacity. Theophanes, it is recorded, disdained the hieratic manuals and their iconographic formulas. He painted from personal inspiration or from nature, and did a view of Moscow on a wall just as Theotocopoulos did views of Toledo. One of the chronicles of the time preserves a miniature of him at work, surrounded by a gaping crowd. In 1405 he left Novgorod for Moscow, where he decorated various churches. Among these was that of the Annunciation in the Kremlin. He worked here in conjunction with Roublev, who must thus, at an early stage of his career, have come under the direct personal influence of a Byzantine master.

The little of Theophanes' work yet visible I was unable to see, owing to the fury of the maenad in charge of the church which contained it. But Professor Anisimov, before he suffered the fate reserved for more rebellious intellectuals under the Tsar's rule and was despatched to an unknown destination in Siberia, delivered his opinion that the frescoes in the church of St Theodore Stratilates, which date from about 1370, may also be regarded with reasonable probability as the work of this Russian Greco. This supposition is reinforced by the fact that the inscriptions are all in Greek, while those at Nereditsa and Volotovo are interspersed with Cyrillic characters. It can only be finally confirmed, however, when the restoration of the church of the Transfiguration has been completed.

Directly I entered the church of St Theodore Stratilates, I exclaimed to myself, without being aware of the above facts, 'Here is Byzantium'; and certainly these paintings, with their accomplished technique and genuine air of the Greek Renascence, may rank with those of Mistra itself. Yet despite the immanence of Byzantine inspiration, the Russian genius of the dance is present in them also. Here, in fact, for the first and last time before the final divergence, the fusion of this genius with the Mediterranean capacity for intellectual, three-dimensional design has been fully achieved.

The colours, which are impregnated with that impalpable suggestion of interior light proper to the Byzantine masterpiece, derive from the same palette as those in the Peribleptos at Mistra (late fourteenth century). Their range is the spectrum of a pearl – pink, bistre, wine-red, love-in-the-mist blue, a bright grey, and white. The last two, in conjunction, foreshadow the development of the later Cretan school and its ultimate flower, El Greco. The finest composition of the cycle is the *Descent into Hell*, in the western apse. Here the mobile Christ, with hands outstretched in expansive gesture, is framed, but for one retarded foot, in a circular aura of two greys enclosing a white ground – the triple aura of Hezychast speculation. On either side of him those of the Old Dispensation rise from their tombs in supplication; while above the aura clustered angels uplift the cross. If such a scheme lacks precedent in purely Greek iconography, the interwoven symmetry and rhythms of the design are nevertheless products of a Greek mind. The delicate heightening of flesh-contours with imperceptible touches of white is also very Greek, particularly when applied to the bulges of the foreheads, down the noses, and beneath the eyes, in the manner of the mosaicist. This prevails throughout the church. In the upper zone of the cupola, the orb-holding angels, clad in royal vestments and alternating with six-winged cherubims, recall the art of the Greek court in the golden age. At the same time, the free and graceful movements of the white-robed soldiers on the *Road to Calvary*, combined with an architectural background in Western perspective, indicate the growth of a new humanism, coincident with that of Italy, which reached its climax in the Pantanassa at Mistra in 1428. The frescoes of St Theodore Stratilates, in fact, represent an interlude between the Peribleptos and the Pantanassa, and in some respects between the Mistra and Cretan schools, an interlude whose monuments, in Greece itself, are lacking. Meanwhile, the development of the Russian tradition continues. The compositions are freer, the figures less static, than those of Greece; and in the colours there lurks, beside their intrinsic light, a hint of that opalescent shimmer whose full glory was reserved for Roublev in four decades' time.

In addition to the frescoes described above, historical evidence suggests a possibility that the scene of the *Dormition* painted on the back of the Donskaya Virgin may also be the work of Theophanes Greco. This icon is now in the Tretyakov Gallery in Moscow. Having examined the back of it at some length, I found it difficult to convert the possibility into probability. But there exist also two other and larger icons, about five feet square as far as I remember, which the most recent Russian authorities are disposed to ascribe to Theophanes. One, representing the *Crucifixion*, is in the museum at Novgorod. Unfortunately it was late in the afternoon when I got there, and there was little time for detailed attention; I noticed only a chocolate robe whose folds were illumined with high-lights of pale azure. The other, representing the *Transfiguration*, is now in the Tretyakov Gallery in Moscow, whose curator, Professor Nikrasiev, expressed a strong belief in its ascription to the Greek. Its colours exhibited those shattering, angular contrasts and fierce lightning effects which are usually associated, in Greece, with the Cretan school – the same azure lights applied to robes of rusty red and honey yellow; red lights to olive-green; slate to wine-pink; while the Christ himself, etched in gold, is framed by an aura of light grey-blue, gold, and white. Professor Nikrasiev, before giving his opinion, asked mine; I dated the icon from the fifteenth or early sixteenth centuries. But now it is evident, after seeing the paintings of St Theodore Stratilates, that the Cretan style, which reached its height at the beginning of the sixteenth century, had already begun to develop at the end of the fourteenth. The icon of the *Transfiguration* may therefore be the work of Theophanes, and the colours common to both it and the paintings of Novgorod may have been subjected, on a panel designed for close inspection, to purposeful exaggeration. For the colours used, apart from their method of application, are essentially the same in both. It was these colours which Roublev undoubtedly inherited, through his Greek master, from the short-lived spring of the Byzantine Renascence, and which he now, in the first decade of the fifteenth century, put to a further use.

Andrew Roublev was a monk in the Andronievsky monastery in Moscow. The first mention of him is in connection with Theophanes and the decoration of the church of the Annunciation. In 1408 he was at work in the church of the Assumption at Vladimir. About 1410, it is thought, he painted the great icon of the *Trinity* for the monastery of that name at Sergievo, where it remained, until after the Revolution, in the iconostasis of the monastery cathedral. Little more is known of the life of Roublev, and nothing more of his work. Yet his influence changed the whole character of Russian painting, and he attained a prodigious, almost legendary, fame in his own country. In 1551 a church council, condemning innovations in icon-painting, proclaimed the style of Roublev as the true standard of artistic Orthodoxy, to be followed in perpetuity.

Until 1920, justification of Roublev's fame in terms of aesthetic talent was somewhat lacking, even to the eyes of Russians. Kondakov, for example, in his book on the Russian icon published by the Oxford University Press, doubts whether the panel of the *Trinity* was from Roublev's own hand, and has no inkling of its real artistic value. For Kondakov had left Russia before the icon had been cleared of its nineteenth-century overcoating. Even now, the numerous foreign visitors to Russia seldom see it. Until 1929 it was at Sergievo. Then it was removed to the Tretyakov Gallery, where the central heating immediately wrought more damage than five centuries of cold and damp. The pieces of the panel warped and the paint cracked down the middle. When I saw it, it lay on the restorer's table, so that I was obliged to stand on a chair and look down on it from above. The view was a revelation. Before me was the greatest masterpiece ever produced by a Slav painter, a work of unprecedented invention, to which nothing in art that I could think of offered any sort of parallel. It was not that I saw a greater painting than any I had seen before; but simply that here was one which differed, in its greatness, more than I had thought possible from the accepted canons of greatness.

The panel is roughly four and a half feet square. It depicts the Trinity in the form of three angels seated at a table – a theme often found in Orthodox iconography and based on Abraham's entertainment of strange guests. The background is light in tone and was probably once white, but has now an indeterminate texture of dirty cream. On one side rises a tower, on the other a hill, both light in tone and distant; while in the middle, though to the right of the central angel's head, stands a nearer tree, green, flat, and formal. The central angel is visible to the knees only; the others have their legs in front of the table. All three of them present a scheme of colour whose simplicity of equilibrium seems paradoxical beside the rare and lyrical splendour of the resulting whole.

The central angel and that on the beholder's right wear full-sleeved robes, round which cloaks are draped to cover one arm and shoulder. On the central angel, these garments are respectively of rich flat chocolate, tinged with red, and of a brilliant lapidary blue, a colour so emphatic, yet so reserved, that in all nature I can think of no analogy for it. The angel on the right wears a robe whose tint is of this same blue, but whose intensity is less. Across this is draped a cloak of dry sapless green, colour of leaves at the end of summer, whose high-lights are rendered in light grey-green shading off into pure white. The angel on the left wears a robe of reddish mauve lit with pale translucent slate colour, over a white vest. All the faces and hands are nut-brown, modelled only by variations in tone of the same colour, and outlined in black. The outspread wings, whose feathers are denoted by thin gold lines, are a flatter and paler brown, something between tea and toffee, which strikes a mean plane between the figures and the tree. Each head is encircled by a plain white halo which was formerly, though not perhaps originally, encased in metal.

The first simplicity of this scheme resolves eventually into something not so simple. The composition has an inner construction which is welded from the contrast not between colour-fields alone, but between tones and textures. While the middle angel asserts its focal claim with such positive affirmatory force that the eye almost recoils, it is precisely because the side angels are able to absorb this force and dispute it that the eye, instead of recoiling, is entranced by a vivid interaction. This process results, chiefly, from the cloaks of the side angels. The colours of these garments have been described in general terms. But in reality there is no describing them; one might try, with equal success, to analyse the palette of Rembrandt's flesh. The reddish mauve and the pale slate, the leaf-green lit by grey-green and white, are seen to comprise on examination of the miracle, not merely these, but all the colours of the pearl spectrum. They shimmer, like hills over a desert in the evening. Such ethereal transparency, enclosed by broad, flat colour-fields, has its own mobility and force, which curb the affirmation of the central figure and balance the design equally.

Long and close as I looked, I could not be certain how Roublev achieved this effect. I could only suppose it was by use of small brushes and many pigments. But I was certain enough that the method, whatever it was, has produced a painting which has no like in European art.

Even in the faces the touch of genius is apparent. He has followed the formula, has eschewed the use of colour on flesh to a point even in excess of it. Yet the faces live and their earnest, downward glances bespeak a vital, if supernatural, intelligence on the part of the strange neuter creatures that bear them. Though Roublev was master of all he inherited from the Greeks, of formulas and colour alike, his real inspiration was Russian. The poetry of the country lives in his paint, the strength of it in his design. Yet in his monkish gravity lurks something greater than melody and dance, something extra-national, which belongs to the world. Until Roublev, Greek art can claim the authority of a parent over Russian – the latter produced nothing that approaches the mosaics of the Kahrieh. But in Roublev the slowly matured independence of the child was finally proclaimed. This proclamation was final in another sense also. For it was not until the literature of the nineteenth century that the Slav genius again scaled the heights discovered by an obscure monk, whose one memorial is a panel of three angels.

Roublev left a school, whose icons betray his aims, but not his genius; almost at once, imitation of the master degenerates into formula. Of his ultimate effect on wall-painting, the frescoes of the monastery of Theraponte, done between 1500 and 1502 by the master Dionysios, must be the criterion. Photographs of these paintings reveal an art of sweeping design and grand invention. But photographs are not enough, and the monastery lies so encompassed by marshes in one of the northern provinces that no one I asked in Moscow could even tell me the name of Kirillov, its nearest station. The best I could manage, in quest of Roublev's successors, was a visit to Yaroslavl, whose churches were decorated in the middle of the seventeenth century. The churches themselves have many beauties, as I shall tell. But their frescoes speak death to the Byzantine Orthodox tradition. Here are all the faults of Russian art redeemed by none of its virtues. Formalism unchallenged and uncomprehended has become the ally of insane elaboration and peasant garishness. It remained for the eighteenth century to create a secular tradition of painting, and for the nineteenth to produce such accomplished, if synthetic, realists as a Verestchagin and a Repin, together with that last nauseating throwback, whose very name is an impiety, the neo-Byzantinist Vroubel.

*

It is possible to object that the above survey, in omitting all reference to the icon schools, takes a very limited view of Russian painting. The objection is just; for icons comprise the great bulk of Russian painting before the sixteenth century, while frescoes are comparatively rare. But the two arts are essentially different. Many of the fresco-painters, it is true, achieved nothing but a moribund formality; many of the icon-painters, on the other hand, created works of the greatest beauty and feeling. But the fresco belongs to the grand tradition of art, while the very nature of the icon condemns it to perpetual approximation with the crafts. The fresco-painter, unless he is out to produce a mere wallpaper, as at Yaroslavl, must necessarily exercise some talent for spacing and movement and balance, some attempt at three-dimensional composition over an area and plane which vary with each individual church; however ungifted, he must invent, to achieve his object at all. The icon-painter, however gifted, need never invent; if the impulse to do so is in him, he is restricted as a rule to the refinement of detail within a narrow convention. Such refinement, especially in the Novgorod school of icons, has often amounted to genius. But that genius has inevitably been limited by, or at least adapted to, the lesser medium in which it worked. Roublev, who was also a fresco-painter, refused to be thus hampered, though his panel of the *Trinity* is technically an icon. He was born of the grand tradition and continued it.

During my stay in Russia, with so much to see of politics and people, I dared not adventure into the labyrinth of the icon schools, for fear that, while my visa lasted, I might never emerge from it. I did see, notwithstanding, some noted individual icons, whose present state and whereabouts deserve a cursory mention.

The paintings in the museum at Novgorod have been selected and arranged with as much discrimination and taste as a private collection. The better known and much reproduced examples of the Novgorod school are elsewhere; many of those now in the museum were undiscovered before the Revolution and have only been gathered in from the surrounding churches during the last ten years. That this should have been possible is a testimony of at least one service rendered by the Revolution to art. I had not time for detailed study. I can only say that the chief impression made by the collection was one of uniform *quality* which in colour and emotion surpassed even the finest icons of Athens and Mount Athos. The most famous icon in the collection is the fourteenth-century painting of St Theodore Stratilates in white top-boots. One early panel stood out from the rest on account of its unique secular theme – that of the Novgorodians sallying out to fight their enemies the Suzdalians before the walls of the town, with the course of the battle depicted in three zones and the skies filled with flying arrows. Every icon seemed to have been picked for its perfect condition, and indeed the majority of them have been conserved rather than injured by the layers of grease and smoke that had accumulated on them. I visited the restoration room near by. A large panel of St Nicolas Lipna, dated 1294, lay on the table under the care of a single man. Its restoration was nearly finished and would have taken, when complete, a year and a half of this man's life. I met no man in the Soviet Union more content with his lot.

In the museum of the Pechersky Lavra in Kiev, towards the end of my journey in Russia, I saw the oldest icons in the world. These were brought from Mount Sinai in the eighteenth century by the Russian Metropolitan Porphyry. They date from the sixth, and are executed on small panels in the wax painting that obtained at that period. One represents SS. Sergius and Bacchus, between whose two heads is that of Christ in a medallion; another, St John the Baptist; and a third, the Virgin and Child. All three bear a close relation to the Fayum and Coptic tradition of portraiture. The brushwork is bold and impressionistic, greens and pinks being used on the flesh; the eyebrows are raised and the eyes themselves stare unnaturally. An explanatory notice informs the visitor that in the year 392 the Emperor Theodosius forbade the placing of portraits on mummies. Consequently, icons of sacred personages were done in the same style and used instead.

Before the Revolution, the most famous of all holy pictures in Russia – and the most efficacious in its transmission of human prayers to the authority competent to grant them – was the Iberian Virgin of Moscow. This stood in the Iberian Gateway, a double, twin-spired arch that adjoined the Historical Museum and gave access to the Red Square. Owing to the increase of motor traffic, this ancient structure had lately been pulled down and an inscription erected, above the site of the Virgin, which reminds the passer-by of Lenin's familiar tag: RELIGION IS THE OPIUM OF THE PEOPLE. When I was in Moscow, the icon was still preserved in an obscure chapel. Thither one evening I was conducted. A service was in progress beneath the low barrel-vault, attended by some fifteen people. The Iberian Virgin hung on the wall at the farther end, and I was eventually able to creep up and examine it with the aid of a taper. Artistically it proved disappointingly wooden and seemed to date from the sixteenth century. But I was pleased to have seen so remarkable and revered a relic of old Russia.

Not long after my return to England, I received a letter from Moscow to say that the Iberian Virgin had suddenly disappeared. Rumour insists that it has been sold to Greece. I have written to Athens inquiring, but can get no confirmation of any such transaction.

The chief collection of icons in Moscow is in the Tretyakov Gallery. During my visit this was in process of rearrangement, but Professor Nikrasiev kindly allowed me access to it, and I wandered about a small room turning over the heavy panels like the pages of some gigantic wooden book. Two formalized Virgins attracted my attention. The first was the Donskaya, dating from the fourteenth century. Virgin and Child incline towards each other with expressions of love and sympathy. But the expressions are fixed and the faces too rounded, like an apple in an advertisement. This is no likeness of a woman, but a likeness of a likeness. Over the head is draped a mantle of deep chocolate, beneath which, framing cheeks and neck, bursts forth a veil of ultra-marine so bright that the eye, in this case, does recoil. This blue is richer and more allusive than that employed by Roublev on his middle angel. The second Virgin, known as the Smolenskaya, is a huge, extra-life-size composition, terrifying in its crude, rigid majesty, like the carving on a Red Indian totem-pole. Again the Virgin wears a chocolate mantle, beneath which hangs a slate under-veil lined with vermilion. The face is apple-red and brown; the nose resembles a large church key and the eyes are like black peas. This icon is primitive in the true sense of the word, and seemed to show what Russian art might always have been had the tradition of Constantinople never come to it.

For the tradition of Constantinople, as I looked about, stood incarnate on an easel before my eyes. Another panel of the Virgin I saw, which is believed to have been sent from Constantinople by the Emperor Constantine Monomach in the middle of the eleventh century, which was certainly in existence by the middle of the twelfth, and which is undoubtedly the work of a Greek painter emanating from the sphere of the capital during the golden age of Byzantine art. During its first two centuries in Russia this icon remained in the cathedral of Vladimir and is known as the Vladimirskaya or, in Western parlance, as Our Lady of Vladimir, under which title a monograph on it by Professor Anisimov was published by the Seminarium Kondakovianum of Prague in 1928. Eventually it became the Palladium of the Russian state and monarchy, and in 1395 was transferred to the Kremlin, where the two sheaths of gold that used to encase it are now among the state treasure. After the Revolution it was disencumbered of these ornaments and subjected to expert restoration. This discovered that the original paint had survived only on those parts which had been always exposed, namely, the two faces.

Already, from Professor Anisimov's colour reproduction, I had gained some idea of the beauty of these faces; but the reality, the sudden view of the picture on the easel, opened a new experience in art, just as Roublev's *Trinity* had done. To describe the colours that make the Virgin's face, the apple-red and translucent sepia-green of cheeks and neck, the touch of pure cold white on the nose, the glowing vermilion of the lips and the corners of the eyes, the unfathomable purplish darkness of the pupils and of the compact lines that mark the upper eye-lashes – to write these details is merely to transcribe the score of an unheard symphony. Even technically, there is no other picture like it, for it is the only painting of the high imperial art of Constantinople which has survived. Furthermore, and apart from academic considerations, it is one of the very few paintings in which an ecclesiastical formula has ever been made the vehicle, without modification or extension, of as profound and touching a humanity as art has ever been able to express. This humanity exists not within the limits of the convention, or in spite of it, but through it, in the language of it. In one sense, then, it is no longer a convention. Yet it is the fact of the convention which augments, by its impregnable reserve, the vitality of the emotion beneath it. The emotion is simple enough: a mother caresses the child whose cheek is pressed to hers and whose pale gentle fingers fondle her neck. But simple emotions endure through the ages. In those grave, whiteless eyes and sad small mouth live the eternal sorrows and joys and the whole destiny of man. Such a picture can bring tears to the eye and peace to the soul. I have known no other picture so able. When I took leave of Our Lady of Vladimir, I gave her my constant devotion. For me, she has set a new standard to the old religious painters, and how vivid this remains I know by the fact that certain pictures I used to hate have now, in my mind, forfeited even the dignity of a separate existence.

VIII

YAROSLAVL AND SERGIEVO

While Veliki Novgorod retains something of the character of early Russia before the Tartar invasion, the monuments of Yaroslavl commemorate the expansion of commerce that marked the seventeenth century. The town had been altogether ruined by the Tartars in 1237, but was colonized anew by Ivan the Terrible with merchants imported from Novgorod. It lies on the Volga, 150 miles north-east of Moscow. With Europe by Archangel, and with Persia by the Caspian, these merchants traded. The English built a naval shipyard there; Dutch, Germans, French, and Spaniards followed them. Great prosperity came to the town, and found expression in a series of churches whose spacious proportions and richness of architectural decoration had no rival in the Russia of their time. Unlike those of fifteenth-century Moscow, these exhibit little foreign influence. The native aesthetic, so long nourished by the Italians, was now putting forth its own flowers, before the Italians should arrive again with the canons of later classicism.

Since the inception of the Five-Year Plan Yaroslavl has again come to the fore, thanks to its position on the Volga and on the main lines from Moscow to Vladivostok and Archangel. The ASEA, a Swedish engineering company, had until 1932 a factory there for the manufacture of electrical machinery – the only foreign concession left in Russia at the time. My guide and I had made no preparations for our visit beyond deciding which train we should catch. This took us to Spolye, where, at six in the morning, we were met by a Swedish engineer. He drove us to Yaroslavl in his car and installed us in the flat of his manager, who happened to be ill in Moscow. My gratitude for this kindness was increased when my guide discovered that the local hotels were not only uncomfortable to a degree that alarmed even him, but were absolutely full.

After breakfast, we took a tram to the middle of the town, and asked our way to the once famous churches. Even the aged, to whom our inquiries were chiefly directed, appeared to have forgotten their Maker, and gaped unhelpfully as I mouthed the names of Ivan Predetchi and Ivan Zlatoousta – Johns the Baptist and Chrysostom; for my guide was such a militant atheist that these superstitious sounds were beyond him. In despair, we mounted a sledge, whose giant driver, wearing a full-skirted black coat tied with a red sash and trimmed with white astrakhan, drove us to a ruined church which he said was the cathedral of the Prophet Elias. So it might have remained, in my imagination, had not two officials also driven up at that very moment, who informed us that it was not. We must go, they said, to the Museum Chancellery in the Spassky monastery, where they would give us all information. To the Spassky monastery we went, a white-walled enclosure guarded by massive square towers with wooden conical roofs. The courtyard was also in ruins; for there was a lot of fighting at Yaroslavl in the Civil War. Its single inhabitant asserted with glee that the Museum Chancellery was elsewhere. At the same time a sentry tried to confiscate my camera. So I gave the driver a prod and we drove off at a gallop. Suddenly I recognized the real cathedral of St Elias, having already seen a photograph of it. The Museum Chancellery was opposite. On entering, we were told that a committee meeting was in progress and could not be disturbed. I ventured to suggest that it could be disturbed, and, dragging my guide with me, burst into its room, followed by a protesting janitor. Thereupon the necessary officials placed themselves at my disposal, showed me a number of Slavonic manuscripts and told me how to reach the monuments I was in search of.

The nearest was the cathedral of St Elias, whose five domes, outer galleries and detached bell-tower with conical roof exhibit the chief characteristics of the Yaroslavl style. This was built in 1647; the domes are green; the outside is covered with plain whitewash. But within, the frescoed walls reveal a jungle of sacred themes in the brightest colours, which are still enclosed in the schematic compartments ordained by the Byzantine Church, and thus represent the last and most fantastic offspring of the Orthodox tradition of Christian art. This was the only interior we had access to. I was glad to have seen it, but had no desire for more, since the interest of the paintings was hagiographical rather than artistic.

Our next objective was the church of St John Chrysostom in the suburb of Korovniki. This place is separated from the town by a tributary of the Volga, across which a herring-gutted iron bridge, known as the 'Amerikansky Most', carries the trams, while sledges take a short cut over the ice. The churches of Korovniki – for there are two – are overtopped by a huge leaning bell-tower, octagonal in shape and topped by a dormered cone. That of St John Chrysostom, which was founded in 1649 at the expense of two merchant brothers called Nejdanovsky, is decorated with brick patterns which take the form, on the base, of a blind arcade conceived in that squat, bulbous manner associated in England with Tudor bedsteads. Mingled with these patterns are panels of the local faience, and at the east end the three windows are surrounded by wide curving frames of the same material. As an architectural medium this faience can only be compared with the Mexican *azulejos*. Later in the day we found an even more lavish example of its use, on the church of St Nicolas Mokri (1672), where the smaller onion-shaped cupolas are entirely formed of chevron-like tiles in peacock blue and green varied with a deep wine-red. Here the same window frames again appeared. Both these and the panels, and occasionally even the cornice of a porch, are done in high relief, to the extent of two inches. The colours, which are very pure, are for the most part blue, green, and yellow, on a white ground.

Thence we drove to Toltchkovo, another suburb, where we caught sight of another campanile, still more oblique, and rising in octagonal tiers like a chocolate wedding-cake. From each tier glittered a row of gilt balls, upheld by a series of pinnacles. This, we knew, must be the church of St John the Baptist (1671). But how to reach it no one could tell us. At length we stopped at the lodge of a paint factory, where two sentries and a posse of comrades disputed our passage, convinced apparently that I was a professional *saboteur* sent by the British Government to upset the paint-front for 1932. My guide, by this time, was convinced of my disinterestedness – having seen me literally reduced to tears by the cold in my fingers while photographing on my belly in the snow at Korovniki – and calmed their fears by telling them, with a pitying glance in my direction, that he had been unable to drag me to a single factory and that all I cared about in this world was churches, churches, churches. Finally I offered them each a Gold Flake, and entrance was granted. I also lit one myself, and in five minutes might have been seen, after all these precautions, perched on a large tank of inflammable oil and smoking hard, while I adjusted my camera. This questionable behaviour, let me say at once, was due to absent-mindedness rather than a desire to give my life for the destruction of the Five-Year Plan. The church itself proved worth the effort. Above a structure of rich chocolate-coloured brick decorated with ribs and roundels of cold green faience, the five scaly onion-domes on their tall stalks shone out over the snowy landscape in a sudden ray of sun, as though the melted gold, deep and vivid as the middle of a buttercup, were actually running down them.

Owing to the shortness of the winter day, combined with the reluctance of the inhabitants to leave their beds, there is only time in Russia for one meal in every twenty-four hours. This takes place when we have tea. That evening I was to dine with the Swedish engineer who had met me at the station. At half-past four he fetched me from the manager's flat and we walked about a mile to his house. Here four other Swedes, also tenants, awaited us. Each had his own room, frescoed – in the style of the *Bystander* – by his own hand. 'Mr Byron,' said the engineer in an earnest, indeed apprehensive, tone, 'we hope you are not a teetotaller.'

After a tiring day out of doors in extreme cold, when the face has flushed and the body suddenly relaxed in the warmth of a comfortable room, life can offer no more supreme content than the first sip of some God-given stimulant. The divine beverage on this occasion consisted of port, brandy, and vodka mixed. There followed *zakouska*, eaten with vodka alone. With the vodka came beer, and with the beer the meal itself and port. This was the dinner. After an interval, those invited in afterwards began to arrive. They were all Russians and the only ones I ever met under normal conditions. First came a lady and gentleman, the former of refined aspect and restrained dress, whose uncle had formerly owned the house in which we sat. For them green chartreuse was brought out. Then followed a youthful doctor with a twinkling eye, accompanied by two ladies of a different type. One of them was his wife; 'but', I was told, 'it makes no difference'. The doctor played the piano. The ladies and gentlemen took the floor. The piano was succeeded by the gramophone; the drinks succeeded one another. The doctor gave us a dance, squatting on his haunches and kicking his legs in front of him. The furniture began to disintegrate under the berserk assaults of its owners. The doctor and I, though lacking a common tongue, engaged in earnest conversation: he pointed to his wife and pointed to the stairs. The refined lady and gentleman went home. At half-past two, when the party had lasted ten hours, I did likewise, guided through a mile of suburbs by one of my hosts, whose mirth, despite the uncertainty of our progress over the frozen hummocks, had suddenly evaporated into a tearful melancholy.

The next morning I had an appointment to see over the ASEA factory at a quarter to ten. I arrived on time and so did my friend the engineer. The others were still in bed, and their various chiefs were wondering if an epidemic had struck the house. This foreign factory, I say with pride, was the only factory in Russia that I visited. The afternoon I spent by the shores of the Volga. That night I left for Sergievo, bearing a feeling of eternal gratitude towards this oasis of merriment in the desert of grim purposes.

We were due to arrive at seven o'clock. I awoke at eight, somewhat alarmed lest we had passed our destination, only to learn that we still had ninety kilometres to go. Soon after, the delay was explained by an overturned goods train whose engine lay on its side, faintly breathing, like an expiring elephant. This was very convenient, since it had begun to snow, and the warmth of my flea-bag was preferable to a long wait in a wayside station. We reached Sergievo – now called Zagorsk – at ten o'clock, and walked straight to the monastery. Seen across the valley, behind a curtain of gently falling snowflakes, the clusters of domes, encircled by a white wall with fat red-washed angle-towers and over-topped by Rastrelli's belfry, 320 ft of pink-and-white baroque arches, seemed more like a painted back-cloth than a thing of three dimensions, substantial and inhabited.

Nor was this illusion altogether unjust. These monasteries and

Kremlins that flash their colours over the gloomy landscape are, in truth, a back-cloth to the modern stage, and redeem the play, if the audience be a foreign traveller, from the monotony of a fore-doomed industrialization. The Troitskaya Lavra at Sergievo is one of the most famous of them. Founded in 1340, and always the object of imperial favour, its corporation of 100 monks became the owners of half a million serfs, so said the lady who showed us round between pants of indignation. After the Revolution the monastery became a museum and a haven for savants, but was now deserted. The savants had been accused of a plot and were dispersed, some to 'manure Socialist fields', others to populate the Ural towns and the lumber-camps.

The peace of the snow-covered courtyard, large and irregular as two Oxford colleges, with its churches, refectory, and lines of cells, was broken only by the cawing of crows in the bare trees. Beside the entrance to the blue-domed cathedral, a squat tomb, half hidden by the trunks of a small coppice, still shelters the remains of the Tsar Boris Godunov. We were shown the Metropolitan's apartments, where the furniture used by Peter the Great remains untouched. And then I asked to see what was formerly the greatest treasure of the monastery, the embroidered sheet or banner presented to it in 1499 by Sophia, wife of Ivan III, Princess of Constantinople – so the broidered inscription calls her – and last historic figure of the dethroned family of Palaeologus. My request evoked first pretended ignorance of any such object, then petulant annoyance, and finally acquiescence, on condition that I made no attempt to accompany the curator to the store-room where the sheet was now hidden, as it was in such a muddle!

After a wait of two hours, I was able to examine the precious relic, a large panel of faded silk embroidery in which patches of a deep rose-crimson stand out against the remains of a blue background. A series of familiar themes such as the *Annunciation*, *Ascension*, and *Pentecost*, surrounds a central rectangle which depicts a *Hetimasia* or *Preparation of the Throne*. Two narrow columns, stretching from the lower corners of this rectangle to the bottom of the banner, contain the inscription worked in metal thread. This was kindly transcribed for me by an old man, the last of the savants, and runs as follows:

In the year 7007, in the time of the pious Grand Prince Ivan Vasilevich and that of his son the Grand Prince Vasili Ivanovich and the Archbishop Simon Metropolitan, this cloth was made by the intention and command of the Princess of Tsargrad [Constantinople], Grand Princess of Moscow, Sophia (wife) of the Grand Prince of Moscow, who prayed to the life-giving Trinity and the miracle-working Sergius and affixed this cloth.

Zoë – or, as she was afterwards known, Sophia – Palaeologina introduced the ceremony and aloofness of the Byzantine court into Muscovy, and it is significant of the importance attached to this link with the Roman succession that, thirty years after her marriage, her maiden title should still have taken precedence of her husband's.

When he had finished, the old man and I had an argument about religion. The old man, whose great years seemed to render him impervious to the terrors of proletarian censorship, said that religion, whatever its form, must always be necessary to mankind. I suggested that the necessity was now filled, in modern Russia, by the new Christ in the Red Square. 'Perhaps,' he replied, 'perhaps.'

At the station, later, I caused a commotion by taking a nip of vodka from a bottle I had bought in the village shop. Such licence is not allowed in public. On getting into the train we heard people saying that they thought they would risk the front coach, despite the accident of the morning and the appalling disaster that had taken place near Moscow two or three days before at a cost of nearly two hundred lives. The train was a local one. There were no lights, the seats were of wood, and the wheels, I felt convinced, were square, not round. The atmosphere was like some unsavoury anaesthetic. A Red soldier fell asleep on my bosom. Myself reclined on the ampler person of an old peasant woman. So we returned to the capital.

IX

THE UKRAINE

The first really surprising impression that Russia had made on me was when, after leaving the Polish frontier, I sought the dining-car and found myself embowered in a coppice of cyclamens, each of which was obscured by an enormous white bow. These bows were not so incongruous as they sound. For the coach itself was a survival from the same epoch of taste and resembled, both in ornament and dimensions, the dining-room of the Ritz Hotel in London. Indeed, these enormous broad-gauge caravans that lumber across two continents are the traveller's first indication of the Russian's inherent hankering after a kind of megalo-comfort. It is a pleasant vice, and a sympathetic one to the Englishman. I enjoyed those interminable journeys, with their ceaseless accidents. The wagons-lits seem to have come through the Revolution without a scratch, brass intact, velvet undimmed. The conductors have come with them, pleasant old fellows always ready with a glass of tea from the samovar in the corridor, and proud of their clean white linen. Even the ordinary 'soft' carriages, which hold four, are by no means unpleasant; choose an upper berth and you have control of the ventilator in the roof. My best journey was from Leningrad to Moscow in the *Red Arrow*, which passed three other trains bound for the same destination and exceeded an average of thirty miles an hour. In the middle of the night I was awakened by two comrades having a dormitory feast beneath the light of a standard lamp in a pink silk shade. Their mumbling gossip was not at all to my pleasure, and I was obliged to shout to the conductor before the interloper would remove himself and leave my berth-mate to go to bed.

A week's journey in the Ukraine, with which my stay in Russia ended, gave my companion and myself a taste of railway travel as a pastime which may or may not have been typical of the country, but was certainly varied in its excitements. The actual process of departure from Moscow involved us in several days' unremitting effort. My visa had expired; worse still, I had omitted, on arrival, to register with the police. The Foreign Office was easily placated, but not the police, who insisted that I should be out of the country by 18 February. There ensued a detailed examination of my notes, diary, and the books I had bought, on the part of the customs, who finally stamped, packed, and sealed them in a manner designed to reassure their fellows at Odessa. Lastly, a Turkish visa was necessary. But the getting of this produced a pleasant surprise. For the Turkish officials, generally so palsied and tiresome, had been inspired to a brusque efficiency by the fabulous incompetence around them.

After so much turmoil, the actual start of our journey, by the 7.35 p.m. to Harkov, seemed like Nirvana itself. Owing to the vagaries of a rival train, which had accidentally escaped from the station on to our line, our actual departure was delayed an hour. We arrived at Harkov correspondingly late next morning and at once conceived a dislike for the town, which is without feature except for a good modernist post office and the Palace of Industry. The latter lies on the outskirts of the place, and when complete will form a circle of skyscrapers, joined by bridges, in the middle of an empty plain. Even now, with only one-fifth of its circumference built, its appearance is that of an industrial 'folly', whose architect has tried to go one better than Stonehenge. We also discovered that the only hotel was full. All they could allow us was the temporary use of a suite containing the luggage, though not the person, of a French duchess. We borrowed her bathroom to shave in; but delicacy forbade us to appropriate her bed, and as there was nowhere else to stay, we decided to go on to Dnieperstroy that night, to see the dam. This was a departure from our programme, which had been so arranged as to avoid the Five-Year Plan. But foreseeing the questions that would be asked at home, we now concluded we ought to have something to say on that subject.

Before leaving, we lunched at the 'Dynamo Country Club' outside the town, a spacious institution approached by two modernist lodges and having its own stadium where a few of the members were engaged in a desultory game of ice-hockey. The walls of the dining-room were severely panelled in the modern French style with woods of various colours; the lighting was in glass strips, flush with the wood and running up the walls and along the ceiling. But the designer responsible for this elegant severity could scarcely have foreseen the addition of a whole forest of barrel-trunked palms fifteen feet high and tied, once more, with giant bows. When, too, each table sported a dead chrysanthemum also tied with two and sometimes three white bows, the room itself resembled more a deserted florist's than an essay in collectivist psycho-furnishing. The food, apart from these impediments, was delicious – Ukrainian borstch with cream, kidneys and potatoes, and tangerine salad. Then we drove to the station, where we found ourselves ushered into the Tsar's waiting-room. For our guide, foreseeing difficulty in securing sleepers at such short notice, had given the authorities to understand that we were persons of high importance, on whose comfort would depend the future course of relations between Russia and England. Our conversation with the station-master, who came hurrying along to pay his respects, was truly royal in character:

'Sixty trains per day before the war and 115 now? You don't say so!'

'Certainly; and in summer there are 129.'

'What strides!'

'The place has grown since the capital was moved from Odessa. In 1913 there were only 286,000 inhabitants. Now there are 600,000.'

We acted as though we could hardly believe our ears, with the result that, when the train came in, a whole compartment was emptied of protesting passengers to make room for us. In the corridor hung a notice offering prizes to travellers and transport workers for sensible suggestions anent the management of the railway. Before the end of the week we had several suggestions to make.

Sleep that night came fitfully. At 3 a.m. the train almost broke in half and I received a sharp blow on the temple from an iron door. We were now at Alexandrovsk, and on descending found ourselves engaged in a life and death struggle with a mob of maddened peasants, who had been waiting several days to find a place on a train. It was a horrible scene; old women, bent and weeping, were knocked to the ground; we had much ado to extricate our luggage, and then guard it. At last a car was found, just vacated by the duchess, who was returning from the dam to her violated suite. This took us several miles across country to the new town.

Morning revealed brilliant sunshine, a hotel which, though but lately finished, was already falling to bits, and an apparition of poached eggs. After eating these we walked through the building town, a scene of indescribable confusion, but tranquil compared with the dam itself. Here, on the great elevated highway that spanned the frozen river, two streams of black and muffled humanity were striving to maintain their opposite courses, shrieking engines drawing heavy goods trains threatened toe and heel alike, sentries wrapped in greasy fleeces menaced each errant passenger with their bayonets, and a wind like a jagged razor whipped across ears and lips. For about three-quarters of a mile – the breadth of the river – we continued thus, deafened and terrified, balancing precariously on ice-covered rails and catching horrid glimpses of the sluices below, where the water came roaring down from under the ice, as the frozen boards of the footway creaked and gaped. At length, in the head office on the farther bank, a conclave of officials and engineers awaited us. Their brains, they said, were ours to command. What, precisely, had we come to study, and what statistics did we need? Such questions left us speechless; it would scarcely have been polite to have admitted that the only reason for our presence at Dnieperstroy was that of the duchess's luggage at Harkov; but remembering a similar occasion on the Sukkur barrage in Sind, I essayed some feeble questions: sluice-gates, forty-nine; three locks on the left bank; nine turbines of 90,000 horse-power. The officials were not deceived. With admirable tact they changed the subject by asking us what we should like for lunch.

Armed with a special pass, I departed to take photographs. Owing to the position of the sun, this meant returning to the bank whence we had come, and reluctant to face the terrors of the bridge, I decided to entrust myself to the ice, promising to keep carefully to existing tracks, since the rate of unexplained disappearances had lately become alarmingly high. Suddenly, as I reached the very middle of the river, a cannon started to fire; blinded by the glare, I could scarcely see where I was going, and now I began to imagine that the whole surface of the river was about to shiver and crack beneath this fusillade of noise. Then my eyelids froze together; this, at least, I reflected, had been spared St Peter. Tottering forward, I reached the bank at last, to be greeted by a man of wild aspect, who jumped out from behind a slag-heap, and after demanding a cigarette, which I gave him, ran away as though I were a leper. I now walked for a mile down-stream in search of a vantage-point. In the distance, the dam stretched across the river like some huge grey fortification, partly hidden by clouds of steaming spray. Trains, diminutive as those in film collisions, crept along its top. From the forty-nine sluice-gates came the water from under the ice, swirling down the rapids formed by two rocky islets, and bearing on its surface a spate of tiny ice-floes, round and white as polar lotuses.

We lunched in a sort of seaside villa, one of a row built for the now departed American experts. The food, elaborately dished and served, was admirable. Flagons of vodka were followed by Crimean champagne. The more we swallowed, the more argumentative everyone became. We Europeans, we said, were possessors of a cultural and political inheritance which had accrued during two thousand years, and which we now saw no reason to throw away. The Russians replied that it was merely a class inheritance. In that case, we maintained, we required no further justification of a ruling class. Finally, our host, who was an educated man of delightful manners, said that whatever one might think of socialism in the abstract, in practice one could not live in Russia to-day unless sustained by a belief in it. We then turned to country sports. Game, our host informed us, was by no means free. He belonged to a club in order to shoot, which cost him sixty roubles a year; as his salary was 6,000, this, he thought, was not excessive. He regretted that he had not got us a hare for lunch. In the old days they used to hunt hares and foxes with borzois; but not now; it damaged the peasants' corn.

In the evening we attended a concert given by a Ukrainian choir. The programme was in two parts: the first, traditional; the second, and longer, ideological. The latter was rendered the more tedious by the presence of a composer, who set about teaching both performers and audience some feeble revolutionary ditties of his own composing. At the end of the concert, the distinguished foreigners were handed a visitors' book, for signatures and comment. This is the usual procedure among these vain redeemers. At the dam we had confined our praise to the cuisine, feeling that the duchess had done enough for the engineering with the words 'Œuvre des Titans!' Now we wrote that, admirable as the singing had been, we could not help regretting that it should have been wasted on such deplorable material. It was a little uncivil, perhaps, and caused some dismay, but we felt the necessity now and then of sounding some note other than the Shavian parrot-song which all English visitors to Russia are expected to utter.

Midnight found us once more at Alexandrovsk, seated on a hard bench in the station-master's office. The train was two hours late; its electricity had failed, and there was only one candle, which we stole. But as was usual in my experience, the bed-linen was clean and the conductor did his best to make us comfortable. Not even the inevitable accident disturbed our sleep.

Back in Harkov again, we received a call from the director of the Opera. He wore a coat of Siberian stag, whose hairs rattled like straw and rained to the ground as he moved. This he had acquired while making a film in the Arctic. Had the film been a success? we asked. 'Oh dear, no – not nearly enough ideology in it.' He preferred his present job. Classics were classics and could not be interfered with.

After dinner, eaten to a band, we started for Kiev, on a journey which proved the eeriest of them all, and confirmed in me a suspicion that the chief value to Russia, and to the world, of the Five-Year Plan will be its unassailable witness to the futility of materialist economics. This time it was the heating that had failed. I sat huddled in my flea-bag. We had two strangers with us: one a member of the secret police in horn spectacles, who looked like Harold Lloyd in the rôle of Torquemada; the other a nondescript, who suddenly announced that he was getting out at Poltava. What a name for one's destination, I mused, and pictured Charles XII fleeing in his litter. It was our fourth successive night in the train. When we woke, the sun was shining and the train had stopped. An accident, of course, we knew. But this time it was something to wake up for. The hind coach of a local train in front of us had become derailed owing to overloading. As we and the other passengers stood bareheaded in the snow, a single engine steamed majestically past us down the line carrying away nineteen bodies in a luggage van. Forty more were injured and our remaining whisky allayed the misery of a bearded, bleeding old peasant.

There seemed little chance of continuing that morning. At the back of our train was a special coach with wireless aerial and Packard car attached, containing the President of the Ukraine. From here we were able to borrow hot water and make ourselves soup. At last, as dusk fell, we steamed into Kiev along the banks of the Dnieper. From a wooded hill, the golden domes of the Pechersky monastery flashed their famous welcome over snow and forest and the huge frozen river – no welcome of hope to faithful pilgrims, but a message of impotence and desuetude in a world of trained cynics.

The chef at the hotel was an artist, and also a friend of our guide. He gave us a dinner of fabulous excellence – for which, and for its fellow the next night, the manager tried to charge us £50. Afterwards we went to the theatre where Stolypin was shot in 1911, and saw *Prince Igor*. This one performance was worth a whole week of the pretentious Bolshoy Theatre in Moscow. The audience, too, was different; its faces were more cheerful, its clothes less devoid of amenity. Next morning we met the duchess, face to face, in the hall of the hotel. 'I'm leaving for Poland this moment', she said. 'Come and see me in Paris.' Her scent, which lingered, was a cheerful reminder of class privilege.

The treasures and monuments of Kiev are many, as befits the earliest and most civilized of Russian capitals. Our first visit was to the cathedral, which was built in 1036 on a Greek model, but was so restored in 1705 by the Hetman Mazeppa that its architecture is now interesting mainly as an example of Ukrainian baroque. Inside, however, the main apse has retained its original mosaics, which are dominated by a great Virgin. This figure, which seems but mediocre in photographs, revealed to us a masterpiece of Byzantine art in its highest epoch.

According to Professor Vassilievich, the surface of the vault which bears the Virgin comprises not one curve but three; so that if a section of the structure were cut through from the roof and observed from the side, it would resemble the sketch opposite. The top curve contains the head and shoulders, the middle curve the belly and thighs, and the lower curve the knees and all below them. This device saves the figure from an appearance of toppling forward, and prevents the head from assuming a size disproportionate to the rest of the body. An Italian would have suited his drawing to the vault. The Greeks chose to adapt the vault lest it should distort their drawing.

The colours of the Kiev Virgin are unique in Byzantine mosaic, and unique, therefore, in their effect, among all works of art. The figure stands alone, without scenery or fellow – an apparition of majesty in the gold emptiness of its quadrant. The arms are uplifted from the elbows, in austere mediation between man and God; the knees bend and the feet are planted apart. A voluminous robe permits the contours of the legs. From the shoulders depends a mantle, which is swathed diagonally across the bosom and drops fanwise to the level of the knees behind, in a cascade of angular creases. This mantle secretes its colour in a tone of unfathomable darkness, on which the high-lights of each crease repeat, though with more glitter, the gold of the background. But the robe beneath the mantle, together with the sleeves that protrude from it, are invested with a tint whose radiant singularity no one that has seen it can ever forget. This tint is a porcelain blue, the blue of harebells or of a Siamese cat's eyes, an adamant, extrusive colour that stands clear from the aureate haze of the vault to proclaim its wearer's invincible personality. Below the robe, shoes of royal scarlet complete this proclamation. Round the waist is tied a cord of lilac pink, whose brightness exactly equals the brightness of the blue and which strikes a mean between that colour and the scarlet of the shoes, thus forming, despite its tiny area, the pivot of the entire composition. On the cord hangs negligently a little gold towel with a fringe. The sleeves have tight, patterned cuffs, also in gold.

On the curving wall, immediately under the vault, appears the *Double Communion*. The Apostles, six on either side, approach with loping tread a canopied altar, at whose either corner a separate Christ dispenses the two elements. The draperies of the Apostles are grey, buff-yellow, and white, sewn with double seams of an emphatic red. Christ wears a dark blue mantle above a gold robe. Faces, hands, and feet are rendered in shell-pink, and the whole mosaic has a fresh and airy quality which contrasts with the overwhelming, solitary grandeur of the figure above. In a second zone, below the Apostles, stands a row of Early Fathers, hieratic figures which have been restored from the hips downwards.

The cathedral contains, besides other more fragmentary mosaics, a superb Byzantine relic in the shape of Prince Yaroslav's tomb. This potentate, whose daughter married King Harold of England, died in 1054 after bringing the Kievan civilization to the height of its early splendour. His tomb is a monumental sarcophagus, about nine feet long, which lies in a dark chapel half-hidden by the encircling walls and by a floor-level which has encroached considerably on its original height. In general form, with its acroteria and sloping roof, it resembles those ark-like porphyry coffins that once held the Byzantine Emperors and now stand in a row outside the Museum at Constantinople. But in this case the material is white marble from the Proconnesus, and the whole visible surface is richly carved in the style of the sarcophagi at Ravenna, though with the addition of later motives. Russian authorities concur in dating the tomb of Yaroslav from the sixth century, and presume it to have been brought from Kherson on the death of the prince.

At the west end of the cathedral, on either side of the main entrance, are two broad spiral staircases, whose walls were painted in the eleventh century with scenes of secular life in Constantinople. The rarity of such scenes, even in manuscript illuminations, is notorious. And when we found the iron gates leading to each staircase locked, we promptly sent our cards to Professor Vassilievich, who lived in a house near by and was, we were told, engaged in the reparation of the paintings. Though it was a 'sixth day', and therefore a holiday, the Professor most kindly emerged from his leisure and eventually devoted a large part of the day to showing us round the town.

The paintings on the staircase were discovered about the middle of the last century, when they were ruthlessly restored. After three years' work, one series has now been almost wholly disencumbered of its accretions. It begins with hunting incidents, such as a man shooting with a bow and arrow at an animal in a tree, or a rider on a white horse being attacked by a lion. Farther up appear individual portraits, equestrian and otherwise, framed each by two columns and surmounted by the badges of the Hippodrome factions, of which the most frequent is a black crescent on a blue circle. These, it is thought, must represent the faction champions. Then comes the royal box, an extension of the Great Palace, tenanted by the Emperor and Empress, and also the box of the diplomatic corps, whose occupants appear to be Persians. Other spectators of high rank are grouped in a series of loggias. The entertainment offered by the Hippodrome games comprises a man in Turkish fancy dress, three horsemen chasing a wild horse, mummers in odd costumes, men playing pipes and harp, and a boy climbing a pole balanced on a man's shoulder after the fashion described by Liutprand during the Christmas dinner of the Emperor Constantine Porphyrogenitus. Various graffiti have lately come to light, which are in Greek, and from which it may therefore be supposed that the artist was a Greek, painting from memory the scenes he had actually witnessed.

Accompanied by Professor Vassilievich, we now drove to the monastery of St Michael, whose church contains an uninspired twelfth-century mosaic of the *Double Communion*, a copy, probably by Russian artists, of the same theme in the cathedral. More interesting proved two red-granite plaques of mounted saints in low relief, which date from the twelfth century and have a Middle Eastern look. Each plaque depicts two riders affronted: one, SS. Theodore Stratilates and Mercury, the other SS. George and Demetrius. The first pair tramples a dragon; the second, a man in armour, who may represent Julian the Apostate. Thence we continued to the monastery of St Cyril on the outskirts of the town, whose few remaining frescoes have already been mentioned.

Later in the day, Professor Vassilievich took us to the Académie des Sciences, where we bought the first and only volume of its newly started Annual, showed us the old bookshops, and introduced us to such friends as he met in a manner which seemed quite abnormal after the ferocious isolation of Moscow. It was like an afternoon at Oxford. Even at the present time, he said, there were 50,000 students in the town. He talked of his boyhood and the Civil War, when Kiev was captured and recaptured fifteen times, and once three times in a single day; sometimes, for nearly a week at a time, it was impossible to go out for the street-fighting. After dinner, following his advice, we went to the cathedral to hear the Saturday evening service. Scene and singing had a tragic grandeur. From her glowing golden vault the giant Virgin gazed upon the packed congregation with eyes nine centuries old, while the basses boomed like water-beasts in the jungle and the trebles wildly rose. At the climax of the service the sacristan, with whom we had made friends in the morning, beckoned us behind the iconostasis, where the priests, in gorgeous copes, were performing their private evolutions about the altar. It was with some embarrassment that we profaned these mysteries. But their sacred character was lessened by the sight of each priest, whenever his turn came to be exposed to the public gaze, running across the bema and combing his hair before a draped mirror evidently kept there for the purpose.

One more journey lay in front of us. There had, of course, been an accident on the line, and the train, which was due in at 6.30 p.m. and had made us hurry over our dinner, arrived eventually at 1.45 a.m. There was no further accident that night. But early next morning the wheels of the coach in front of ours were observed to be on fire. We waited an hour, while they removed it, in a wayside station. Snow was falling in a thick curtain; through it, a loud-speaker fastened to the station roof was relaying an old gramophone record of Peer Gynt. It was our last day in Russia, and the sound of those tinned melodies whinnying their glorious message of scientific culture through the snowflakes, over the broken train, to the white unpeopled landscape, served as a melancholy but precise epilogue.

There was still time for one more mishap: another train got ahead of us by mistake. Already the ship was due to have left. At Odessa we drove at racing speed along the quays, while the sun set like an expiring furnace across the frozen sea. The ship had gone – but it was believed that she might be found elsewhere taking in oil. Bundling some customs officials into one of our two cars, we pursued the ship up the coast like a gang of bandits.

At one o'clock in the morning I looked from my porthole. We were moving, crunching through the ice-floes in the wake of an ice-breaker. The lights of Russia receded. Then we reached the open water, and already the wind seemed a little warmer.

PART II

TIBET

I

THE AIR MAIL

The journey here described may with some justice be called unusual,
since, apart from the survivors of the Younghusband expedition and
certain officers of the Indian Army and Government, they are comparatively few who have accomplished it. Travel within the Tibetan
frontiers involves obvious difficulties, of which one is an unpredictable
degree of physical discomfort. But such a journey as ours, when
regarded as a journey among journeys, can make no claim to be
considered unique or even remarkable: the difficulties were overcome
with moderate effort; the knowledge gained was such as to satisfy
only the personal curiosity of those who sought it. In thus unloosing
a second torrent of personal anecdote I have but one purpose and
excuse; which is, if I can, to please the reader with some pale reflection
of the quality of pure enjoyment which became known to me during
my first visit to Asia Magna. To travel in Europe is to assume a
foreseen inheritance; in Islam, to inspect that of a close and familiar
cousin. But to travel in farther Asia is to discover a novelty previously
unsuspected and unimaginable. It is not a question of probing this
novelty, of analysing its sociological, artistic, or religious origins, but
of learning, simply, that it exists. Suddenly, as it were in the opening
of an eye, the potential world – the field of man and his environment
– is doubly extended. The stimulus is inconceivable to those who
have not experienced it.

If, as I think must be so, the European can attain this experience
most vividly in Asia, it is to Asia north of the Himalayas that he
should go. There the very face of the earth, the atmospherics, clouds,

and colours, are absolved from all known criteria. And there, in Tibet, alone of the world's political compartments, have the effects of the scientific revolution not yet intruded on the outward picture of every-day life.

From an early age the fact of Tibet's existence had coloured my thoughts, fastened there by 'Y for Yak' on a zoological alphabet. Later, in course of some military operations with my school OTC near Goring, a friend and I fell to concerting fabulous schemes for our future betterment: a visit to Tibet was one; but, we agreed, the most fabulous. With the coming of responsibility the purpose waned, as other purposes such as engine-driving had waned before it. Until one day came a letter from India, tempting me with 'a trip to Sikkim'. Sikkim? – the atlas showed a small state in the Himalayas bordering on Tibet. Obviously, I might even see a yak in Sikkim. But why Sikkim? Why not Tibet?

Modern literary travellers are divided into those to whom expense is no obstacle, and those who profit from an absolute lack of any money whatsoever to achieve picturesque suffering and strange companions. I myself escape these categories. Unaccustomed to starvation, and preferring, at all times, luxury to squalor, I had neither desire nor intention of beachcombing my way to Central Asia. Simultaneously, to effect even the preliminary voyage to India under conditions of normal comfort seemed a matter of prohibitive cost. Yet the phantom, once invoked, would not be laid. Go I must, and set myself to will the means. How they occurred, by what slender fortuity, was an event that still leaves me breathless when I think of it.

I had been asked to join a party for supper after the theatre. It promised little entertainment: at first I refused; then went unwillingly, and still more unwillingly to a subterranean night-club. There I sat, scarcely able to keep awake and preparing an abrupt good-bye, when there entered an acquaintance, who informed me that Lord Beaver-brook was in search of new writers. This particular acquaintance I had not seen for two years, and but for my weak-mindedness in sitting up when I should have been asleep, might not have seen for another two.

It was already plain to me that since the initial difficulty of reaching

India at all was to all intents and purposes insurmountable, I had best aim at travelling by the most expensive route possible. This was the Air Mail, which had then been only a week or two in regular service. If Lord Beaverbrook wanted new writers, he might want new subjects also. Let me offer both.

Next day, thanks to the good offices of our mutual friend, I visited Lord Beaverbrook. Undeterred by the exuberant presence of Lord Castlerosse, I treated my host to several profound thoughts (hastily formulated in the taxi) on the more effective welding of our imperial ties; observing, though without undue emphasis, what a vista of possibilities had been opened by this new route to the East. My seed, though I did not know it, fell on a rich plough. For a fortnight later Lord Beaverbrook's Empire Free Trade Campaign burst on the public.

I pursued this advantage. Numerous conversations followed. I even attempted, without success, to write on my chosen theme for the *Evening Standard*. But my plans got no further, and the theme was outside my knowledge. Meanwhile, if I was going to India, the time was rapidly arriving when I must come to a decision as to dates and make arrangements. At length, one sunny June morning, I sat with Lord Beaverbrook in his garden overlooking the Park, and I asked him in plain terms whether he was prepared to pay my passage to India in return for some articles. He knew, as I knew, that no articles on such a subject could possibly be worth £126 in the open market of journalism. But with a generosity which the march of politics can never efface, he assented, walked indoors, and reaching for an ivory telephone, gave the necessary instructions to his office.

I informed my family of the good news, and feared some possible objections on their part to the hazards of the new route. My mother, however, could think of nothing but the drawing-rooms of Anglo-Indian relatives. All she asked was that I should not bring home a Buddha. My elder sister supposed that now I should have to become a sahib. '*Are* you a sahib?' she inquired dubiously. My younger sister, recalling the field of my previous activities, muttered under her breath: 'Now it'll be tribes instead of monks.' My father remained acquiescent, merely toying with the probabilities and pains of sunstroke.

During the ensuing weeks my parents' ears were filled with the precautions taken by past and present administrators of the Indian

Empire, men and women of all ages and complexions, to preserve their health. One had worn a tummy-belt for forty years; another had taken a nightly dose of quinine over the same length of time. One thing was certain: my instant demise could be averted only by a miracle; and the chances of that miracle would be dangerously handicapped by a first arrival in the hot weather. Reluctantly I submitted to various inoculations. The aeroplane was to leave on Saturday. On Friday morning I enjoyed the important sensation of a farewell lunch at the Ritz, attended by Miss Tilly Losch. That evening numerous friends sent me telegrams, couched as though I were going to execution. My ticket lay fatting in a breast pocket, a book of coupons for lunch in this country, dinner in that, and transit in between. I spent till midnight fitting clothes, medicaments, and stationery into a kit-bag and a blue Revelation suitcase.

The morning of Saturday, 27 July brought a feeling of relief, as though it were the first day of the holidays. Whatever the horrors in store, at least they could be met passively, and without the exercise of that wearing initiative demanded by the packing of an unprotected bottle. At nine o'clock I reached Airways House in Charles Street. Body and baggage, I weighed two and a half pounds under the permitted complement. At the aerodrome we hurried through passages and barriers, and emerged from a door to find the *City of Wellington* buzzing and roaring on the threshold; its three enormous propellers threatened our hats with their wind. I crept up the diminutive gangway to my seat. A door shut. And the machine cantered across the aerodrome, turned, galloped back, and rose above a sea of small red houses.

My first sensation was one of suffocating depression. But for a quarter of an hour in a tin and canvas Flea, which looped the loop for an extra 7s. 6d. and fell in half the week after, I had never flown before. And I now beheld myself in a dark cabin scarcely five feet across, twisting about in a constricted wicker space, and convinced that my whole being would soon disintegrate altogether under pressure of sheer noise. A long dormant home-sickness rose within me, an ache for train or boat, the old and comfortable friends of travel. A trip to Paris might be borne. But to contemplate the continuance of this inferno of drill, buzz, and roar, and these attitudes of a strait-jacket, for eight days on end was to relinquish faith in the beneficence of earthly fate. My mother's good-bye assumed an aspect of tragedy. I dreamt of the lazy days on deck that might have been, or the blue velvet of a wagon-lit, to take the place of these preposterous cretonne curtains, over-waisted and functionless as those of a doll's house. When Air-Marshal Sir Geoffrey Salmond, seeking to levitate himself from the chair behind, accidentally rapped me on the head, I all but turned and knocked him through the aeroplane. Only the merry-go-round motion of the bumps provided some relief, which was increased to pleasure by the sight of several passengers at their cuspidors.

As we rose to between three and four thousand feet, the patchwork of English fields, heavily embroidered in elms, disappeared in a haze. A line proclaimed the Channel, and, after half an hour's gloom, another the coast of France. Here the patchwork was cleaner, strips and squares of ripened corn interspersed with larger and more irregular shapes of green velvet woodland; occasionally a white road showed like a lining beneath, with sometimes a stumpwork of trees along it. One o'clock found us at Le Bourget, lunching beneath a wallpaper of inebriate birds. Those around us ate delicious omelettes. We, coming from England, were treated to a parody of our national beef.

At two o'clock we embarked again for Basle. At lunch I had made the acquaintance of a professional journalist, named Butcher, who said he loathed flying, but flew everywhere for copy. He was now sick. Eventually hills appeared, and clouds, the latter suffusing the cabin with an odd winter light. Then the town lay beneath us, and we glided down to the Birsfelden aerodrome, where the customs house was adorned with a series of excellent modern frescoes, depicting 'Porterage'. Hence a bus took us to the Hotel Euler. The drive revealed the 'Crewe of Switzerland' as a charming, shady town, with many old houses, fountains, and flowerbeds. The local zoo was advertised with posters of seals.

From the hotel I went to the Kunsthalle, which, though officially shut, was in fact open. The barkings of a dog brought its master, who, on my explaining that I had come by aeroplane especially to see El Greco's *Laocoon*, admitted me to the galleries. Unfortunately this picture was no longer there. It has since appeared in London. The main interest of the collection was the Holbeins, which included the famous miniature of Erasmus in old age, and a water-colour of Edward VI of England holding a small, flap-eared dog. The keeper drew my attention to the phantasies of his fellow-citizen Böcklin, who enjoyed a great vogue about 1880.

After dining on the terrace of the hotel, and surrendering the requisite coupons from our tickets, the party, now depleted to five, proceeded to the station, accompanied by various officials of Imperial Airways carrying the sticks, coats, and parcels that had been left behind. 'We have to treat our passengers like children,' they observed resignedly. The train was in; wagons-lits were reserved; we disposed our baggage; but there was no engine. This arrived three-quarters of an hour late, and then rushed through the Alps at an immense pace, interrupted by halts of such violence that on one occasion I fell out of bed.

Morning dawned in northern Italy. More of the company's officials, smartly uniformed in blue serge and gold braid, met us at Genoa. 'They don't half run the houses up here,' remarked one passenger, who had not been in Italy before. After traversing the untidiest port in the world, we came to a small barge, the property of the SANA (Società Anonima Navigazione Aerea), where poached eggs and strawberry jam lay inviting on a table.

Already the heat was sweltering. Out in the harbour glittered the white Calcutta flying-boat, the *City of Rome*, with a small Union Jack fluttering from its cockpit. After a slight delay, caused by the checking of the mails, we went off in a launch. The Union Jack was furled; the hatch closed; we were away. The rise of a flying-boat, particularly when there is a swell, resembles all that Luna Park just fails to achieve. The engines roar; the floats on the wings dip, first on one side, then on the other; at each wave a great bump lifts the machine. The speed increases, clouds of spray lash the portholes; till suddenly we have exchanged elements and the sea is beneath. After circling a good-bye to the seaplane base, we set off to the south, leaving the coast of Italy on our left. One of the party, Captain Bennett-Baggs, whose stature was such that he exceeded in personal weight the full quota allowed each passenger with his luggage, took the second controls.

A pleasanter and more intimate atmosphere now prevailed. The portholes once opened, it was cooler; the noise was less, the engines being set behind, on the wings; and the seats of inflated leather allowed freer movement. Outside, the wings gleamed white against the lapis of the Mediterranean 500 feet below, and the floats beneath them looked like huge silver fishes accidentally caught out of the deep. From time to time the wireless operator sent us messages: Elba on the right, Leghorn on the left. In due course, we passed over Ostia, circling a salute to the seaplane base, where we could see the Dornier-Wal machines lying each in its little dock. According to schedule, we should have lunched there; but the water was too shallow for a safe descent. Instead, the engineer now produced a typical Italian lunch of ham, salami, chicken, new rolls, cheese, Russian mushrooms, nectarines, and wine. These we ate from tin trays, which slid up from the backs of the chairs like prayer-book racks. There were two forks, three glasses, and one cup, to assist us.

Another note arrived, asking if we wished to fly over Vesuvius and look down the crater. We did. But when the Bay of Naples came round the corner, a cloud was covering the top of the mountain. The town and its dependencies, stretching in a circuit of thirty miles round the shore, presented a gorgeous panorama in the golden glitter of a southern afternoon, as we passed between Ischia and the mainland, flew over Posilipo, and came spirally down upon the harbour. New officials met us. The customs obliterated themselves. On the bus, we talked of Mussolini as Mr Smith, and of the pleasures of Capri in yet more cryptic terms.

After a bath at the Hotel Excelsior, I drove out beyond Posilipo, and off the main road down a one-way track enclosed between the high mud walls of vineyards. This led to a gate, within which rows of painfully watered carnations bespoke the Englishman's determination to carry his home with him. P. was in the drive, clad only in vest and trousers, and abounding in classical lore. Here was the rock, like so many rocks in this neighbourhood, where Vergil wrote the *Aeneid*; there the palace of Lucullus, its painted rooms still intact; beyond, the tunnel which Sejanus, minister to Tiberius, cut through the rock to the same main road, rather than use the drive which my taxi had reluctantly negotiated. The R.s must endure it, as the tunnel is a national monument, and must therefore be permitted to fall into decay.

Having undressed, we descended the cliff on which the villa stands by a series of other tunnels and quarried steps, to bathe. It was like a home-coming to float once more on the buoyant waters of the Mediterranean, and swim with an ease that two years' absence from the sea had made me forget. We plucked a fat sea-urchin from a rock, which the gardener later identified as a female. At dinner, the food was from the sea, the wine from the garden. Mussolini was here referred to as Mr Jones. P.'s brother, then in the Air Force, said that before coming out to Italy he had received rigid instructions not to speak to, or be spoken to by, any member of the corresponding Italian service, for fear of being thought a spy. Afterwards, we sat looking over the bay, a semicircle of quivering yellow stars in the blackness. Up in the sky hovered a stationary comet. This was Vesuvius: the railway its tail, and the observatory its body.

Recalling my obligations to the *Daily Express*, I made ado to return, eventually leaving in a pony-cart drawn by a diminutive brown Pegasus, which had no thought for the ravines that yawned beneath each corner. A tram was waiting on the main road, which took me back to the hotel. I sat up till one o'clock composing an article, and rose again at five to type it.

Unbuttoned, unshaven, and unfed, I clattered into the hall at a quarter past seven, to find the other passengers already waiting. At a quarter to eight we were off again, crossed the instep of Italy with an occasional bump, touched the southernmost point of the Gallipoli peninsula, and, an hour later, landed in the harbour of Corfu for lunch. I had last spent seven hours of an April day here, painting an island, which had then been green and yellow. To see it now dull brown gave me a shock. Above us, the lion of St Mark spoke of Venice. An argument with officials ensued, who forbade us to disembark our cameras, though we could see a party of German tourists busily taking photographs on the cliff above our heads. It was as though the fact of travelling by air had invested us with supernatural powers of espionage. To settle the matter, I produced a *laissez-passer* from the Greek Minister in London; whereupon, to the astonishment of the rest of the party, I was hailed as a 'friend of Greece' and permitted anything. During lunch, Sir Geoffrey Salmond said that he might be old-fashioned, but that *All Quiet on the Western*

Front was not a book to leave in the drawing-room. Butcher replied with a perk of surprise that all that sort of thing was ended now, and wasn't he a bit behind the times? To which the Air-Marshal sighed: 'Well, I suppose there are drawing-rooms and drawing-rooms.' He then recalled that Corfu had once been British, and what bloody fools we were the way we always gave a good thing away. It was on the tip of my tongue to hope for a similar restoration of Cyprus from the Labour Government, but I was too content to be in Greece again to bother with an argument.

After examining an Italian Dornier-Wal monoplane, and a French machine which was painted an aesthetic orange and bringing mails from Beyrut, we flew round to the back of the island to see the Achilleion, the palace built by the Empress Elizabeth of Austria, and later vulgarized by the Kaiser. Then we continued southward along the coast, till an easterly turn took us inland over flat marshy country. Being anxious to take a photograph of Byron's death-place, Captain Stocks, the pilot, invited me into the cockpit, where I perched my feet on two aluminium platforms behind him. As I stood, my head and chest were above the wind-screen, and, since the propellers were behind, could remain there without discomfort. Below us, a marshy plain stretched into the distance; to the left, mountains; to the right, mountains; in between, patches of water reflecting the blue sky; and all the land emitting that subtle rosy glitter which is Greece. And here was I, on my fourth visit in five years, arriving in the sky – arriving not with rush and hurricane, as may be imagined; but moving with measure and circumstance through the blue vault; the great wings spreading like a house behind me; and the pilot at my feet finding it superfluous to exercise more than the slightest control over so rational and self-sufficient an instrument of locomotion. The sensation was superb and like no other. A ship is always on the water, a dependent, humbler than the humblest wave. This proud vehicle, on this unflecked, sunny afternoon, asked no visible substance for support. Standing with head bare, drunk with the wind that tossed my hair and ran over my skin beneath a fluttering shirt, I travelled as sovereign of the universe, a solar emperor.

As Missolonghi approached, I descended from my perch to the space intervening between the cabin and the cockpit, where the wireless operator sits. Here was a porthole from which, at a whistle from Stocks, I achieved a successful picture, taking care to keep the bellows of the camera out of the line of the wind. The wireless operator, who assisted, was Mr Stone, familiarly known as 'Sparks', whose personality kept me happy during the whole voyage. His round eyes and small piscine mouth suggested some ever-present outrage, until, at short intervals, the whole face would expand into a coil of smiles as ripples spread over disturbed water. The face is a sad memory, for Stone, with Pembroke the engineer, was drowned when the *City of Rome* sank with four passengers just outside Genoa in the following October.

At length we reached the Gulf of Corinth, flying close round the great obelisk of a mountain which stands at its entrance, and which, for those on shipboard, is the first real view of Greece. There lay Patras, spattered white over the opposing shore; there Lepanto, a brown village beneath us; there, across the peacock water, the S P A P railway running along the coast. In an hour we were over Corinth. The same trains were in the station; the same restaurant where I have eaten so many odd things on so many odd journeys; the same slag-heaps whence I had paddled on my second day in Greece. The Gulf curved round to meet itself, to end, but for that diminutive incision which leads to the Aegean. Along the Canal and over its bridge we flew, while a toy train puffed laboriously across it, and a still more farcical boat crawled stealthily along the bottom of the reft. At length, as we rounded Salamis, the chimneys of Piraeus hove in sight, followed by the Acropolis and the twisted cone of Lykabettus.

In Athens, to my disappointment, Imperial Airways had arranged for us to stay at the Acropole Palace, a new hotel having a bathroom to each bedroom, but situate in a low, slummy quarter of the town, and lacking that maturity of personnel which is essential to comfort. A flood of reunions awaited me. I learnt that the bookshop had sold fifteen copies of my last book. Dr Zervos presented me with a basket of Mocca coffee which had actually grown in Mocca. Later we assembled at the Hotel Grande Bretagne, where Stocks, Bennett-Baggs, and the Air-Marshal were already installed in the bar. Dinner we ate at Mr Rompapa's open-air restaurant in the Zappeion gardens, newly surrounded by an artistic trellis-work. At midnight

I dropped asleep as I sat. The other party sat drinking till four o'clock.

On Tuesday morning we left the hotel at the comparatively reasonable hour of half-past nine. Just outside Piraeus we circled low over a capsized fishing-boat, a grisly wreck in the crystal blue water, and wirelessed a description of it to the mainland. Butcher, the Air-Marshal, and myself were now alone. A following wind brought us to Suda Bay in Crete by half-past twelve, where a welcome effusively and lavishly English greeted us. For the company had stationed here a yacht, the *Imperia*, formerly the property of numerous millionaires, and able to ride any sea in case of a forced descent in bad weather. A bathe from the side, which, like all Greek bathes, will live in the memory for ever, was followed by a six-course lunch set at a table whose posy of flowers might have come from an English garden. Our appetites were sharpened by the witticisms of Captain MacLeod and Chief Officer Horn, who had lately been described in the English Press as 'Adams in an Eveless Eden'.

That afternoon Captain Stocks again permitted me the joy of sitting in the cockpit. The White Mountains, legendary home of the human vampire, were cloudless, and he decided to fly across the island and through them by a broad pass, which I had already traversed on foot two years before. Stocks had told us how, one evening in the dark, he was attempting this course, when the altimeter stuck; the pass was approaching; he was unable to make the requisite height; until, frightened and desperate, he knocked the dial, and the hand jumped up three thousand feet. Such were my own sensations now. With the nose of our great winged ship tilted upward, swaying slightly, dropping suddenly, leaping up again, we made as though to crash into the huge barren hill-side, as the vineyards and cypresses gave place to a speckling of rock and scrub. Stocks tapped the altimeter, which this time did not shoot upwards. On which – though it afterwards transpired that my apprehensions were simply the result of optical delusion, and that we actually had plenty of room – we turned, avoiding, as it seemed, the encircling mountains by a hair's-breadth, and executed a broad spiral to increase our height. Then we went straight for the pass. Still my optical delusions persisted. At every bump, as the mountain currents tossed us from side to side and the wings dipped up and down, the escarpments and rocky slopes leapt into threatening proximity. I looked down. There was the road up which I had motored on a cold October morning; there the house where I had found my mules; there the village where an escort of police had joined me; and there, cleaving the pass itself to a depth of a thousand feet, the airless gorge down which I had picked my way, a black thread twisting and bulging as it led down towards the sea. We were over. Suddenly the island dropped away from us, and the smoother southern slopes, arid brown in the summer heat, fell down to the village of Sphakia, where I had slept the night in a policeman's blanket already inhabited. From the top of Mount Ida on our left to the bottom of the sea fifteen miles out the earth's surface drops some 23,000 feet. As the island receded behind us, it seemed as though any moment might see us engulfed in this appalling abyss. Slowly and safely we descended, till the flat blue sea gradually developed a warp and woof, and at last each wave could be personally distinguished. We were heading southward for the coast of Africa.

There was something impressive about this transition, in the space of two hours, from one continent to another. From Spain, the change is not so great; the coasts resemble one another. But here, as the line of dead orange limiting the inky sapphire sea stretched interminably on into the distance, it was plain that this was a land like no other, endowed with different shapes, colours, and lights, a vast land of black races and of strange self-centred cultures that have remained isolated from the great movements of taste between Europe and Asia. As the aeroplane circled over the harbour of Tobruk, a burnt plain of measureless extent was disclosed, rippled but never hilly, and merging, fifty, a hundred, a thousand miles away, into a horizon of opal mist. I looked involuntarily for Capetown. I seemed to recognize the place. Then I thought of Egyptian art, and the recognition was explained.

Tobruk, the only landmark for hundreds of miles along this desert union of land and water, is the capital of the Italian province of Cyrenaica, and the centre of a sponge-fishery conducted by the Greek divers of the Dodecanese. The town consists of an area of mud shanties, interspersed with one or two official buildings and guarded by a wall fortified with barbed wire, outside which no Italian dares venture.

Only recently, said Stocks, he had arrived to find the quay covered with dead and wounded. Into a crowd of Arabs and negroes, gathered on the one pier, and tattered and draped in the proverbial colours of the East, we stepped ashore. Tea was waiting in a small café, behind which, adjoining a courtyard filled with embarrassing domesticities, was the Imperial Airways' agent's bed- and sitting-room. The latter he placed at my disposal, whence, after composing another article for the *Daily Express*, I emerged in a stream of perspiration to bathe. The Governor, a depressed man wearing pince-nez, kindly lent us his Ford, and also, since we were proposing to leave the town, supplied us with an escort, lest a hostile force (silhouetted, on camels, as in Purilia) should appear from over the horizon and steal our clothes. As we drove along, bent and ragged old Arabs, seeing the official flag floating from the mud-guard, favoured us with the Fascist salute, which looked more than usually ridiculous under such circumstances. The agent told us afterwards that they have a deadly hatred of the Italians, and that the latter are literally not permitted to leave the town at all except in the bathing season, and then only for a distance of 500 yards. The water was delicious; but not Greek.

Sir Geoffrey Salmond was staying at the Residency, and Stocks, Butcher, and myself dined alone on a verandah overlooking the harbour. The agent, who was only nineteen, had written out an elaborate menu. Stocks talked of his early trips during the inauguration of the service, of the difficulties of obtaining petrol, the lack of mechanics, and his own consequent sleeplessness. The crisis had come when a hungry débutante, returning from India with her father, had reached up into the rack and gobbled down the crew's lunch. Butcher said that the Air-Marshal seemed a wiry man for his age. Stocks said *tough* was the word. We gave him much credit for his charm of manner towards the personnel of the route.

As we left Genoa, there had appeared in the sea below us a yacht similar to that stationed in Suda Bay, which was then on its way to Tobruk for the accommodation of passengers. Unaware of this, however, an enterprising inhabitant had taken and furnished a house in the back of the town, in which we were now put to sleep. Through the windows came the sound of dervishes' drums. The rooms were tall and clean, and boasted mosquito-nets and plush-covered chairs. On being called at half-past four, I discovered a cement pool filled with cold water, and was able to enjoy a bathe.

After breakfasting in the same café, we took off at five minutes to six. The colour of the water was astounding – a sharp, deep scarab-blue, beside which even the Greek sea seemed pale. Inland, the desert stretched for ever, with no sign of a human being. We crossed the Italian frontier, a range of low hills, and dropped a bundle of news-papers at Mersa Matruh, where we observed, painted in large letters on a roof, HILLIER'S GUEST HOUSE. It was here subsequently, after two successive accidents, that the Maharani of Cooch Behar dried her clothes and slept, while William Gerhardi bound up the heel which the propeller had all but removed. The weather had been rough; the *City of Rome* had sunk that very week. Stocks, who had fortunately escaped that disaster owing to illness, was their pilot. In trying to take off he struck a buoy. After two or three hours a rescue machine arrived, and they set off again, only to hit a reef. Water rushed into the cabin; and they all emerged on to the roof, whence a boat took such of them as the propellers had left intact to shore again. I was in Calcutta at the time, and my letters arrived stampless and stained with sea-water.

At a quarter past eleven came the beginnings of Alexandria. As we passed Lake Mariut, an extraordinary illusion presented itself. The water, owing to its excessive saltness and the angle of the sun, shone absolutely white; while a long shadow, probably caused by mist, exactly coincided with its farther shore. The effect was that of a snow-clad hill rising against a November sky. Beyond, the town stretched enormous. We circled over the harbour and came down in front of King Fuad's palace.

On the quay we parted from the Air-Marshal, who was continuing his journey by Air Force machines. Sadly I said good-bye to Stocks, who had been a host as well as a pilot, and whose visitors' book, now at the bottom of the Gulf of Genoa, we had all signed. I shook hands with Pembroke and Stone. And turned to find Mr Casulli, an acquain-tance of three years ago, waiting to greet me with a gleaming La Salle car. Having lately been reading those scarce and entertaining publica-tions, E. M. Forster's *Guide to Alexandria* and his *Pharos and Pharillon*, I anxiously inquired the site of the old lighthouse, whose ground reflector, illumined by a giant bonfire, was one of the wonders of

Antiquity. As we drove along the sea-front, the tall houses, with their weathered, plum-coloured bricks and ancient timbering, were strangely reminiscent of our own Tudor architecture. At Mr Casulli's office the cashier bore the appropriate name of Athanasius. Mr Casulli talked of the horrors of the cotton-market. Then we drove out to his house to lunch – a palatial residence decorated in the Victorian Arab style and set in a garden of flowering shrubs and trees. Madame Casulli said that her children's English governesses always insulted her because they were not supplied with English food.

II

THE DESERT LANDS

The new aeroplane was timed, according to our information, to leave at two o'clock. Aboukir aerodrome is some twenty miles from Alexandria. Mr Casulli drove his La Salle at between sixty and seventy miles an hour through the burning heat, past his own farm, where he grows bananas, dates and cotton, and breeds Arab horses, till as far as King Fuad's palace, where the road, no longer subject to royal criticism, changed character and obliged him to slow down. We reached Aboukir with five minutes to spare, to discover that the mails from the *City of Rome* had not yet arrived. Consequently there was a delay of an hour. The other passengers, who were also waiting about, included two directors of the French air mail from Marseilles to Beyrut, and a Persian boy returning to Teheran after four years' school in York.

Eventually we took off at three o'clock in the *City of Cairo*, a powerful machine, able to climb on two of its three engines. The route lay over the northern border of 'the Wilderness', that land where the children of Israel wandered and suffered and children of Christian education continue to do likewise. Very strange it looked in the afternoon light, a sea of dunes, each rotund hummock casting an elliptical blue shadow on the golden sand, till all were absorbed into a horizon of jagged, opalescent mountains. The villages were few – small clusters of square mud buildings accompanied by occasional palms and sparse scratches of cultivation. Sometimes camels were returning to them along tracks dotted serpentwise among the dunes. Even from a thousand and two thousand feet, every footprint was visible.

We reached Gaza for tea. The Imperial Airways' hangar and hostel lie some way out of the town, on the site of the various battles which took place here during the war, and of which the Turks generally had the advantage. A former gunner was among the passengers, and as he had been badly wounded on this spot, and had not seen it since, we allowed him to indulge his reminiscences. The British trenches, which we later visited, were still littered with bones and shredded clothing. Live bombs are also found, which the local gipsies use for killing fish, to the outrage of resident sportsmen. That we were now under the beneficent shadow of a British mandate, was recalled to me by the following conversation:

R.B. (*to the* HOSTEL SUPERINTENDENT): That's a nice spaniel you've got there.
SUPERINTENDENT: Yes. Damn good with birds.
R.B.: Have you been shooting much round here?
SUPERINTENDENT: Don't you *know* that the grouse season doesn't open till August the twelfth?

The hostel was comfortably planned, a double line of one-storey buildings containing bedrooms, shower-baths, a dining-room, and offices for the staff and mails. In front, a garden was in the making, a geometrical arrangement of whitewashed stones, in which bananas, cypresses, and one eucalyptus had been planted among tree-geraniums. Here tea was waiting, surrounded by arm-chairs.

On my suggestion that we might bathe, the superintendent produced a car, and Butcher, the gunner, and myself motored down the seven miles to the sea. The Frenchmen declined to come; they had had 'assez de transport'. On the way we passed through the town, which, as my readers will remember, was formerly a stronghold of the Philistines. Amos, Zephaniah, and Zechariah heaped their curses on the place; 'baldness is come upon Gaza,' asseverated Jeremiah. While Samson, very rightly threatened by the inhabitants for practices inimical to public morality during his first night's sojourn, snatched away the town gates. The scene of this exploit is now identified as lying on the left of the general store. Historians may cavil. But they cannot, we were glad to learn, question the survival of Delilahs.

By the time we reached the shore, twilight was deepening. A furious orange sunset marked the limit of the sea, against which a three-masted brigantine lay anchored in silhouette. We hurriedly undressed beneath a thatched shelter, and avoiding the melon-rind with which the shore was strewn, stepped into water which was almost too hot to be refreshing. Slow oily waves lifted us on to the jagged edges of concealed rocks. A fisherman's line became entangled in my legs. It grew wholly dark. On the way back the driver informed us that he had just spent £5,000 on planting and maturing a grove of Jaffa oranges.

Dinner was nasty and inadequate. Since, however, the hostel superintendent had only just recovered from one nervous breakdown, and avowed himself threatened with another at the prospect of exposure in the *Daily Express*, I told him that the catering was beyond all expectation. The Frenchmen were patently dissatisfied. But as there was no single person present with whom they could communicate unless I chose to assist them, they suffered in silence. After dinner we agreed that the French understand the English better than the English can ever understand the French.

On Thursday morning we were called with tea at five o'clock, and then told to go to sleep again as the mail train from Port Said had broken down, according to its usual custom. At seven we breakfasted off kippers, which Captain Alcock, our pilot and brother of Sir John, had brought from Alexandria. Then the arriving mails were found to be heavier than expected, and the aeroplane had to be relieved of a corresponding amount of petrol. By this time the superintendent was positively haggard. We took off at eight o'clock, flew over Bethlehem, caught a glimpse of Jerusalem such as Richard Coeur de Lion must have had, and came to the sinister depression of the Dead Sea where the Jordan, a sluggish stream, leaves it, carrying a bed of green up the landscape in much the same way as it does on physical maps. In front, the Moabite mountains expanded before us. The formation of the whole country was most extraordinary, resembling a giant architecture. Domes and towers, temples of ribbed ornament, bulging chimneys, obelisks and cenotaphs, façades and dorsal roofings, were endlessly repeated, to form a natural municipality of impalpable burning rock, from whose bottomless streets wraiths of opal colour came floating up the vast cracked perpendiculars. What wonder that the Chosen, crawling ant-like about their pastoral pursuits, evolved the forbidding deity for which this landscape must answer posterity, as the coasts of Greece answer for the evolution of form and sense?

By degrees the cliffs and canyons grew less, till they merged into a sandy plateau strewn with black stones. Here, for no apparent reason, we suddenly began to descend. The explosion of rockets, which the pilot sent out to find the direction of the wind, sounded like an engine failure. Alarm was dispelled by the sight of a small metal circle, such as usually communicates from the pavement to the coal-cellar, set by itself in the middle of the desert, up to which we manoeuvred in a storm of sand, and which in fact gave access to a tank of petrol. A quarter of a mile away stood the fort of Kasr Kharana, a ruin, in whose upper chambers skeletons lay still in their clothes. 'Hah! des cadavres!' muttered the Frenchmen. Outside were Turkish graves, from which jackals had abstracted the contents.

It was now midday, and the heat of the air, as we took off again, seemed scarcely possible, like the conditions of a dream. Even at five thousand feet it felt as though a stream of flames were playing through the window upon the neck and face. Enormous bumps hurled us up and down, to the visible distress of the other passengers, as the wings dipped from side to side, and the aeroplane fell through space like a stone, or leapt towards the heavens with the quiver and thrill of a hunter at a fence. The Persian boy and Butcher frankly collapsed; the gunner was disturbed; and even the Frenchmen, experienced fliers, admitted afterwards that it had been 'une voyage pénible'. We lunched at Rutbah, where the Nairn Transport Company rents a large square fort from the Government of Iraq. Members of the local camel corps, ferocious men with daggers stuck all over them and rifles in their hands, guarded the entrance. Within the courtyard, which was filled with tattered and irrelevant humanity, stood a comfortable and very cool lounge, supplied with weekly papers. The wife of the superintendent brought two tame mongooses to play with the guests. She said that her chief amusements were learning to gallop on a camel and shooting gazelle from a car. I shared a table with the gunner, who, on discovering my first and more exclusive Alma Mater, remarked that he wouldn't have thought it, and proceeded to expatiate on the airs of her offspring out East. I was flattered.

In the afternoon the heat became even greater. It was so unusual, so improbably violent, that I wondered how it was that I or anyone else continued to survive under such conditions. A lake appeared; and then a muddy ribbon, fringed with palm woods: the Tigris. A haze of dust proclaimed the city of the Arabian Nights. We landed for tea. I asked why, of all invented hats, the Iraqis should have chosen the black Victorian forage-cap for their national head-dress. No one knew.

The Maude Hotel, a ramshackle wooden quadrangle, was prepared for our reception. I retired to my room in the interests of the *Express* and wrote: 'The heat is like a joke; the paper shrivels as I type; the glass from which I drink, though filled with iced ginger-beer, emits a sharp warmth.' Attached to my room was a wooden bathroom, which I thought held the seed of hope. But the water, having trickled through half a mile of pipe-line under the desert, was steaming hot, and even after it was poured out took seven hours to become only gently warm.

Dinner we ate in the garden, a spacious enclosure of date-palms, whose bunches of fruit hung ripening below their leaves. Farther down electric lights protruded from their trunks. The food was excellent, consisting of fish from the Tigris, roast duck, and an exquisite almond-ice tasting of cyanide of potassium. 'This hotel has always good food,' said the waiter, with that aristocratic intonation peculiar to Arabs. 'You shall tell other gentlemen.'

As Butcher and I ate, a sound of singing spoke a romantic Oriental message out of the night. Our attention, however, was diverted from its tragic cadences to the idiosyncrasies of our companion, an American, whose name, if the reader will be so kind as to believe it, was Boggins. He was suffering from an accretion of phlegm, and was engaged in fertilizing a cactus hedge near by. 'I've spent the greater patt of the lasst few yearrs in South Amurrica,' he informed us. 'But my company wannted me to come out here' – spit ... splash – 'so I guess I came' – snort; spit ... splash, spit ... splash. 'I believe Crosse and Blackman's are yewerr leading manufacturers of canned goods, are they naht?'

'Crosse and Black*well* is the name.'

'Well, whether it's Black*well* or Black*man*, I guess they're the ones I've heard of,' – spit-spit-spit, SPIT!! ... splash.

The birds in the trees above twittered on, protesting.

At this juncture, like the first whiffs of a gas attack, the fact that

Iraq was officially within the sphere of Anglo-India was announced by two compatriots, who came to join us. 'Give the sahib a whisky,' said one to the waiter. So I *was* a sahib, curious though it seemed. 'What did you think of Alex.?'* said the other. 'My memsahib's there at the moment.' This remark was calculated to inform me that, being married, he was not perhaps the guide to pleasure that I expected. Undeterred, I replied that I wished to see the town. Even though it was dark, my desire was surely natural. Bagdad, like Athens and Rome, is one of childhood's cities. 'What on earth for?' came the reply. 'There's nothing in it but a lot of bloody wogs.' None the less I persisted, and stood myself on the Maude bridge-of-boats. Across the huge river came the strains of an Orientalized tango and the reflection of café lights. Every variety of Arab filed before me – fat and thin, draped and trousered, running madly, pensively singing, Bedouins in 1880 moustaches, the more sophisticated in those of Charlie Chaplin, some women veiled, others (particularly those of substantial bust) in the scantiest of cotton frocks, and children tottering beneath fezes larger than themselves. The streets were filled with dashing horse-cabs.

The party meanwhile had gone to the 'Arabian Nights', a gloomy outdoor night-club, furnished with a proscenium at one end. At the other tables sat Arab gigolos in Palm Beach suitings, Bedouins in those gorgeous trappings which the features of Colonel T. E. Lawrence have rendered depressingly familiar, and a few Englishmen aglow with righteous indiscretion. Tarts in tulle and spangles sat avidly in the background, while our group discussed their pasts and those of every other white woman between the Mediterranean and the Arabian Sea for the last ten years. 'That one, as a matter of fact, really used to haeve a *very* naice little body ... You see the woman with the drum; a bit fat, what? When she came out with the Army of Occupation she was a damn useful bit o' work. Then they tried to send her away, and she married a wog and took his nationality, and here she is for good and all, serve her right ... Soecially, Bagdad's all raight, I can tell you. The clubs are absolutely delaightful ... of course no one but Britishers. There's hunting and poeloe, horses to be had cheap, and all sorts of racing ... What are the new shoews in town now?'

* Alexandria.

147

By this time it was nearly midnight, and as the 'shoew' here had not yet begun, I walked back to bed, observing on the way that the distant melancholies which Mr Boggins had so forcibly eliminated during dinner, had in reality proceeded from the mouths, not of wistful houris, but of large pink gramophone horns. I bathed in the now cooling water. But sleep was banished by the piercing wails of what I could only suppose to be a hyaena in travail on the floor beneath. Stumbling into the courtyard, and out into the street, my pyjamaed figure conjured the porter from the gutter, and he silenced the animal, bringing me a large bottle of beer besides. It was now one o'clock and I slept. At ten minutes past two, I was awakened. After a meal of fried eggs, we drove out to the aerodrome, and took off, in complete darkness, at ten minutes to four. It must be explained that, according to schedule, we ought to have reached Basra the evening before. But owing to the delay at Gaza, and the possibility of water in one of the tanks, Alcock had thought it advisable to stop in Bagdad, and make this early start instead.

On land, it was comparatively cool. But 'hot air rises'. And as we rose also, the darkness became a suffocating inferno. Fortunately the pilot received a wireless message to the effect that a following wind was to be found at an even greater altitude, and was thus able both to increase his speed from 90 to 120 miles an hour, and to relieve our discomfort. The arch of Chosroes at Ctesiphon was concealed from us. And though, by the time we reached Ur, the sun had risen, it failed to reveal the home of Abraham. At Basra, the home of Sinbad, we landed to exchange pilots and toy with a second breakfast at the British Air Force base. Already the sun was sending out a pale, searing heat. Passing over a group of oil refineries and tanks that resembled a village of small gasometers, we came to the head of the Persian Gulf, and reached Bushire, on the north side, about half-past ten, to find a third breakfast awaiting us, this time of fish. We were now in Persia. A soldier uniformed like the Shah stood by the machine. Customs officials, to show their importance, rummaged through every cranny of our luggage. A horde of semi-naked men, brown and black, proceeded with the process of refuelling, mounting by ladders to the upper wing, and there connecting the tanks with the Anglo-Persian Oil Company's wheeled container by means of long hoses. The aerodrome was blistering. As we prepared to leave, the resident engineer begged the pilot to obtain from Karachi a watering-can with a rose, as he had some seedlings for whose health a fine spray was essential. Astonished at the incongruity of man and his environment, we were off again, flying at 5,000 feet along the side of a yet higher range of mountains. The shores of the Gulf presented a desolate and purgatorial appearance on this blazing August morning, lacking entirely the sharp blues and golden cliffs of the Mediterranean. Land and water had been sucked of their colour by the sun, and displayed only a malignant pallor.

During the journey, we ate sardine sandwiches, crumbling with heat, and drank lime-juice and water from an earthen pot, which had kept it surprisingly cold. The next stop was Lingeh, where refuelling was again necessary. Here the heat became a white delirium, dancing over the arid, pebbly dust, hurting the eyes and weakening the breath. A few palms and a group of women stood in silhouette, as upon a snow-field. A cluster of bee-hive domes in the background sheltered a group of wells.

Crossing over to the southern shore of the Gulf of Oman, we were now above the forbidding peaks of Musandam, a huge menacing complex of whittled humps, grey-black against the baleful yellow sunset, and cleft by two titanic fiords, in whose bottoms the water gleamed a pale silver. This extraordinary formation is one of the oldest pieces of the world; it stood before the Himalayas. Alexander's admiral, Nearchus, saw it, but declined to visit it. Pliny knew of it. Even now it is inhabited by a race known as the Shihuh, whose language is unintelligible to other Arabs.

We were above the sea again, when the sun, whose intensity had been steadily increasing since we left Genoa six days ago, was suddenly concealed. The atmosphere became sticky. It was the Indian monsoon, stretching out to meet us. Crossing a lagoon, we circled over Jask, and landed for the night, having flown 1,070 miles that day. At the aerodrome, a strange figure, with the bearded face of a sheikh, but wearing linen plus-fours, greeted us. This was Dr Williamson, a professing Moslem, and known as Hadji Williamson, since he has made the pilgrimage to Mecca. A Ford lorry was waiting for us, a recent innovation, which the inhabitants, accustomed enough to aeroplanes, regarded as the devil. This took us to the house of the Indo-European Telegraph Superintendent, a resident of thirty years in one of the hottest places in the world, whose employers had never troubled to provide him with a means of making ice, though there was a large electric power-house almost in his garden. He was not the first English-man in Jask. Sir Thomas Herbert, visiting the place in the early seventeenth century, wrote the following epitaph:*

> Here lies buried one Captain Shilling unfortunately
> slaine by the insulting Portugall: but that his bones want
> sence and expression, they would tell you the earth is
> not worthy his reception, and that the people are blockish,
> rude, treacherous and indomitable

Atwood, the pilot, and I had thought to bathe. But as it was now dark, and sharks had lately become as plentiful as shrimps in two feet of water, even leaping out to nip people's legs as they walked along the beach, we thought better of it. The heat was most oppressive, envelop-ing the body in a clammy film. After a dinner of stuffed crabs, we went to bed beneath a rush awning on the roof, where a cool wind got up and gave us a full night's sleep.

The following morning we took off at six o'clock, and continued along the inhospitable coast till the Persian boundary was passed and we were over Baluchistan. Range after range of mountains, ramparts of drought and desolation, stretched into the hazy distance, pallid and oppressive. As we passed over a ravine, a sudden bump sent Butcher and myself leaping from our seats almost to the roof of the cabin. At midday we came to Gwadar, where a single tent, a stack of petrol tins, and a pot of tea, were pitched in absurd isolation on a plain of white dust. Not a house nor a habitation was in sight, and the Imperial Airways' agent, a voluble Indian, had taken the whole morning mounted on a camel to reach the landing-place and prepare for our reception. It was exactly a week since we had left London, and we thought of our first lunch at Le Bourget, as we drank the tea. Then we re-embarked for India, flying through a bank of cool cloud. A new coast appeared, arid, but less forbidding. Ten minutes more, said the mechanic. The vision of an American city in the Middle West expanded beneath us. We landed some eight miles the other side of it, ten minutes ahead of the scheduled time.

* Communicated by Sir Arnold Wilson.

A number of dark-faced gentlemen in white leg-draperies, black smoking-caps and umbrellas, surrounded the aeroplane. An English customs officer begged me to inform him if I had brought any gramophones, bicycles, or pianos, and if not, whether I was engaged in gun-running. Some friends of a friend met me with their motor, and pointed my attention to the new airship hangar, the largest single-story building in the world, and constructed entirely of corrugated iron. 'The number of men,' they remarked with relish, 'killed in the process was enormous.' This observation I subsequently published in the Calcutta *Statesman*, to the great indignation of the Karachi Press, who harped on 'Author's Callous Remark' for several weeks. The casualties, it was pointed out, had actually been extremely few. Having inspected the internal height from which the bodies had fallen, we set off for the town.

This, I said to myself, suddenly remembering, is India; and looked out from beneath the hood. Beneath a depressing, overcast sky stretched an asphalt road, black and efficient, whose objectives were conveniently labelled on a white English signpost in black letters. Occasionally a bungalow stood up, carefully shrouded in a front garden. Otherwise the earth lay bare, a dead mauvish brown, sprouting tenuous bushes of cactus growth or small fig-like shrubs with mauve flowers that fluttered in the wind. In the background ran a low railway embankment, interrupted by a horizontal bridge. Above this appeared the distant towers of the English church of the Holy Trinity, the Scottish Denominational church of St Andrew, and the Gothic lecture-hall, all executed in yellow stone. This placid scene was enlivened by a lady in a yellow sari and a gentleman in white draperies on a bicycle, going one way, and a string of camels, evidently afraid of the asphalt, coming the other.

It transpired that my welcomers, without whose kindness I should now have been in tears, had made me an honorary member of the Sind Club, a palace of comfort, good food, and eternal drinks, set in a compound of flowering trees, where I found myself in possession of a suite of three rooms and the usual offices. An inscrutable brown wizard with a white moustache was also at my disposal. 'To-night, of course,' they said, 'you'll only want a dinner-jacket.' Ruefully I apologized for the loathsome contingencies of air travel, explaining that limitations of weight had prevented the inclusion of evening clothes in my luggage. By day I might have arrived wearing a grass loin-cloth, for all anyone would have cared. But the Indian night holds no place for the undressed. The dilemma was solved by my agreeing to dine alone in my room. This I did, assailed by the sensations of a first day at school, and experiencing that singular feature of Indian life, the difficulty of ever lighting a cigarette owing to the unceasing fans. Outside, a military band was playing composite tunes for the entertainment of a 'frontline' dinner. To-morrow was August the Fourth; but that being a Sunday, the dinner was to-night.

I awoke next morning to a whistle of wind that would have alarmed Macbeth's witches, on which were borne the noises of the parrot-house at the zoo: the monsoon and the local birds. Timidly I ventured to breakfast. Nothing could have exceeded the friendliness of the members; my diffidence began to disappear. But the pall of my absent clothes hung over me, and I was motored into the town to a Mussulman tailor, who that evening delivered in my room a white suit with pearl buttons. The appropriate shoes were supplied, with no less expedition, by a military bootmaker named Mohonjee Nagjee.

The week's flight, though I was unconscious of it at the time, had left me exhausted. And in the interval between my arrival on Saturday afternoon, and the departure of the boat for Bombay on the following Thursday, I was content to do little. Various incidents enlivened the days. There was the shock of discovering that *chota hasri*, which I had always believed to be a form of suicide, in fact denoted early morning tea. The men with whom I consorted embarrassed me by asking what I thought of them and their fellows. To which I replied, evasively, that I noticed a sort of sadness creeping over those lately arrived. One afternoon we went down to the harbour to bathe. It was a gloomy scene; heaps of rotting fish lay about our feet, providing food for emaciated dogs; across the water was a pier laden with goods trucks and cranes. The sky was heavily overcast. As I clung to a rusty buoy, the wretchedness of the world was completed by the unavailing efforts of two Indians to land a cow from a boat with a high curving triangle of sail like an old slave dhow.

But during this time my thoughts were really on the journey I had just completed. I see it now as one of the great experiences of a life, a period of vivid, unclouded enjoyment in its revelation of a huge expanse of the world's surface, of unsuspected and unimagined beauties, of heat and desolation beyond credence, of a new pleasure in physical movement. Of the revelation that was to follow, of India itself, I have written elsewhere. The present excursion describes yet a further revelation. India exists, as an entity conscious and distinct, on account of the Himalayan frontier. I was now about to cross this frontier, and to record, with my own senses, the degree of India's separation from the plateau of Central Asia.

III

ANGLO-HIMALAYA

Three persons were involved in the proposed expedition: G., who had already been some months in India and from whom had come the original suggestion of a trip to Sikkim; M., who was sailing at the beginning of September; and myself. Once Lord Beaverbrook had decided how and when I should reach India, M. and I, who were in London, resolved to make Tibet the ultimate and definite goal of our respective journeys to the East.

The first thing to be discovered was whether, under any circumstances, permission could be obtained to cross the frontier between Sikkim and Tibet; and if so, from whom. Inquiries were transmitted to Mr Wedgwood Benn, then Secretary of State for India. He replied that, provided we kept to the trade route, the Government of India would place no official obstacle in the way of our going as far as Gyantse.

It only needed the pronouncement of a Labour Minister on any subject in the Indian sphere to provoke the ridicule of better informed opinion. Insuperable difficulties were forecast by those who knew, they said, what they were talking about from first-hand experience. Apprehensive of failure, and bewildered by the contradiction between authority and experience, I sought the help of Sir Charles Bell, whose works on Tibet proclaimed him endowed with both these virtues. Sir Charles said that since the indiscretions of the last Everest expedition, permits to cross the frontier had been harder to obtain; but that he thought, on judicious application to the right quarters, we should find the way open to us as far as Gyantse, where, ever since the Younghusband expedition of 1904, the British Trade Agent at Yatung had been accustomed to spend part of the year, and where a small detachment of Indian troops was stationed to ensure his safety. A general permission for travellers approved by the Government of India to proceed thus far had been one of the fruits of his mission to Lhassa in 1921. Gyantse, he said, was the third largest town in Tibet. Naturally, I replied we were anxious to go farther, to Shigatse or Lhassa, the other two. But on our discussing the details of the expedition, its probable cost and our earliest possible date of starting, it appeared that, unless we were to be crippled financially by the expense of transport and physically by winter on the Himalayan passes, Gyantse must remain our ultimate objective; and this apart from the evident impossibility of proceeding farther, unless in disguise and at the expense of honour.

Here at last was some concrete and hopeful information. But our satisfaction was quickly undermined by Lord Zetland, who expressed lugubrious doubts. As a former Governor of Bengal, and one who had not only travelled over the first part of our route, but described it with charm and understanding in *Lands of the Thunderbolt*, he spoke with a weight that could scarcely be denied. The Viceroy, he told M., was our only hope.

By good luck Lord Irwin had just arrived in England on leave. Fanned by the conflict of opinion into enthusiasm for a project which he had previously regarded as fantastic, M. now got into communication with Colonel Harvey, the Viceroy's Military Secretary. He was optimistic. He would write, he said, in the Viceroy's name, to Sir Denys Bray, the Indian Foreign Secretary, to Colonel Weir, Political Officer in Sikkim, and to the Governor of Bengal. This was two days before I left England. That same afternoon we telegraphed to G. that if our Himalayan journey was to become a trans-Himalayan one, he would be well advised to postpone the bungalow reservations as originally contemplated. Sikkim, he had given us to understand, was a favourite resort of Calcutta holiday-makers. And since only a limited number of Europeans are allowed in the state at any one time, he had been anxious to ensure that we should be among them in the following October.

No sooner had I reached India and joined G., than fresh prognostications of official opposition assailed us. I therefore wrote personally to Sir Denys Bray, to whom Sir Charles Bell had given me an introduc-

TIBET

tion. He replied that the Government of India would place no difficulties in the way of our proposed journey; but that we must first receive formal permission from Colonel Weir as Resident in Sikkim, a post which, though outwardly insignificant, carries with it the highly important duty of liaison between Lhassa and Delhi. This at last was a definite concession which could not be contradicted and which was soon after confirmed by a letter from Colonel Weir himself, warning us that officers from Gyantse were being replaced about the time of our proposed start and that we ought to reserve in advance accommodation in the rest-houses along the route.

It was impossible to wait for M., and we were obliged to make arrangements without consulting him. In course of a voluminous correspondence with the Trade Agent at Yatung, we settled our dates and stages so as not to interfere with those of the returning officers. We received a frontier pass, accompanied by a list of conditions which we must promise, in writing, to obey. The chief of these were that we should neither fish nor shoot, since Buddhism, despite the carnivorous dispensation accorded Tibetans on account of their climate, objects on principle to the taking of life; that we should not deviate from the established trade route; and that we should subsequently write or publish nothing likely to offend Tibetan susceptibilities without first submitting it to the Government of India. It seemed that not only has the Dalai Lama a touching weakness for the illustrated Press, but that he also shares the susceptibilities of Western nationalism; and that on finding in the pages of a London weekly a pock-marked harridan of great age and squalor facetiously described as a 'Tibetan Beauty', he was provoked to official recrimination. This, and similar unwise pictures on the screen, were the work of what was then the last Everest expedition; and it was generally, though wrongly, supposed that there would be no other such expedition for many years to come.

G. and I, who had been travelling among the temples of Dravidia, now returned to Calcutta, where we fell to earnest preparations for the journey. That we could go, and would go, was settled. But formidable prophecies continued to distress us. These, uttered in all sincerity, only echoed those of Sir Charles Bell and were concerned with the question of physical endurance. Though we had calculated (wrongly as it turned out) to anticipate the Tibetan winter by returning before the middle of

156

November, it was evident that we must expect severe cold. It required some effort to persuade ourselves of this fact: the climate of a Bengal September is such that even to move across the room beneath the blast of an electric fan induces a protracted sweat. Nevertheless, we ranged through the bazaars purchasing mattresses, bales of vermilion blankets, and sweaters. We employed a regimental tailor to make us coats and jodhpurs of a carpet-like material, blackish green in colour, and so impenetrable that each fitting necessitated a cold bath and half an hour's rest afterwards. Wind-proof waistcoats, of the type supplied to the Everest expeditions, water-proof gloves without fingers, Balaclava helmets, water-bottles, satchels, and all else that the polar-tropical nature of our route demanded, were provided by the Calcutta branch of the Army and Navy Stores.

This establishment proved, in the matter of stores, an omniscient and omniprovident godmother to our project. It happened that Captain Noel, the photographer whose jocular sub-titles had so disturbed the Dalai Lama, had lately arrived in Calcutta for the purpose of revisiting the scene of his former exploits. Having arranged a large commissariat, he learned, on reaching Darjeeling, that he would not be allowed to cross the frontier. Consequently, he had returned his stores, and the boxes which had been specially constructed to fit both them and the convenience of mules were therefore available for us. Hour upon hour we pored over lists of commodities potted and commodities tinned, labouring to tabulate a menu for each meal of each day. Eventually it was decided that every week's provisions should be fitted into two boxes, which could be carried by one mule. Each box should be supplied with a duplicate list of contents, one inside it and one with us. Each also should have its own key, and be supplied with the necessary openers. The theory was ideal. But the practice resulted in the contents of every single box being strewn over the floor on our first night out.

At length M. arrived, lucky to have escaped the acrimonious discussions which these attempts at organization involved. His fellow-passengers, he said, had consisted wholly of generals. The wife of one of them, finding on board a young officer who could play the piano to her banjo as it had never been played before, had had him transferred then and there from the Khyber Pass to her own garrison town. Such is the convenience of wireless in imperial affairs.

During the previous fortnight, immersed as we had been in things of the flesh, culture had not been altogether neglected. G., to whom linguistic obstacles are unknown, insisted on our taking Tibetan lessons from a Sikkimese who was otherwise employed as a translator by the Asiatic Society. His long pigtail and twinkling elfin face, the spit of an autumn leaf, endeared him to us; while his sense of humour bore with equanimity G.'s suggestion that the whole language was an invention of his own, composed solely to annoy us. The inflections defeated us entirely. It seemed humanly impossible, when listening to him, to distinguish '*nga*' (meaning 'I') from '*nga*' (meaning 'drum'), or to distinguish either of these from '*nga*' (meaning 'five'). 'Not "*nga*",' he would instruct, 'but "*nga*"'; while we strained our ears in vain to catch the remotest difference between the two utterances. All we could do was to repeat the accursed syllable in bass, baritone, and alto, evoking in reward a pitying grin. Another difficulty was that the Tibetan language is not one language but three: ordinary, honorific, and high-honorific. The first is used towards the common people; the second towards gentlemen; and the third towards the Dalai Lama. It might be thought that these distinctions were merely a question of prefixes. But no: even the roots of the corresponding words in each have no relation to one another whatsoever. Our teacher had no experience of teaching. And as we had no time to master the grammar, our method was to conceive ourselves in situations common to travel in all countries, and then to try and learn by heart the remarks or questions appropriate to each. But as it was impossible to arrive at a single phrase without first determining the social status of the person addressed, and as at that time our acquaintance with class distinctions in Tibet was not extensive, the greater part of our lessons was taken up with rules of etiquette and deportment, knowledge of which later proved of some value. Nevertheless, we gradually progressed to such formidable structures as: 'May I wear your yellow hat?' 'Can I become a monk in your beautiful monastery?' 'But I must first visit my dying mother.' Our success was illusory. During the whole trip we scarcely uttered a dozen words between us. These, at least such as emanated from myself, will be recorded later, with due prominence.

Among the rules of politeness which our teacher impressed on us, none was more essential than that which entails the presentation of a white scarf by a caller to his host on arrival, and by a host to his caller on the latter's departure. These scarves, like the language, are of three grades. But as there was no prospect of our calling on the Dalai Lama we only needed to supply ourselves with two. These we had arranged to purchase in the Chinese quarter of Calcutta, whither our teacher, on the morning of M.'s arrival, conducted us. A deep passage led to several flights of stairs, up which we climbed. The floors were covered with red spittle, product of the betel-nut's encircling leaf; whiffs of absent sanitation floated through half-opened doors. Unwitting, we were ushered into a room filled with sleeping forms, who arose only to display their sores and bandages. Food and tea lay mouldering in yesterday's utensils. Suddenly our teacher remarked: 'In Tibet-side, sir, you won't find the shops and houses clean like this.' Hurriedly purchasing a scarf, which was reputed to have come from Pekin, and was indeed wrapped in a Chinese newspaper, we left the building with foreboding.

M., thanks to the good offices of the Viceroy's secretary, had received an invitation for himself and his party to stay at Government House, Darjeeling, during the final preparations for departure. We had hoped to attend the Darjeeling Knights Errant Ball, the climax of the Anglo-Himalayan season, to be held on 30 September. It would, we felt, have been the Duchess of Richmond's party to our Waterloo. But owing to the bungalows of Sikkim being, many of them, already reserved, we were obliged to start a day earlier than expected, and had to forgo this pleasure. We were invited for Saturday the 28th. I decided to leave Calcutta on Wednesday night, to make the last arrangements and acclimatize myself to the height.

That afternoon, on receiving from the Army and Navy Stores the railway receipt for the transport of the boxes, I noticed that thirteen had been sent instead of the prescribed twelve. It then transpired that G. and M. had gone clandestinely to order a whole case of whisky, with a view to an orgy in Gyantse, where, we were assured, we should not be welcome save as harbingers of debauch. This extravagance recoiled on their own heads, because before half the journey was over they came to dislike the taste of whisky more even than that of water boiled over yak-dung.

The Darjeeling mail, like all trains that leave precisely at the dinner-hour, was without a dining-car. Still holding a bunch of cheese straws, I rattled off towards the north, tortured by the coughs and sneezes of an incipient cold. The heat was extreme, and the fans only served to increase it. Morning brought Siliguri, whence it was necessary to proceed by motor. Actually a mountain railway, two feet wide, reaches Darjeeling. On front of each engine sits a man dropping sand, in case the wheels slip. But this takes six hours, and I had much to do.

India was gone. My car, a crimson American vehicle, lavishly appointed with silver plate and sporting an enormous metal serpent that belched warnings to the corners, was owned by two russet-skinned hillmen, whose round black caps, with their red buttons and twinkling slit-eyes, bespoke the fringe of the Celestial Empire. Their natural humour was apparent in their driving. Birds on the wing we destroyed in flocks. But a cow, similarly threatened, retaliated with a smart clip on the serpent's eye.

The road led out of the station yard, turned a corner, and made straight for a towering rampart of dark, greenish blue hills, stretching this way and that as far as the eye could see. I felt a qualm of disappointment. I had hoped of the Himalayas something more than the Alps. And here, immediately, appeared that hard, uncompromising prussian-blue, the enemy of colour and form in landscape, which our grandmothers delighted to stipple from their Swiss hotels, which explains why the German race have never produced a single painter, and never will, and why there are so many tedious interludes in Wagner's music. In a flash, we were at the foot of the hills. We rose a little. And there, behind us, stretching southward to an infinite unbroken horizon, lay the turgid greens of the Bengal plain. The sun was already in the heavens, a sinister prophet of the midday heat.

On the flat, the railway and the road had progressed side by side. But once in the hills it seemed as though their courses were the outcome of a game of catch-as-catch-can played by the engineers as they went along. The road to Darjeeling ascends seven thousand feet in forty miles, during which the two tracks, intricate as sweet-pea tendrils, intersect three or four times in every hundred yards, and once, or sometimes twice, on every corner, so that the descending train may impale the ascending motor to the best advantage. At every station the chauffeur is forced to stop and inquire what traffic, engine, hand-trolley, train, cart, bus, or motor, he is liable to encounter during the ensuing stage. While the news of his own advent is immediately telephoned to the station above.

The road, for the most part, wound upward through magnificent forest, beneath whose huge arching trees it seemed no more than a footpath. A profusion of vertical creepers, tassels of vegetation thirty or forty feet in length, fell from their branches. Strange plants and shrubs carried flowers that had previously existed only on porcelain or in old ladies' bonnets. Gradually we rose, passing from shade to sun and shade again, while rare glimpses revealed the plains unfolding farther distances beneath. Troops of pigtailed elves, of that rarefied Mongol type assumed by the peoples of the southern Himalaya, wandered by. Such dwellings as appeared from time to time were constructed, as are all the buildings in this romantic region, of corrugated iron and flattened petrol tins, painted red.

Suddenly, round a corner, the snowy back of Kanchenjunga leapt into the sky, a stupendous horizon of glittering vertebrae, packed with cotton-wool clouds, and encroaching on three-quarters of the heavens. Below, a profundity of spurs and valleys, darkly feathered in pines, was lost in shadow like the bottom of a well. The heart beat; the breath came quickly. Until, round another corner, appeared Darjeeling, and all relapsed into hate and misery.

Imagine Margate, Filey, and Bognor Regis wholly roofed in red corrugated iron; distorted into a phantasmagoria of chalets and châteaux, such as even they have yet to achieve; vomited into the tittups of an Italian hill-town; and then lifted bodily on to a long spur, a promontory rising from a sea of depths that seemed to pierce the very core of the world; overseen by the white throne of God, a continent on end, trees, cliffs, and shores of snow five miles high, as the eye travels up them to the blue vault above; and still preserving all the inevitable accessories of our national life: the exclusive clubs, the Anglican, Scottish, and Roman Catholic churches, the Tudor hotel, the seaside milliners, and the polo-ground in the bottom of a tea-cup; streets without motors, but municipally railed; rickshaws pulled and pushed by crowds of ragged Mongols; tiny ponies with saddles like high-chairs for children who can scarcely walk; all the races of the Himalayas: Nepali women with their huge necklaces of gold beads and red flannel, like Lord Mayors' chains; the elfin Lepchas and Sikkimese; emigrant Tibetans, mottled lumps of turquoise in the men's ears, the women's chests hung with enormous rhomboid charm-boxes, silver and jewelled; the clouds, as the morning advances, closing in, arriving mysteriously from both above and below, till the last glimpse of Kanchenjunga is obscured behind a wall of mist, the valleys themselves are lost, and at last, thank God, even Darjeeling is invisible but for the two nearest villas and their front-gardens; such is the conflict of joy and horror at the first sight of Anglo-Himalaya.

Having reached the Tudor hotel, somewhat out of breath owing to the height, I changed hurriedly into a tweed suit, and having made the necessary arrangements concerning the Sikkim bungalows, discarded the tweed suit and retired to bed and a fire for two days, in order to cure a dribbling cold. During this process, Naspati, the local contractor for transport, brought Ah-Chung and An-Den, whom he proposed that I should engage as cook and sirdar, the latter to act as personal servant and overseer to the whole caravan. 'Pö kyeh schingi yüdgam?' I said, meaning 'Do you speak Tibetan?' Their astonishment was profound; but was lessened when they discovered that it was almost all I could say. A sweeper was also produced, to perform the menial offices connected with sanitation. I engaged them and, rising, proceeded to the bazaar, there to fit them with new boots and sweaters.

That night the *maître d'hôtel* requested me to share my dinner-table with others. 'We shall soon have everyone sitting at separate tables,' he complained. Observing that the dining-room held about a quarter of its full complement, and that half the waiters were standing idle, I rounded on him with such ferocity as to shatter his belief in good-fellowship among guests for good and all.

The following day was Saturday. Early in the morning I proceeded to Government House, at the end of the promontory, with my luggage on the backs of ragged coolies. The procession resembled that of an impecunious pedlar. None the less a squad of small soldiers in shorts presented arms at the gates, and I proceeded down a neat Victorian drive, winding through pinched Victorian lawns, whose appropriate conifers seemed about to topple over a bottomless precipice on the farther side. At the end of this vista stood a Victorian seaside boarding-house, beneath which, on a lower level, nestled a less forbidding child.

This was the guest-house, approached by a terraced garden of Iceland poppies, which would have been charming had it not been disfigured by the inevitable commemorative slab, informing the future archaeologist that it had been designed by the Earl and Countess of Lytton. Inside, however, lurked comfort and good taste: flowers in vases, chintzed sitting-rooms, blazing fires, and spacious writing-tables, appointed with sealing-wax and gilt-embossed invitations to guests to order horses or rickshaws at their own convenience. Those of the latter attached to Government House were like small barouches, picked out in red and resplendent with coronets. ADCs heaped us with drinks. We could be in or out to meals as we pleased, provided that notice was given beforehand. It was country-house entertaining in perfection.

The others had arrived, and at lunch-time we were lined up in the drawing-room by one ADC, while another fetched the Governor and Lady Jackson. We were then introduced, ate, slept, had tea, and afterwards received a call from Mr Laden-La, a twinkling Sikkimese with a minute pointed moustache, chief of the local police and a prominent freemason. He talked of Tibet, described his experiences in the Younghusband expedition of 1904, when they lost a man a night from pneumonia, and said that he had been employed on Sir Charles Bell's mission to Lhassa in 1921. He had then stayed behind to organize a Lhassa police force, and had received the rank of general in the Tibetan army. This army had now been disbanded, all but a few regiments on the Chinese frontier, owing to the monks' fear lest its leaders should be planning a *coup d'état*. He was in Lhassa at the time of the Everest expeditions, and when the reports came through of the films shown in Darjeeling by Captain Noel making fun of Tibetan customs, and the Dalai Lama had received his English illustrated papers doing the same, he was sent for by the latter and called upon to explain. At the same time, it appeared, a trio of monks had been persuaded from Gyantse to London without the necessary permission, and had there dressed themselves up for exhibition in the robes of their superiors, a proceeding which had increased the displeasure of the Tibetan authorities. In the period immediately following the 1921 mission he had actually transported two motors over the Himalayan passes, assembled them at Phari, and driven as far as Gyantse in a day. But these had soon been stopped. Conversation then turned on the impossibility of proceeding farther than Gyantse, and those who had tried to do so since the war. General Pereira had arrived at Lhassa from Pekin, and had vowed that not the offer of a million pounds would tempt him to return that way. Dr McGovern had reached Lhassa from Darjeeling in the guise of a coolie, and had subsequently libelled Laden-La, who had obtained indemnity from his publishers.* There was Sir Charles Bell's mission in 1921, during which the permission was obtained for the Everest expeditions, and Mr Kingdon Ward and Lord Cawdor were allowed access to the river Tsango-po or Brahmaputra. A French female Buddhist also reached Lhassa disguised as a beggar, and turned publicist after the event. Colonel Bailey subsequently visited the capital during his tenure of the Residency in Sikkim. This year Colonel Weir, his successor, was also to have gone. But at the last moment a message was sent asking him not to proceed.

The most curious attempt was that of Mr Carpenter, a wealthy American, who had succumbed, in later life, to the doctrines of theosophy. It appeared from his account that there dwelt in Shigatse 'three masters', from whom he used to receive messages, transmitted no one, nor he, knew how. Anxious to visit them, he arrived at Darjeeling and, with the help of Laden-La, composed an ornamental address to the Dalai Lama, which was written on parchment in both English and Tibetan. This was enclosed in a binding of ornamental leather, in which were set, as medallions, two gold ten-dollar pieces. The whole was wrapped in the requisite complimentary scarf, of the third and highest order, being printed all over with prayers; and was then despatched to the British Trade Agent at Gyantse, to be forwarded to His Holiness. Mr Carpenter waited; no answer came. At length, with our former Tibetan teacher as sirdar, he started out with a large train and came to Gyantse. There he waited again. Till at length he telegraphed. An answer came back saying that there might be hope for him in four years' time. Being a man of honour, he refrained from proceed-

---

* We frequently heard it stated by ostensibly well-informed persons that McGovern never reached Lhassa at all. His account of his experiences there may be partially fictitious. But that he succeeded in his objective, all who were in Tibet at the time or immediately after agree. Furthermore, he was an extremely brave man, as anyone who has travelled in Tibet in winter will testify.

ing surreptitiously to Shigatse in search of 'the masters', and returned.

It appears that the only means of making certain of reaching Lhassa at the present moment is to embrace the profession of telegraphist. The telegraph and telephone to India are much valued by the Tibetans, and have to be kept in order. A European was in Lhassa at the time of our trip, superintending them.

Laden-La finally warned us that the villages were full of ferocious mastiffs, who were liable to tear us from our ponies; and that the monks, if we stepped over their lines of prayer-cushions instead of going round them, might be expected to stab us in the back. The dogs were certainly savage, when tied up; when loose they were usually too busy with their amours to notice the casual itinerant. From the monks we received nothing but hospitality and smiles.

We dressed, gulped down cocktails as big as lemonades, and assembled in the drawing-room for dinner. An ADC fetched the Governor and Lady Jackson as before. Two ADCs preceded them in to dinner, while they talked over their shoulders. This was in contrast to the procedure of Lord Irwin, who, when I lunched at Delhi, went in behind his guests. A regiment of *chuprassies*, uniformed in gold and scarlet, wearing blue and gold puggarees, and clinking with medals, formed a double line at the entrance to the dining-room and made salaam as we entered. Simultaneously an invisible band, concealed behind the kind of net used for theatrical waves, struck up a nursery rhyme. We sat down. During dinner the Governor recounted with indignation how the crowds at Dacca, whither he had lately gone on tour, had shouted 'Jackson, go back!' The nursery rhyme gave place to Elgar. The meal drew to a finish. The Governor rose and said 'The King-Emperor', while the band played it and everyone stood clasping glasses of port to their stomachs, each hand trembling at a different pace. When the tune had ended, all grunted 'The King-Emperor' and sipped nervously. Before the utterance had died away, two ADCs had flung down their glasses and marched from the room. The Governor and Lady Jackson followed, still talking over their shoulders. Groups were then formed for conversation, until at length Lady Jackson retired.

A few minutes later an ADC strode into the room, stood to attention before the Governor, and, having waited for the latter to finish what he was saying, observed: 'The house is on fire, Your Excellency.' He then strode out again to telephone for help, leaving us all rather bewildered. Ladies first, thought G., and ran upstairs with a fire-extinguisher. 'Don't come in,' shouted Lady Jackson through the door. G., who had never used a fire-extinguisher in his life, was determined to do so now, and emptied it up a neighbouring chimney. By this time a quarter of an hour had elapsed. The flames – we wondered where they were. Then the telephone rang. 'Is that Government House?' said a voice. 'I'm ringing up to know if there really is a fire.' Meanwhile the Governor was lost. M. and I, shaking with laughter, emerged from the front door in search of the flames, to find him standing forlornly in a puff of cloud that had settled on the drive, upholding an umbrella and blowing wild blasts on a pocket siren. 'I keep on whistling,' he moaned, 'but what's the use? The guard doesn't come.' Indoors the telephone rang again. 'Is that Government House? This is the fire-brigade speaking. Do you want any help with your fire?' The heroic A D C was now half-way to the roof, hanging like a sloth from a drain-pipe and straining every nerve to locate the flames. Suddenly the guard, the fire-brigade, and 120 servants arrived in the hall simultaneously and stood to attention. In face of such forces, further assistance on our part seemed superfluous. But we should like to have seen the flames.

Sunday bore the proper English stamp. At first I cast it off by going for a ride on a polo pony that threatened to precipitate me to the foot of Kanchenjunga at every twist of the neatly gravelled footpath. Then the clouds rolled up and in at the windows. It became dark and cold. G. and M. disorganized the Government of Bengal by staying in bed to breakfast. His Excellency and Lady Jackson set bravely out for church in rickshaws drawn by men uniformed in the colours of the Eton Field. Naspati arrived leading three ponies for our inspection. At his command they cantered gaily up the road; and thenceforth could not be urged beyond a slow walk till induced a month later with whips purchased in Gyantse that would have flayed a rhinoceros.

Midday, there was a lunch-party, which included the parson.

'Do you get much snow here in the winter?' G. opened politely.

'Oh! quantities,' was the reply.

'How marvellous everything must look!'

'Yes; and, you know, it's such wonderful snow.'

'Oh, is it? How?'

The parson leaned forward confidentially: '... *wonderful* for snow-balls,' he whispered.

I sat next a bishop, robed in purple, who kindly quieted my doubts as to whether the Abyssinian Church really had canonized Pontius Pilate. 'Another curious feature of their observance,' he continued, 'is their consecration of bishops by breathing instead of the laying-on of hands. As the Abyssinian bishops-elect often find it difficult to come to Alexandria, where the Coptic Patriarch resides, a paper bag is employed as intermediary. The Patriarch breathes into it. It is sealed, transported to Abyssinia, and there exploded over the bishop-elect's head with a loud POP!!' – and he burst into a thunderous guffaw which astonished the whole table.

We had arranged to leave at ten o'clock on Monday morning, though G. and M., a prey to mounting depression, considered this unreasonably early. The mist was impenetrable; a heavy rain was falling; we became helpless with packing; M. cut his finger – 'for the first time in ten years,' he said, and doubted if he could start. Having said good-bye to our hosts, and numbed our senses in Madeira, we at length set off in a motor to some incorporeal landmark known as the eighth milestone. Nine mules had preceded us; two remained for our personal luggage. As it was downhill, M. elected to walk.

G. and I mounted our ponies. He, I remarked, had the air of a Jesuit missionary about to win a continent. I, he remarked, was the retreat from Moscow. From in front came a mutter of Virgilian cadences, M.'s observations on the local flora. After an hour and a half, tea-gardens and then a factory emerged from the fog and proclaimed Peshoke, where their owners, Mr and Mrs Lister, gave us a delightful lunch. Their visitors' book was a wall, strewn with the names of the famous, each attached to a line denoting its owner's height. From their garden, a precarious terrace in a world of verticality, we could look down two or three thousand feet into the Teesta Valley below, an inky well imprisoning a fleet of porcelain clouds. We had started among rhododendrons and conifers. Henceforth the vegetation was tropical, and M.'s remarks became a saga. Cathedrals of trees, branchless for fifty feet, flanked the winding cobbled descent. Parrots called; cicadas, unceasing treble sirens, riddled the consciousness; sheets of cobweb, containing black and yellow monsters, and crusted with lichen, tilted the hat on the back of the head; butterflies like iridescent bats flitted through the sun-spots; bells and trumpets, red and white, hung from bushes or raised their heads from tangles of fleshy leaves. There was no colour, no atmosphere; only a world of rich, downright greens. At length the Teesta river came in sight, a broad muddy torrent, caught between stupendous walls of forest, and spanned by a suspension bridge. On the other side of this a motor was waiting, which took us up to Kalimpong by an astounding road, the victim of numerous landslides, which in one place looped round and crossed itself on a bridge. My head, which had remained normal at Darjeeling, had begun to hum to itself on descending 4,000 feet to Peshoke; at the Teesta, only 500 feet up, it recovered; now, ascending 5,000 feet to Kalimpong, it began again. Behind us, as the sun set, all the hills turned to black, and only the motionless porcelain clouds caught the rosy glitter.

At Kalimpong, we stayed at the Himalayan Hotel, kept by Mr Macdonald, for many years British Trade Agent at Yatung in the Chumbi Valley, to whom Sir Charles Bell had given me a letter of introduction. He was assisted by Mr Perry, his son-in-law. Our arrival coincided with that of the late Trade Agent at Gyantse, and his wife, who said that the winter had begun a month early this year, as indeed we were to discover. They had with them a Lhassa terrier puppy, which resembled a fluffy brown and white Pekinese. After dinner, Mr Macdonald gave me elaborate instructions as to Tibetan etiquette, the officials to be approached, the scarves and presents to be distributed; and next morning, with the aid of a lama, wrote us a number of letters of introduction, invoking my friendship with Sir Charles Bell. He it was who, at the time of the Dalai Lama's flight to India, dressed the commander-in-chief of the Tibetan army up as a British mail-runner, and thus enabled him to escape over the frontier unmolested by the Chinese troops that were in pursuit.

G. and M., having gone to bed unnaturally early, woke and were wandering about at eight o'clock; but being determined to make a late start, refrained from dressing till half-past ten. They then sat till midday keening over their last bath, last hot meal, last knife and fork, last day on earth. Meanwhile I walked into the town with Mr

Macdonald, and purchased from a fat Tibetan woman with a goitre a Tibetan hat of black felt, heavily embroidered with gold, and possessing four fur flaps, those to protect the ears being longer than the others. Of those of the superior type, which boast a crown of hard silk adorned with a finial of red coral beads, I could find none to fit. Mr Macdonald said that Kalimpong, as the centre of the large Tibetan wool-trade, was a growing place; whereas Darjeeling, being off the main route, owed its *raison d'être* simply to Government House with its legislative and social train. Formerly, Europeans were not allowed to live in Kalimpong. Now, a special development area had been set apart for them. The place is chiefly famous for its propagation of Himalayan arts and crafts, which deluge Calcutta, during the winter season, with nauseating 'fancy goods', and for its orphanages. A child from one of these, born and educated in the Himalayas, eventually obtained a job in Calcutta. When he reached Siliguri, seeing the whole plain of India stretching away before him, he observed: '*What* a football field!' Such is the beauty of British education.

On our return to the hotel, Mr Perry handed me a tin box, containing a wedding present for the eldest son of Rajah Tehring and his newly married wife, a daughter of the former Tibetan commander-in-chief whom Mr Macdonald had assisted over the frontier. Rajah Tehring and his family lived, we were told, on an estate about six miles away from Gyantse. Meanwhile the mules had been loaded, and the ponies sent on ahead to a spot two or three miles along the road, where we joined them in a motor. We mounted; and I was ambling peacefully along in front, when M., looking like a Victorian engraving of Lord Cardigan at the head of the Light Brigade, flew past and disappeared round a corner. The path was only a few feet wide; bottomless valleys yawned beneath it; and he admitted that he had avoided riding for eleven years; but his pony was costing five rupees a day, while ours were only four; so that we concluded he was after his money's worth. After some time, he had slowed down, when a small girl, bobbing up from under a precipice, sent him off again. Then he dismounted, and G. took his place, though not for long. He was lengthening the stirrup leathers, when the animal suddenly leapt into the air, and he fell off into the dust. The saddle-bags, which were really the cause of the trouble, fell with him, disintegrating our lunch. Mercifully, a pot of pickled beetroots escaped destruction. Another mile revealed the pony taking its ease beneath a clump of bamboo. I mounted with trepidation, but proceeded more quietly, as the saddle-bags had now been transferred to a senile travesty of a quadruped whom nothing could disturb.

The path took us from 5,000 feet to 7,000. The hill-sides were largely cultivated. Scanty attempts at afforestation were apparent. We lunched in a cloud, on a flat stone. The baked potatoes had continued cooking against the pony's belly. After another two hours downhill, a green slope appeared. My pony broke into a gallop and brought me to a pink and white building, the rest-house of Pedong. A babel of confusion followed, ponies unsaddling, mules unloading, everyone calling for his possessions, the cook awaiting tea. The store-boxes were opened, but nothing could be found. Eventually whisky, tea, sugar, flour, milk, biscuits, tongue, French beans, and cherries were set aside for the evening. Ah-Chung, the cook, a diminutive pigtailed witch who had ministered to the first Everest expedition, begged us to eat a chicken for dinner. He was carrying several in a wicker basket. Knowing the consistency of the Indian fowl, we thought it wiser to await a higher altitude, where the corpse could keep and soften. It grew dark about five o'clock; lamps were lit; and we slept or read till dinner. The sirdar waited, assisted by a coolie who smelt. M. was now outwardly cheerful.

Owing to misunderstandings, breakfast was not ready till a quarter past nine. The whisky had no cork, and must be decanted into a water-bottle; the pickled beetroots refused to resume their lid; the camera had been packed in the bedding. From outside came the clatter and shouts of loading. These trivial irritations seemed strange at first. As the days passed, and our organization improved, they grew less, becoming merely an unpleasant routine. Below the rest-house lay a village, where a guard, uniformed in dark green with a messenger-boy's cap, demanded our passes. Sikkim, the only Buddhist state in India proper under British suzerainty, does not allow Europeans within her confines without special permission. Having seen we possessed it, the guard returned to dig his garden, and we crossed the frontier.

Our day's objective was Ari, a point exactly opposite Pedong, about four miles away on the wing, nine by earth. The broad cobbled path led steeply downward. A train of 100 mules on their way from Tibet to Kalimpong, each carrying packs of raw wool, interrupted our progress. Trees with the stature of factory chimneys, rank, weeping palms glistering like seaweed, broad-leaved shrubs, plump lilies, stood about us. Overhead, the spiders wove, the parrots called, and orchid tubers dropped serrated sheaves of browning leaves. Land-crabs, encased in black tortoiseshell, edged their way along the gutters. Streams fell down the hill, to rest for a moment in stone drinking-troughs and then go on. From the shadows flitted butterflies of every size and pattern: slowly flapping swallow-tails of nocturnal emerald, lit with squares of iridescent azure, elliptical wings of soft mouse-brown, spangled with a crescent border of sky-blue; purple emperors, exotic and enormous, flashing streaks of iris from their bouncing silhouettes; a shower of hot golden yellow petals rising from a clot of dung; a huge orange-tip sailing white and ruddy gold through the green depths; a flag of red, white, and yellow netted in black veins; all floating through the patches of sunlight, and then disappearing among the sinister, indistinct shapes of the vegetation.

On reaching the bottom of the valley, being now very hot, we bathed in the river, lying horizontally on the surface of the water and clinging to successive boulders, till the current tore them up, and we were swept down to others. Such was the speed of the water that the impact of head and body created a waterfall in itself. A thousand feet above, we came to the village of Rhenoke, where a state visitors' book was presented for our signatures. The resthouse at Ari was set in a garden of pebbled paths, surrounded by rose-bushes and chrysanthemums in flower. Beneath, the valley fell down, and rose again to disclose our resting-place of yesterday. During dinner, *marwa*, the local drink, was brought. It consisted of hot water, poured on a crush of millet, which was contained in a segment of bamboo a foot high and three inches wide, and sucked through a reed. The taste was indefinite, and the alcoholic virtue remote.

Next morning, we descended into a valley as dank and rich as yesterday's, and then followed a river upward. Stupendous, overhang-ing faces of mountain stood about us; at every turn it seemed as though there were no way but to attack them; yet still the river wound on through some unforeseen cleft. The vegetation increased. On the opposing hill the tops of the trees glittered in the midday sun, while all the rest was black: bananas like torn green flags; the tangled ribbons of the seaweed palm; huge ivy shapes; starry bunches of magnolia leaves; and round us, as we rode, the festoons of orchids and ferns, and a kind of creeper, having itself a trunk, whence depended great herring-bones of green oil-cloth leaves. The river was now below us, a foaming thread cleaving this inverted arboretum. Above, the sky was reduced to a mere triangle, whence fringes of cloud came encroaching on the rim of our prison. Then suddenly the bottom of the hills widened into a valley, where there was a village and a number of monks were chanting in the upper room of a house. The river was with us again, and had lately engulfed the road. Slithering down the aftermath of an avalanche, we crossed it on two tree-trunks, while the animals with some difficulty stood up against the current. Then began the ascent we had been expecting, a series of hairpin twists on a perpendicular face. After two hours of sliding and panting, we came to Sedonchen, as the clouds settled down for the night. Below the rest-house, through increasing mist, appeared the broad-eaved roofs of low houses, the villagers trailing about their affairs, sheep huddled in a tiny square, whence white prayer-flags fluttered sadly from their masts, and a wool-train arriving to be unloaded for the night. Beyond there was nothing. The whole scene was perched in space. Gradually the edges of the farther houses were swallowed up. The night increased. A perceptible cold made us shiver. We had tea, and then dinner. The latter consisted of Ah-Chung's chicken, potatoes, onions and carrots, 'cling' peaches, and a sardine savoury.

IV

INTO TIBET

The morning of Friday, 5 October, disclosed a view such as only the Himalayas can offer, range after range, peak after peak, filling the distance, with Kanchenjunga, on the right, making tentative bows from its place in the sky through the floating clouds. Below, the hill up which we had climbed was too steep to be visible. But the village was there, which seemed slightly surprising, after its disappearance the night before. The wool-trains were setting out, the fluffy, hide-bound packs being loaded, and the animals defiling one after another down the path and out of sight. During the morning, we met others, varying from thirty to a hundred mules, usually on some precipitous turn of the narrowing path, which obliged us to stand patiently and wait till they were past. The leaders wore collars of heavy bells, and were decorated with scarlet yaks' tails. Many had little head-pieces, shaped like those that elephants wear, and embroidered with cabalistic designs in bright colours. The men in attendance wore either the usual Tibetan robe of dark maroon serge, loosely caught at the hip, or else a species of plus-four made of the same local stuff. On their feet were high felt boots with canoe-shaped toes, appliquéd in red and green over the instep, and tied round the back, where they were slit, with brigand's garters. The effect was frequently completed by a Homburg hat several sizes too small which was affixed to the top of the head by means of the pigtail.

The ledge to which Sedonchen clings lies 6,500 feet above sea-level. Above, the path zigzagged inexorably up a continuous perpendicular face, the cobbles becoming rougher, and the precipices, falling sheer

173

from the narrowing footway, more unnerving, though their full menace was lost in a sea of grey cloud, whence came the noise of cadent, invisible waters. The luxuriant vegetation, which the last two or three days had made familiar, disappeared. Silver firs stood up, strangely ornamental. Other conifers, jagged and torn with age and wind, rose gaunt from the mist. Below them, walling the path to a height of twelve feet, grew woods of rhododendrons, their leaves, in star-shaped bunches, varying in length from two inches to ten, and coloured with a bluish grey unknown to the English varieties. The textural effect of the fine leaves against the broad, the innumerable permutations of a daisy pattern, broken by thin-elbowed branches, angular as strung bones, was one of great beauty, recalling the minutiae of Chinese ivories, save for the impalpable colouring and the wraiths of mist. Suddenly, out of a cloud, a solitary Tibetan emerged, dressed in a padded, full-sleeved robe of weathered red, which reached to the knees and gave an illusion of pregnancy, since the stomach, where it was caught across from shoulder to opposite hip, was used as a pocket. On his head he wore a tall conically crowned hat, with its brim, broad and scalloped, turned up in front. His face was parchment coloured, the eyes narrow, and the lips and cheeks very red, a typical Tibetan characteristic, giving the appearance of a sinister waxen doll. On his back he carried a frying-pan. From his waist hung a silver-sheathed knife in the place of a bayonet.

The ponies, panting and steaming, seemed on the verge of collapse, when the trees and rhododendrons gave place to a gloomy silhouette of huts through the darkening fog. Being in advance, I practised a Tibetan sentence upon two women and a baby, who said it was four miles on to Gnatong. The road now ceased to climb and branched off to the left; we had risen 5,000 feet in four miles, the latter being marked by mile-posts. Our other companion was the single telegraph wire to Lhassa, attached to trees or posts as convenience demanded, and during the stage we had just completed, carried vertically up the mountain-side with tantalizing directness, while we wound from side to side of it. Soon after the village we passed the tree-limit, and at half-past twelve came to Gnatong, 12,000 feet up. Having been unable to sleep the previous night, I had lit a candle and read a book by Edgar Wallace. This work, though forming part of a sixpenny edition, was

encased in a lavish gilded binding, and was prefaced by an announce-
ment that the editors of the series were anxious to place within reach
of the proletariat not only the classics, but an ornament to the home.
In commercial compensation, the paper used resembled an antique
blotter, and the type was barely distinguishable. As a result, I had
developed a headache, which was now considerably increased by the
height.

Gnatong lies in a cup of peaks, a place of about twenty houses, which
include a telegraph and post-office. At the rest-house, recently
constructed, we ate our lunch and warmed ourselves by a fire, paying
a fee of eight annas each for the privilege. Afterwards we sent a telegram
to Yatung, announcing our arrival on the morrow: a premature precaution. I posted some letters in time to catch the downward mail,
which had crossed the Jelep La that morning, and which we later met,
four runners of nondescript appearance.

It was now five miles to Kapup. The scene was almost Scottish in its
colouring; yet the colours were richer and more precise. Across the hill-
sides, whose tops reached into the clouds and were lost, lay great expanses
of dank yellow grass and the dank yellow leaves of dead flags, scattered
with black boulders, and interspersed with tiny rustling streams. From
this yellow sprouted clumps of a short star-leaved plant, of a lucid
pinkish red. In addition, the slopes were covered with patches of dwarf
rhododendron, small-leaved, and growing to the height of gorse. So
that, as a whole, the receding hills alternated between dank yellow
starred with autumn red and a rich, inimitable blue-grey green, a fright-
ening, melancholy colour, merging into the acrid purplish blue of farther
valleys darkened by hibernating clouds; while here and there escarpments of square-jutting rock, black and grey, increased the gloom and
inhospitality of the scene. A vulture flapped from a knoll to join its
fellows, crouching lumps of feathers, with their naked heads and necks
moving in and out like those of comic dolls. As we ascended farther,
my headache reduced me to the borders of insanity, and my pony had
to be led. The turn of a corner disclosed a lake, a smoky, forbidding
sheet of water, long in shape, and lying a thousand feet below us. Far
away, a pink speck proclaimed the roof of the Kapup rest-house. Above
it, towering into the sky, a yellow tendril threaded its way up the purple
silhouette of mountain – the road over the Jelep La into Tibet.

The rest-house, down to which I staggered in a condition of gibbering sightlessness, had two rooms only, in which fires were already blazing. Ah-Chung, who had gone ahead, had fever; but managed, none the less, to cook our dinner of steak and kidney and plum puddings. I went to bed, to listen to the hammers on my skull; but ate, and felt better for it. In the next room G. and M., elated with rum, turned their thoughts and conversation to London, but not their charity. So presumably people think and talk when marooned on that disappearing phenomenon, the desert island.

As we ate dinner it began to rain. Every drop, echoed and magnified by the corrugated-iron roof, filled us with a mounting apprehension. At half-past eight I went to sleep, and consequently woke at three. Despite an aluminium hot-water bottle dressed in a small pink vest, five blankets, and a great-coat of that nineteenth-century consistency which can, and had, come through forty years unblemished, I was cold. It was 13,000 feet, I said, as I twisted from side to side and ground myself into the coverings. But the cold came up through the mattress, which was thin. The noise of the rain was like rifle-fire. The wind howled. When day broke, the surrounding peaks and the pass over which we had to travel were obscured by falling snow. We lay in bed irresolute, till the sirdar came in to say that both cook and sweeper had fever, and that in any case it was impossible to start. That this was not so we knew. But we agreed with him.

After a breakfast of sausages, potatoes, tomatoes, poached eggs, scones, and coffee, we settled down in front of the fires. The single book-shelf was furnished with several copies of the *Revue des Deux Mondes*. M. read *Wolf Solent*, a soil-reeking novel by J. C. Powys, which he said harmonized exactly with our present surroundings. G. lay on the floor, his now perceptible beard protruding from the rim of a yet more ponderous tome, *The Mind and Face of Bolshevism*.

Lunch was welcome, as it is on rainy days. In the afternoon, impelled by the gloom and a temporary cessation of the rain, G. and I walked up the village street, which consisted of two shacks and a seat. The rain then began again. Having collected some rhododendron seeds, and had a glimpse of the lake, we returned.

That night the stars showed, and the morning brought a cloudless sky. The snow-spattered hills glittered in the sun. Leaving before the others, I urged my pony towards the pass. The slope was gradual, and the ground dotted with large trumpet-like gentians of indescribable blue. A bird, inky blue, with a rusty tail and a white spot on its head, hopped from a boulder. Wagtails, half white, fluttered about. Then I was in the snow, two or three inches of it. Till suddenly two cairns appeared, one on either side of the path. Dismounting, I looked down, and across, to Tibet.

The scene, as became the moment, was spectacular, revealing terrestrial conformation on a scale that the eye had never witnessed and the imagination never dreamed of. Vanished for ever was the prussian-blue of Anglo-Himalaya and the Alps, that immanent, formless tint which oppresses half the mountains of the world. A new light was in the air, a liquid radiance, presage of scenes with which the whole earth offers no comparison. Here was no gradual transition, no uneventful frontier, but translation, in a single glance, from the world we know to a world that I did not know. It was only a glimpse. Not for three days, till we were out of the Chumbi valley, was the reality upon us. But I knew, as I looked, that here was a land where natural coloration, as we understand it, does not apply, a land whose effulgence affirms intent more positive and less explicable than the fortuitous convenience of warmth and light.

From my feet the mountain fell away, sheer down, till the path hid itself underneath, and only reappeared a thousand feet below by the side of a lake, a cold tarn, dark green like a slab of inlaid ice. This was contained on a precarious landing, whence the mountains rose in a circle, falling back to the dorsal ridge on whose lowest point I now stood. The lower slopes supported scattered regiments of dark green firs. Beyond the lake a valley formed, falling down, down, down into a haze of wooded declivities, until, forty miles away, a new range stood up, a heathery buff colour of chocolate bloom, with every valley black, and every spur agleam, in the radiant morning sun. The eye moved upward, to come to rest, far above its own level of 14,300 feet, on a wavy line of snow, a glittering girdle to the blue sky, whence two sparkling white peaks, the grandiose Chomolhari and another, thrust their heads above a puff of cloud into the firmament. On either side the clouds were gathering; I was barely in time; within ten minutes the peaks were gone. Then, as I still looked, a line of men came crawling up the mountain-side beneath my feet, so diminutive, so absolutely small against the surrounding heights and distances, that my pony and I, silhouetted on the summit with India at our backs, seemed of colossal stature. Their approach disclosed a party of Bhutanese coolies, bearing heavy loads, and hung with curious household utensils. The majority wore dark glasses, and one a finely woven straw hat shaped like the lid of a dirty clothes-basket. The party immediately climbed on to the larger of the two cairns, where they remained busy for some minutes rearranging the large branch that stood from its midst. This was hung with prayer-flags, tattered pennants of various colours, to which the coolies were adding their own, taking care to ensure their being well placed. Then they went off, and I was left alone to gaze.

After an hour the others arrived, and behind them some of the servants, also furnished with appropriate prayer-flags. During the first part of the descent it was impossible to ride. We could only slither down the snow, and then the mud, till we came to the lake and the trees began. Yet we were afterwards informed that the two elephants in the Dalai Lama's zoo at Lhassa had crossed this way. The milestones were no more; and the path, even now that the valley proper offered a more rational foothold, was more obstacle than assistance, as though some giant in his course had been playing football with the boulders. We passed occasional villages, small hutments in the forest, their broad-eaved wooden roofs held down by stones, and adjoined by large open stables. A river accompanied us; yaks, black and silky as though caparisoned in Victorian hearth-rugs, grazed by its side. On the slopes around us the autumn colouring attained an incomparable richness and variety. Flowing golden larches; duller yellow maples; shumack of flaming red; innumerable blue-grey rhododendron bushes, the smaller bearing occasional orange flowers; huge silver firs, their tops broken with age and storm, which gave place, as we continued, to pines with brushes of bright green needles; flowering shrubs of many kinds, tenuous and spiky; and clumps of Michaelmas daisies to remind us of the same season in England; all stood about us, as we walked, rode, or slithered, crossing and recrossing the river by delicately engineered wooden bridges.

There accompanied our party a youth on a grey pony, whose frisky paces, unhindered by stones or mud, were our envy. Summoning my few words, I engaged him in conversation. Was he Tibetan? No,

Bhutanese. Where was he going? To Rinchengong, round the corner –
the corner indicated being a mountain-slope the size of Skiddaw.
Wasn't there a monastery there? Yes, and he was going to be a monk.
What was his name? Dambü. Thereafter, words failed me.

I was ahead, and having rounded the intervening mountain, had
caught sight of the roofs of Rinchengong, when a noise of drums
proclaimed some event. Turning a corner, I was confronted by a
religious procession.

It produced a curious feeling, almost fear, this first contact with
persons, clothes, and observances of utter strangeness. For many years
I had thought about Tibet, read about it, and gazed longingly at
photographs of its huge landscape and fantastic uniforms. None the
less, the reality came as a shock.

The valley had widened a little. In front, and all round, the hills rose
up, covered with dank yellow grass and the bright green pines. In the
middle distance appeared the roofs of Rinchengong, approached by a
few patches of cultivation. Between these, hemmed by two tumble-
down stone walls, came a troupe of about forty women and children.
The latter waved and laughed; the former carried on their backs long
boxes containing the sacred books. They were dressed, as the majority
of Tibetans are, in a coarse serge of mauvish purple. Their black hair
was done in the manner of Nurse Cavell's. The faces were well filled,
the mouths often sensual. The skin was ivory; but the cheeks and lips,
like those of the man we met among the rhododendrons, were brilliant
apple-red. This painted effect is the distinguishing characteristic of the
Tibetan appearance, and at first seemed strangely unnatural.

In the midst of the women and children walked numerous monks,
shaven-headed, and swathed in the manner peculiar to Buddhist
monks, in thick red serge; some striking thin, slightly barrel-shaped
drums; one beating a large cymbal. Occasionally they wore hats,
astounding shapes, high-pointed cones of red, or Phrygian caps of the
same colour. This was evidently the red-hat sect. At the head of the
procession moved a benign grey-headed figure, who smiled as I dismounted, but in reality told our servants to take us round another way.
In the rear, borne in a palanquin, came a golden image preceded by a
scowling fat monk. One might have been the Virgin, and the other a
priest, in an Italian village.

Rinchengong lay on both sides of a new and larger river, which was crossed by a wooden bridge supported on two horizontal piles of huge beams, each layer protruding farther from the bank than that below it, so that the topmost ones almost met beneath the middle of the footway. The houses were of two and three storeys, tall and solid, with heavy square windows paned in glass (twenty years ago there was only paper) and set in richly carved and coloured wooden frames. The ground floors, entered by massive double doors, were used as stables; the upper, beneath the roof, were open and stored forage. In the centre of the town rose a magnificent *chorten*, an onion-like erection rising from a square base and supporting a spike of brass that glittered in the sun like gold. This was surrounded, as is usual, by a plantation of peeled masts, twenty feet high, down each of which a single narrow flag, printed with the prayer *Om Mani Padme Hum*, was tacked to within six feet of the ground. Nearby stood a rectangular edifice, like a large stone chest, about twenty feet long, eight high, and five broad, through an arcade in which could be seen a row of prayer-wheels, revolving reels a foot high. Along the outside, innumerable little painted plaques bore the faded image of Buddha. These *chortens* and *mendongs* are to be found in all the Tibetan villages, and sometimes standing by themselves on frequented paths. As we passed out of Rinchengong we observed an old man, with two wisps of white moustache depending from the outer corners of his mouth, seated on his doorstep slowly turning a brass prayer-wheel, which revolved, as he waved its handle, by means of a small weight on the end of a chain.

The way continued along the banks of the new river, the Chumbi, a broad, tearing volume of water flecked by little waves. Cultivated fields stretched from hill to hill. There were even patches of flat grass, on which my pony alone could be induced to gallop. In the villages, each with *chorten*, prayer-masts, and *mendong*, the inhabitants gazed fixedly at us, their ruddy faces sometimes breaking into smiles, sometimes not. The telegraph wire was still with us. We lunched by the river-side. The scene, for the moment, might have been in Canada. At three o'clock, after travelling eighteen miles and descending to 10,000 feet above sea-level, we came to Yatung, a large place with a main street flanked by prayer-masts, and overlooked by the bungalow and Union Jack of the British Trade Agent, and the tin barracks, complete with *pissoir* and football field, of his twenty-five Indian soldiers. The rest-house lay opposite, across the river, set in a paled garden of hollyhocks and Japanese anemones. Its interior disclosed unexpected luxury: brocade curtains, padded arm-chairs, reproductions of Gainsborough, Romney, and Franz Hals, an original and somewhat unfortunate still life, numerous books and more copies of the *Revue des Deux Mondes*, evidently the former property of a political officer. Over the mantel-piece hung a coloured portrait of the Prince of Wales, clad in the golfing fashions of 1924, and holding a cairn terrier.

The following morning brought a steady downpour of rain. Being rather tired, we did not start till late. Two or three miles out we encountered an official of the local post-office, who said that beyond Gautsa, our day's objective, snow was falling.

'Gyantse you're going to, are you?' he continued. 'My God, your faces will be in a state.'

'We've got cold cream and vaseline.'

'They're no good. If you do use them, rub 'em off before you go into the sun . . . Well – good luck! I don't envy you. Cheero!' And we parted.

The rain was falling steadily. There was a darkness in the air. Above the path, on the right, stood a line of ruins, the old Chinese barracks which fell into desuetude after the recall of the imperial troops in 1911. We passed along a soggy plain, the bottom of an elliptical cup of hills, in which the river broadened into a placid stream and yaks were nibbling at the sedges. A bridge crossed the river and a path led up to a monastery on a ledge in the opposite hills, a new building restored out of all picturesqueness. It was here that Lord Zetland and Mr Laden-La consulted the oracle as to the fate of the war; to which, after exhibiting a series of spasms, he gave a Delphic answer of no great perspicacity. We had hoped for his advice ourselves with regard to certain domestic problems; but had learnt, before starting, that he had lately been seduced by a woman in a wood and consequently relieved of his duties.

Beyond the plain the valley narrowed into a forbidding gorge. Now we were level with the river; now 300 feet above it; now it was bounding and foaming above us. Gigantic peaks, inclining from our very foot-falls, towered into the remaining sky. The path was steep, a series of rocky steps, interspersed with pools of mud. The raindrops trickled slowly down the long red hips and haws of Chinese roses. We fell into a trance of gloom, as the wet percolated down our necks and up our sleeves. Time had ceased. The ponies picked their way of their own accord. At length, almost unknowing, we arrived at Gautsa, a scattering of wooden huts, which seemed as though half sunk into the ground for fear of the sombre ramparts about them.

That afternoon, before the light went, it began to snow here also. It continued during the night and the following dawn. When we awoke there were six inches on the ground, and half as much on every branch and boulder. It was impossible, the sirdar said, to start. That might be; but this time we were not to be daunted. G. and I were muffled in our carpet suits, helmets, mackintoshes, and fingerless gloves; M. had brought his winter-sports clothes and looked like an illustration in the *Tatler*, save that the smile was lacking. The path was invisible; we were advised to leave its discovery to a mule; and Ah-Chung, enveloped in a mackintosh with a frilled hood, set off ahead like some cardinal on his way to a session of the Inquisition. In view of its superior strength, my pony had been loaded anew with the saddle-bags. Alarmed at the rattle of tins and bottles, he set off at an angry pace, heedless of the snow's foundations, and lurching and slipping, passed the mule-train. As we rose to 13,000 feet, the snow deepened to a foot, and the trees gave place to bushes. The path, high above the river, became a ledge. A frightful desolation hung in the air, as the snowflakes floated persistently from the bilious leaden sky, down from above, past, and down again, to the river miles below, which had become a trickling black ribbon in a world of white, enclosed by stupendous white escarpments that allowed it no banks and rose sheer from either edge of the water. Only the water's distant rush and trickle broke the tingling silence. Should we get through? should we get through? The question became an obsession. We were mounting. Would not the snow be deeper at the top, once out on the Phari plain? To be baulked, to turn back in face of all our preparations, to have stood on the threshold and been barred, to admit that an inch or two of snow had got the better of us – these threats drummed my mind. Not a footfall had we seen; we were entering the unknown; the plains might be full of huge drifts in which we could move neither back nor fore and should only freeze to death; and the servants were plainly apprehensive. Suffering was tolerable. But not failure, even though it entailed a hero's death.

The path was now scarcely more than a yard wide. Beneath it, the precipice to the river was increasing in depth, and the pony was picking its way more gingerly, when suddenly the whole ledge was blocked by an avalanche of snow that had left a dirty track on the white slope above. Thankful for my high Cretan boots, which I had brought from their native island as a mere curiosity, I set about to trample down the snow, which was soft and, as it stood, came to the height of my chest. The pony, following at reins' length, decided to make a rush for it, and in doing so let its hindquarters fall over the edge. I pulled it back till it was firmly embedded in the drift, and continued my trampling. This was not easy, owing to lack of breath and superfluity of clothes. Eventually I made my way over, piling up a rampart on the outer side, to prevent further alarms. Immediately in front lay another similar obstacle, rather larger, into which I delved spasmodically, while the pony stood alone, looking slightly supercilious. After half an hour the train came in sight, like a string of black insects crawling slowly up the white slope. At the first drift Ah-Chung dismounted and led his mule. The next fell heavily and had to be relieved of its boxes. However, the grooms and muleteers, having come thus far, displayed an admirable determination; and after much digging and stamping, both obstacles were negotiated.

A little farther on, where the bottom of the valley had rejoined the path, we reached a solitary hut, outside which a mail-runner was waiting. The downward post from Phari had not arrived. Our hearts sank. We decided to wait a little, while the men drank tea out of tin mugs, and we did likewise. Ten minutes later the four postmen appeared, and after them a large wool-train. Both said that, once out on the plain, the snow grew less. We set off again, this time with a definite track to follow.

At length the valley widened, the snow ceased falling, and the mountain-sides fell back at a more gentle incline, till we were riding over an upward-sloping plateau. Over its brow came two men mounted on yaks, and leading another packed with their belongings, uncouth silhouettes as they plunged through the snow, the riders flinging the single rope attached to the nostril from one horn to the other. We met at a bog, whose presence was discovered by the sudden disappearance of the mule bearing G. and M.'s luggage. Its head remained visible, and it was rescued. But the suitcases were immersed. The sun began to shine in a vague way, but not vague enough to prevent, after an hour or two, a strange burning feeling in the nose and the sirdar's going snowblind. But for Ah-Chung, our servants seemed to have come ill-provided for the trials they must have foreseen. Half of them had no glasses. That morning one of the grooms had been left behind owing to his having neither boots nor shoes. He did not catch us up till the evening before we reached Gyantse. And on the journey down, when conditions were worse, I was forced to distribute my own shoes and stockings to others.

We reached the plateau proper, and knew that we had reached Tibet. The snow, save on the surrounding hills, gave place to bare earth and stones. A great herd of yaks was grazing – calves, cows, and bulls, their deep shaggy black unrelieved save by an occasional streak of white up their bushy tails. Beyond them rose the huge twisted cone of Chomolhari, 24,000 feet high, whence jagged cubes and triangles of overhanging rock where the snow could obtain no hold, protruded nakedly. The earth around us was pitted with small holes, dwellings of the marmot, a peculiar animal between a rabbit and a rat, which sat on its hind-legs, whiskers a-quiver, till our actual approach, then disappeared over its threshold.

At last, beyond a stretch of cultivation, Phari Jong, or Castle, stood up, an impressive mass misty grey in the afternoon light, its perpendicular lines slightly convergent and gathering to a squat central tower-storey. A few wisps of smoke proclaimed the town. The castle seemed nearer than it was, as things do in Tibet; my pony had gone lame; and it was another hour before we reached the rest-house compound. This contained also a post-office. The postal service from Gyantse to Phari is bi-weekly, and accomplished by mule; between Phari and India it is daily and on foot. The service is maintained by the Indian Government at a cost of between £5,000 and £6,000 a year. The receipts we did not discover. It is much appreciated by the Tibetans, whose own arrangements between Lhassa, though daily, are not so certain. Rich inhabitants of the capital and of Shigatse frequently send their letters and parcels to the Gyantse post-office by private messenger. Their volume is increasing, since communication with China, whence Tibetans draw most of their amenities, is become more and more precarious overland, and the route by Calcutta and the sea is preferred.

Despite our exhaustion, both physical and mental, we hastened to despatch the letters of recommendation with which Messrs Macdonald and Laden-La had provided us, to the Jong, accompanied by the requisite scarf. Each Jong is the seat of two Jongpens, administrative officials with magisterial powers over certain districts, who are supposed to act as a check on one another. The occupants of the Phari office, probably young officials beginning their careers in Lhassa, were absentees, as often happens, and their powers were delegated to two representatives. In about half an hour these arrived in person, one cadaverous and tall, the other plump and short, both lacking numerous teeth, and wearing the single ear-ring, four inches long, of turquoise drops jointed in gold, which is the mark of all persons of substance. Their robes were of the usual purplish cloth. On their heads they wore ordinary black-and-gold caps, with the fur flaps turned up windmill-fashion, and underneath long pigtails. We were told later that they were very poor. We presumed them to be the victims of grievance or neglect, since they opened the conversation by suggesting that we should take a letter for them to the Dalai Lama, the reason being that all correspondence arriving by the ordinary channels is carefully scrutinized by secretaries before being presented to His Holiness. We could only regret that we should have no opportunity of delivering it.

The following morning I awoke in a condition of physical misery such as I have never experienced before or since. Phari, 14,300 feet above sea-level, is possibly the highest town in the world. My head, yesterday quiescent, had begun to drum and throb as though an hydraulic machine were pumping all the blood in my body into it. The cold was bitter. In addition, my whole face was a suppurating jelly of yellow liquid, which nothing could stanch, and which dripped through my beard over the sheets and on to my clothes, as I fitted my body into them with palsied movements. Though it was only six o'clock, and barely light, the sirdar suddenly announced that the castellans had arrived again. Mopping my face with a handkerchief, I emerged into the sitting-room, to find the naked corpse of a sheep lying on the table, accompanied by a number of eggs. We pressed them to tea, and then raw whisky, which they sipped with as much distaste as we ourselves.

They accepted, as return presents, tins of ginger-nuts, smoked salmon, sardines, and chocolate. As my pony had not recovered, they promised to find another.

We were anxious to visit the Jong itself, and encountering the taller castellan on a dung-heap an hour later, I framed the request in Tibetan. An emissary was appointed to lead us. The town was unprepossessing, as all travellers have found it. The houses, constructed, save for a few solid buildings on the outskirts, of turfs, were scarcely above the level of the ground; so that columns of smoke came wreathing out of holes in what seemed to be mere platforms of earth, about the height of the shoulder. Stacks of yak-dung, in round kneaded pats, lay everywhere; for we were out of the wood area, and had had to pay heavily for our fires at the rest-house. The streets, seven feet wide, were runnels of filth, and strewn with bones and pieces of bloody hide. Enormous ravens, croaking and disgusting, crouched on the house-tops or flapped a few feet above our heads, as though in appetite for ourselves. Stocky black mastiffs, fortunately tethered, barked at our approach. Yaks, ponies, and mules were tied by the hind-leg in open stables.

The Jong, which was shelled by the British in 1904 and has since been repaired, proved considerably smaller and less substantial than its excellent lines had seemed to warrant. Ascending by a flight of steps, we were ushered through a doorway four feet high into a low room, whose ceiling was supported by a wooden crutch-pillar in the middle. Though it was not distinguishably clean, there was no smell and the windows were open. One of the castellan's wives, assisted by numerous servants, gave us tea from a blue enamel kettle in glasses marked MADE IN JAPAN. This, though boiled with milk and sugar, was 'English' and cheered our spirits. Should we be passing this way again? We must come and see them. She was a pretty woman in a somewhat solid way, and her complexion clean and fair, with the usual blush on the cheeks. After twenty minutes we took farewell, mounted our ponies, and set off over the plains.

V

THE PLAINS

This account must now enter upon that stage familiar to all readers of Tibetan travel-books, in which the desolation of the country overwhelms all other impressions. While the eye is dazzled with colour and form of such intensity and glitter, and on such a scale, that it seems as though our drab and commonplace planet had been exchanged for the moon or some other heavenly body, an unwilling, clandestine fear lurks in the shadows of the stranger's being, as though he were threatened with gradual but total extinction, with that cessation of being or becoming which Buddhism teaches to be the goal of man and his perfecting. Readers of Tibetan travel-books may find little excitement in our short journey, carried out under conditions of comparative comfort over one of the most frequented highways and one of the most comparatively hospitable parts of the whole Tibetan plateau, a journey accomplished by British officers several times a year as part of their normal routine. What is this beside the laborious and dangerous incursions from the north and east, where the altitude and savagery of the country surpass anything on earth, of Huc, Prjevalsky, and Pereira? None the less the slow ride of 150 miles over the frontier reveals enough of Tibet and of the character of the landscape to invest with reality the monotonous, agonized records of those more adventurous explorers, whose words fail them to paint the horror and beauty of their journeys. Tibet, for us now, is no longer the 'land of mystery', a piece of dark brown on physical maps, gripped by an unholy hierarchy, and possessing no amenities of life beyond devil-dances and butter statues; but a physical, aesthetic, and human definition as implied by the words

France or Germany. Henceforth it exists on the map of our intelligence as well as of our atlas. If, say the newspapers, this or that is happening in Tibet, this or that means something. In Terra del Fuego it does not. This or that, moreover, is invested with a particular romance. We see again the parched distances, the damson hills and gilded rocks, the encroaching snows, the yaks ploughing the pale dusty earth of the valleys, the threshers singing on the outskirts of the four-square farm-houses, the laughs of the passers-by, the burning turquoise sky, and the pop-eyed clouds. We have a part in the country. We wish it well.

From Phari the way led over three or four miles of plain, through the street of a village, and then sloped gradually up to the Tang-La, an imperceptible pass 15,300 feet in height, and the summit of our journey. As we rose, patches of snow reappeared; while the enclosing hills were covered with white down to their junction with the flat. On the right, Chomolhari, grown enormous, towered over us, rising, as it seemed in the clear air, from only a few hundred yards away, a massive cone whose jutting, naked peak, wrenched round the wrong way, threatened to crash from the clouds 9,000 feet above upon our heads. Beyond it, as we descended from the pass and inclined towards the north-east, a subsidiary range, jagged outline of unbroken white, stretched away to the north, its depressions filled with swollen, shining clouds. There are no clouds like these clouds. Shaped like those of Chinese landscapes, the dancing light, the very essence of light, neither silver nor gold, but *light*, fills their underneaths and middles with sharp, three-dimensional shadows, so that their protuberant white bodies assume a reality that could be tossed and caught, if only reached. A pink pervades them: complement of the sky, the oppressing ultra-marine sky, dark as the interstices of waves, near as the speckled visions beneath the eyelids – a pink which is on the snow as well, and on all the land, an emphatic tint of unearthly propinquity. In the foreground, reflecting these marvels, ran a small river, broken by diminutive islets and crossed by a humped bridge. Beyond, the ground rose in a kind of terrace at whose top stood a Tibetan rest-house. Through the double doors of the outer wall appeared a square compound of stables and a house, where our men stopped to drink tea. The lame pony stopped also, and I had to go back for it.

An interminable flat, ten miles long, now confronted us, across which the metal telegraph-posts expanded into a single dotted line. These were not so incongruous as they sound; for Huc recorded lines of black poles traversing similar plains for the guidance of travellers. Over to the right, towards the roots of Chomolhari, a donkey lay recumbent while a woman beat it, and its foal ran this way and that in perplexity. On the opposite horizon, where low hills began again, a strange glacial formation, the top of some stupendous range, flashed like a sheaf of crystals in the blue. As our eyes strained ahead in pursuit of the posts, till the hills circled in, we could distinguish Tuna, a scatter of black rectangles, whose details became clearer as the hours went by. The tedium of our progress seemed insupportable. I yearned for my life's terror, a horse that would run away. Mounted on a species of small dog, having the appearance of an autumn chrysanthemum and the shoulders of an eel, over which my saddle and myself were continually falling on to its neck, I jolted along, sometimes inducing a series of rapid stumbles by dint of simultaneously lashing one rein about the head and the other about the tail. G. and M., though higher off the ground, were in no better plight. By a disastrous oversight we had brought neither whip nor switch. For four days on end not a bush nor a twig did we see; and after Samoda there was only a prickly scrub, which tore the hands and broke at the first blow. The duration of our stages was made half as long again, and the tedium correspondingly increased, by this circumstance.

Tuna, where the Younghusband expedition lay encamped for a whole winter, is 14,700 feet above sea-level, and commands a square view of the entire Chomolhari range. As the sun set, shadows of a frigid, incalculable blue gave new form to the great extended mass and its dominating peak. Seated on a chair in three greatcoats, I sought to sketch it; but a steely, icy wind drove me in. By the light of a lamp I continued, till my head began to ache. During the night my whole skull seemed to be splitting into sections like the pigs of an orange, among which I took a new shape as the Governor of Bengal attending a garden-party under compulsion, and dressed in a mackintosh designed by Bert Thomas, whose drawings in *Punch* I had been looking at.

The morning, which came at last, was the crisis of the expedition. My own face, for which I had constructed a mask out of two handkerchiefs, had ceased to drip, and was now covered with yellow scabs, which adhered unpleasantly to the surface of the beard. But those of M. and G. had liquefied in the night, and they arrived in my room to breakfast, speechless with despondency. The cold was intense; the room was filled with the odour of yak-dung and lamp-smoke; my head was pounding; and I had whispered to myself, during the despair of dressing, that if – if either of the others were to suggest an about-turn, I should not oppose him. To endure this pain for three more weeks would be merely the weak-mindedness of the strong.

M., his face dripping, unshaven, and crinkling with nausea as it opened to receive a piece of tinned sausage, spoke the first reproach that I had ever known of him: '*Why* have you brought us to this horrible place?' – as though it were any more my doing than his. Whereat G., employing the dogmatic tone of an Early Father, an-nounced: 'I am going straight back to Phari.' It was that tone that saved us. 'You can,' I said resentfully, though ten seconds before I would have followed him. 'I'm going on. Anyhow I rather want to see Lake Dochen.' I had no such desire; but as we should reach it that morning, it seemed the nearest incentive. 'Well?' we both inquired at once of M. 'I'm so wretched,' he replied, mopping his face and pushing away the sausage, 'that I'm indifferent. But I don't like not keeping to my plans.' 'Grotesque weak-mindedness!' snarled G.; and to me: 'If you want to see Lake Dochen, GO and see Lake Dochen.' Thereafter no more was spoken. Outside the window the noise of the loading mules went on; then stopped. They had gone. The sirdar cleared away the breakfast; Ah-Chung was on his mule. We put on our scarves, gloves, and helmets and, mounting, continued northward.

We now left the Tuna plain, and, turning a corner of mountain, came to another, containing Lake Dochen, whose waters, after a long expanse of marsh, revealed themselves in a series of peacock blue and green diagonals, stretching out towards the same Chomolhari range, which seemed to follow us as we moved, though the peak was now at our backs. We were anxious to make good time, as we had set ourselves a double stage of some twenty-five miles. At an angle of the lake stood the bungalow of Dochen, a mile over half-way, which M. and G. decided to avoid, in order to take a short cut across the lower ground by the lake. Feeling exhausted from want of sleep, I wished to eat in comfort at a table, and, taking the saddle-bags containing our joint lunch, proceeded to the bungalow, outside which a huge train of ponies and their grooms was waiting. Entering the door, I encountered Captain Smith, the British Trade Agent at Gyantse, who was on his way down to Yatung and had halted for the same purpose as myself. His companion, the doctor, galloped off to stop the others. Meanwhile I drank greedily at some Ovaltine, and felt nourished for the first time in weeks. Captain Smith, politely averting his eyes from my swollen face and purple lips, said that these altitudes did not suit him either, and that he hoped never to see Gyantse again. The doctor, returning, said that if they didn't, they didn't, and there was nothing to be done about it, which depressed me. During lunch, another officer, McLeod, came in: he had shot a gazelle, which was outside, in process of dissection, that he might give us a haunch – a tiny animal, about three feet high, with horns like a duiker's. Smith said afterwards that we all looked pretty bad, and that he wondered at the time if we should get through.

'Oh, you've got a Tibetan hat, have you?' remarked the doctor as we made to depart.

'Yes,' I answered. 'It's almost saved my life. D'you like it?'

'Well, I shouldn't wear one myself, you know – not warm enough.' Saying which, he assumed a scanty tweed thimble. As the Tibetan hat is presumably the warmest hat in the world outside the Arctic Circle, he evidently considered me a traitor to the Anglo-Saxon decencies.

'Personally, I like Tibet,' he continued. 'The Indian troops at Gyantse are frightfully keen on hockey. I really get all the games I want. It's a bit lonely sometimes. But as I say, I get all the games I want.' And he shrugged his shoulders with a gesture of perfect satisfaction.

We went our way, they theirs, to our envy, at a canter. That morning I had acquired a second pony no bigger than a dog, also orange and decrepit. A third was now produced, similar in appearance, but of a different spirit. To my surprise it trotted smartly away from the bungalow, and, turning the corner of the lake, proceeded up its western shore. After about seven miles we came to a river, flowing out of the lake in a westerly direction, evidently to a lower level. This had created a gorge, into which I turned, finally losing sight of Chomolhari. Above the path a squat square tower, slightly tapering and built of coarse brown stones, bespoke the strategic significance of this point in the route. Coming to a village, where the gorge widened, I mistook it for

Kala, and, on reascending from questioning two farm-women, fell in with a party of riders who were evidently in a hurry to be at their destination before night fell. Some were carrying guns; saddle-bags of reddish brown hide bounced from their high, carpeted saddles. They rode mules, which trot very quickly, without the jolting of a horse; for no Tibetan ever rises in his stirrups. I had offered a cigarette to the one beside me – a present which, being forbidden by law, is always welcome – and was continuing at my normal pace while he stopped to light it, when suddenly he passed me at the gallop, and my pony, like a Gadarene swine, set off after him. The reins were rotten, and would have broken had I exerted any strength. Up and down the narrow path we clattered and thundered, till at last I and mine slipped off it into two feet of water. This made no difference to our speed. Then the sacking under the saddle fell off, one girth broke, and I came to rest sitting on the animal's ears in the midst of the whole party, who looked extremely surprised. My competitor had retrieved the sacking, and now reaffixed the saddle. Kala was upon us, and he pointed my way to the bungalow.

Immediately I sat down the blood in my head began to pound with a violence unknown to the previous days, and I relieved the monotony by picking my face. The others arrived, and as soon as mirrors were forthcoming, did the same. We were now without speech of any sort, or the desire for it, and moved about our occupations with a desperate fortitude. It was remarkable what a vivid interest the face could provide. Every evening henceforth it was our first concern and recreation on arrival. At first in small pieces, caked with ineffectual grease; then, where there was no beard, in great streamers, skin after skin peeled off, leaving us with raw, wet complexions like a rabbit on the brink of the pot. Only the lips remained impervious to our pains, ringed with sores that made every bite a martyrdom. The most remarkable feature of our joint appearance was G.'s nose, a prominent organ, which assumed a colour to warm one's hands by.

That evening at Kala we ate the gazelle's haunch, which was excellent, with French beans and mushrooms. How many more days? we asked; and went to bed.

Kala gives its name to another lake, where the British Trade Agent's party had shot a brace of geese, one of which they had very kindly left behind for us. We only caught a glimpse of the lake, as the road led off in the opposite direction, across a plain six miles long, whose surface was covered with star-shaped cracks like the bottom of a dry pond in summer. Since leaving Lake Dochen, the landscape had changed; we were now below 14,000 feet; and the glacial effects of the Chomolhari range and the lake had given place to deeper and more tangible colouring. Damson, brown, and gold, the hills rose above us as we reached the end of the plain, their tops sugared with a blueish snow, and their colour, unlike the misty depths of a Scottish glen, intensified by a microscopic clarity of detail which revealed every pebble two and three thousand feet above our heads. Behind, the blue of the sky pressed forward. The hills were very close. A huge conformation of sharply outlined boulders, slides, and checky strata rose above our heads, colour of gilded caramel satin, tinged with pink: a dark tone in itself, despite the blaze of sun that covered it; behind which, as my eye reached its rim, the sky appeared as dark again, comparatively, as a pool of ink soaking on to a clean sheet of blotting-paper, and yet losing none of its colour of powdered lapis. Words are inadequate to describe the effect. The light was such that the colours had assumed a relationship and tonality outside the normal ken. And as the sun, vilely near, beat upon us, and the mind strove to believe the scenes that confronted it, the desolation increased. After leaving Phari, we had found ourselves on the moon; there was something credible in that; we have all imagined the moon. But neither we nor anyone else had ever imagined this. Save for our ponies' hoofs, and the bone-like rattle of dead irises, a ponderous silence hung from the mountain-tops as we rode through the middle-day, and the sharp outlines of the stones grew blacker and longer. 'Oh for a tree!' groaned M. from the depths of a temperament that finds beauty only in luxuriance. 'What a country for motor-racing!' murmured G. 'I shall tell Segrave.' 'Well, it won't see me again,' replied M. sharply, 'till there's a wagon-lit.'

After Samoda, where we stayed the night and ate the goose with a tin of sweet corn, there were no more plains. The road, imperceptibly but surely descending, led through a series of valleys, more hospitable in appearance, where the sun blazed hotly and there was little air: on either side the same golden brown hills, with their tops now almost clear of snow; overhead, from one summit to another, the sagging blue firmament; fields of cultivation; yaks, two at a time, straining forward to drag their wooden ploughs through the dry baked earth, each team directed by a fur-hatted, high-booted peasant; in the distance, square white farm-houses, their perpendiculars still convergent, and furnished at the four corners with small turrets, whence groups of sweet-pea sticks gave the prayers of the inhabitants, untidy shreds of rag, into the universe. Around stood the farm-buildings, and beyond them, walled enclosures stacked with corn, in which threshing-floors had been cleared, and men and women, up to their waists in golden chaff and straw, were jumping and beating to release the grain. As they worked they sang long-drawn rhythmic utterances on one or two notes, filled with a cumulative solitude, as though the hills themselves were speaking. These chants of the ploughmen at work, borne miles along through the clear air and the dancing light, from where, between river-bank and stony hill-side, two long black specks and one upright one could been seen moving slowly to and fro over a given limit, ring through my head still, recalling for ever the land and its people.

A short distance down the valley, at Samoda, we passed an old monastery, backed by a tall square tower, whose temple and outer courtyard were in process of reconstruction. A nondescript crowd gathered on the roof and laughed at us as we rode by. As the valley expanded and twisted into another, a series of ruins, all of brown stone, black-shadowed and conical, were visible from a farther slope. Adjoining a farm-house in the distance was a walled grove of yellowing willows, the first trees since we left the Chumbi Valley above Gautsa. A butterfly flitted frivolously across the track. That evening we stayed at Khangma, where the telegraph-wire was tapped, and we telephoned to Captain Blood at Gyantse. Next morning the valleys continued and the sun grew hotter. A red-leaved berberis dotted the hillsides. In the river swam fish three inches long. On its banks hopped huge iridescent magpies and speckled, crested hoopoes. Mules, outspanned, were grazing on a stretch of grass, while their drivers lay, as they had spent the night, in the shelter of their loads.

Suddenly river and path converged to enter the 'red-idol gorge', passing beneath the string of prayer-flags that marked the gate to this place of sanctity. The walls of the gorge, of a brilliant golden stone, displayed an astounding geological formation, like a mighty pile of sandwiches and buns. At the bottom every rock was heaped with miniature cairns, built of marble fragments. Down the vertical face of one enormous boulder had been carved the life-size figure of a Buddha, painted in red, white, and cold blues and greens, and sheltered by an arbour of loose stones. Then the gorge widened into another valley, and we reached the bungalow at Saugong, to find that Captain Blood had already sent ponies to bring us into Gyantse on the morrow. There, for the first time since Phari, my head ceased to ache. We were now below 13,000 feet.

The rest-houses between Phari and Gyantse, whose hours of tedium and misery are stamped indelibly on our memories, are of a Tibetan rather than an Indian type, and externally at least resemble the other Tibetan rest-houses which we saw, and which complete the routes to Lhassa and Shigatse. The ever-guiding wire comes to rest at a low square enclosure, not unlike a Tibetan farm-house, though more kempt in appearance. A double door gives entrance to a courtyard, cloistered with kitchens, sleeping-places for the servants, and shelters for stores awaiting further transport. Outside, a few men are standing about, perhaps loading or unloading their animals. The women attached to the establishment, dressed in the same coarse stuff as the men, and possibly wearing the astonishing semicircular hoop of the Gyantse head-dress, or a jacket embroidered with swastika and crescent, stand or sit in the remains of the afternoon sun, dropping and catching their spools of yarn. Tiny children, in miniature serge robes, play at their feet, or practise their woollen slings in the direction of straying yaks. The traveller arrives, dismounts painfully, and with his knees unable to straighten, shouts 'Chowkidar!' for the caretaker. His pony is led away to a stable at the side. He traverses the courtyard, where, if the altitude and season permit, dwarf hollyhocks, marigolds, and cornflowers are growing in pots, and enters the bungalow at the back, which strikes cold after the sun outside.

Two doors on the courtyard give access to two main rooms, behind which are two smaller ones, and off them two bathrooms containing washstands with tin basins, tin wash-tubs, and rickety commodes, small and rusty. The other rooms have a bed and a fireplace each, the latter a hole in the wall of such depth that all the heat is effectually conserved in the chimney. In the smaller rooms are a table, wooden chairs, and a bookshelf containing Edwardian novels without covers, whose beginning- and end-pages are gradually disappearing, copies of the *Journal* of the Royal Geographical Society and the *Revue des Deux Mondes*, and a bound volume of *Punch*. The walls, to the height of four feet, are washed in shiny pillar-box red, a colour that came to sicken us, above which they display a cold green. Between these two runs a band of red, blue, and green stripes, each three inches in width and picked out with gold. Over the doors and windows hang curtains of a charming Tibetan stuff, coarse and hairy, and printed all over with little crosses like a medieval tabard. This is made in many colours, the prettiest patterns being red crosses on yellow and red on white. These curtains can serve as supplementary blankets, and even, if the clothes are wet, as Roman draperies. On the floor lie Tibetan carpets, possibly ten feet square, of bold colouring and Chinese design, which bear a singular resemblance to those found in the more cultured residences of suburbia.

The caretaker hurries in, places a wisp of some dried scrubby-looking plant in the fireplace, shreds a yak-pat on to it, piles others above, and thus makes a fire, which, if it is to exude a yard's radius of heat, must be re-fuelled every ten minutes. The pronunciation of the word 'yak-pat' troubled us at first; till we evolved the refined form of 'yappet'. In the same way our Swedish biscuits, entitled by their makers 'crisp-breads', became more euphemistically 'crippets'.

As it grows dark a turmoil without announces the arrival of servants and mule-train. The luggage is hastily disposed in the wrong rooms, then changed about. The sweeper, muffled to the nose, crouches in the courtyard, filling the lamps from Ah-Chung's can of oil. These, when brought, are of two varieties: one with a glass chimney, the worst make to be had, which either flickers dimly, or else, when turned up, emits a volume of smoke like an oil-well on fire, so that the whole room is clouded with fluffy black smuts that form a paste in the nostrils during the night – the glass having cracked meanwhile, putting it out altogether and leaving us to indemnify the caretaker; the other of an ingenious German type, without a glass, but burning a certain proportion of air, which is impelled into it by a ticking clockwork that runs down now and then, and again leaves us in sudden darkness. In the wake of these uncertain luminaries come tea and scones, with butter, jam, and milk out of tins. This meal reveals what the Press calls a human touch. Thanks, it appears, to the forethought of the late political officer in Sikkim, Major Bailey, and his wife, each bungalow is furnished with several specimens of Goss ware, whose municipal heraldries bring poignant reminders of happy romps at Dolgelly and improving afternoons at Stratford. It was intended, however, by the donors, that the reminiscence should eventually be reciprocal. For the initial letter of each mother-town represented corresponds with that of the Tibetan village in which its offspring is now situated. Thus, should I ever, during this present incarnation, succeed in penetrating the fastness of KINGUSSIE, my imagination will at once jump back the intervening years to the cosy hospitality of KHANGMA. Similarly, SEAFORTH shall transport my spirit once again to sweet SAUGONG, and SEAFORD to SAMODA. The most whimsical choice has been that of BARNARD CASTLE for PHARI JONG. Major and Mrs Bailey, to whom, in all seriousness, gratitude is due for the real comforts of the bungalows, have introduced a new spice into the art of travel.

After tea, and the facial operations described above, the time comes for rum. Rum is G. and M.'s preference, since their whisky, which has necessitated another mule, they find too disgusting to touch. Hot water, richly flavoured with morsels of yak-dung, is added, and also sugar. We crouch by the fire, sipping and shivering, heaping the yappets into their insatiable hole. Follows dinner, arranged by G.; the bedding is unpacked and made; hot-water bottles are placed within. We say good-night, unwillingly shed our numerous clothes, which are becoming increasingly smelly and dirty, block the chinks of doors and windows, and leap chattering between the sheets. Next morning, apart from my particular headache, which fortunately did not recur on the return journey, we awake to a sensation of profound nausea. A vapour of breath, yak-dung, and lamp-smoke obscures the room; a blast of freezing air rushes in with the sirdar as he brings the pot of tea, without which life must be immediately extinguished. When dressed, we seek the bathroom, where the sponge crackles with ice, and we gingerly wash our hands and the tops of our eyelids, submitting to other unmentionable operations entailing laceration and frostbite. And then people say but the Tibetans are so dirty, aren't they? They may be. But at least they preserve their faces. There can have been no one in the whole country so filthy, so utterly repulsive to look at, as ourselves by the time we arrived at Gyantse.

VI

THE PLEASURES OF GYANTSE

The joy of life had returned. My headaches were gone. It was the last morning of the journey. We were mounted on stocky Chinese ponies, resembling those of Mabel Lucy Attwell, which set out to cover the remaining fifteen miles at a canter.

Some four miles from the bungalow stood a monastery by the road-side, a small country-house in appearance, flanked by a walled grove of willows and poplars, outside which boy-novices in tattered red robes were threshing. The road led on into a broad cultivated valley, over to one side of which lay the larger Naini monastery, a scattered complex of buildings, enclosed by a wall and extending up into the crevices of the hinder hill, a conical mass of golden putty crowned by a ruined fort. From a distance the foremost buildings, a temple of the usual raspberry red, and others of gleaming white, seemed insignificant; but this was mainly owing to the absence of windows as a standard of magnitude. On approach they towered above myself and the attendant groom, disclosing a massive wooden door about fifteen feet high, evidently intended to withstand attack. Inside this we were confronted by a cave containing three diabolical pot-bellied images, life-sized and ferociously coloured. These were protected by a wire netting, presumably against the pigeons, whose ordered postures formed an extra cornice to the adjacent temple. Beyond this stood three huge *chortens* surmounted by elaborate finials of terra-cotta tiles. The rest of the monastery consisted, as far as I could see, of a wilderness of small houses, adorned with window-boxes of marigolds and other flowers. Not a soul was about save for one decrepit figure carrying a pitcher, who informed us that nothing could be seen. We therefore returned to the road, where we met a monk wearing above his red robes a tall peaked cap of lemon yellow.

After passing through a defile in the hills we came out on a broad plain, no barren waste, but broken into small fields by an elaborate system of irrigation, and scattered with farms and country-houses. On all sides the rampart of mountains continued. But on the right, and far away on the left, at the ends of the plain, they seemed to fit into one another like the wheels of a cog, thus permitting the routes of Lhassa and Shigatse. In front of us, as the road descended in a westerly diagonal, a great fort could be seen, springing from a peaked eminence, and behind it a wall of deep pink strung in a wavy line from summit to summit to summit of the foot-hills. These were the Gyantse Jong and monastery. Behind again towered a range of heather-coloured mountains, beyond which the top of an occasional snowy peak glittered in the blue.

The road was now alive with traffic, and I felt like a medieval notable as I cantered round the bends and over the little bridges, with my groom behind me. Drivers of pack-animals hastened to remove them from the course; male riders dismounted in respect; female reined in to one side. The farms and small country-houses, of white composition ornamented with dark cornice-bands, bore an unexpected resemblance, save for their corner turrets and prayer-flags, to their European counterparts, being set in plantations of osiers and poplars, and approached by drives, and sometimes by pretentious gateways. At length we came to a river-bed fifty yards in width, in which a fair volume of clear blueish water was swirling along, and which was crossed by a broad, unrailed bridge, supported at close intervals on massive, diamond-shaped piers of loose stones about twelve feet high. Beyond this lay the town, a scene of striking beauty: in the foreground, clumps and rows of poplars and willows, each one a shower of bright golden leaves, an exquisite colour, like that employed in mosaics; the Jong, built out of its hill, a twisted, squat cone of putty-coloured rock whose lines of black shadow were gathered to a climax by great faces and tiers of masonry, converging one above another to a single flat cupola; behind, the red monastery wall, looped from hill to hill like a scenic railway, and fastened at each apex by a squat white tower;

beneath it the huge complex of monastic buildings, walled again in front and centring on a crimson temple and a vast white *chorten*, the latter being surmounted by a pointed golden tower that flashed in the sunlight and carried on the colour of the trees; behind again, the hills, a back-cloth of flat purple; the flat blue sky; and last of all, immediately above the Jong, a single cloud, a puffy Chinese thing with a black shadow to its belly.

The rest-house, I judged, lay to the left towards the Jong, and evidently some way out of the town, which was half hidden by the latter's hill. The groom, however, guided me to the right down half a mile of road neatly gravelled in grey, and enclosed by an avenue of incipient poplars. At the end of this lay a mud fort and mud barracks in the *Beau Geste* style of architecture, the headquarters of the British Trade Agent, when in residence, and his escort. I galloped up with a flourish, entered a courtyard, and, ascending to an outside balcony, found G. and M., who had refused to visit the Naini monastery, seated with Captain Blood in a room with an incredibly ugly wallpaper, but comfortably furnished. The first book that caught my eye was one of regulations for court dress. This interesting work, if not wholly essential to life in Gyantse, was probably connected with one of those periodic examinations which now afflict the life of soldiers and drive them to an early dotage. Blood gave us tea; then conducted us back past the bridge to the rest-house, an enlarged version of all the others, where there was a separate bedroom for each of us. Its dining-room led out on to a verandah and a garden of grass, enclosed by poplars and a wall.

Our first concern was to shave – a sickening process, with only four skins instead of seven, and ten days' growth to remove. We also bathed, seated in front of our respective fires. When we met for tea, we struck one another as quite good-looking, and sleek as suburban knuts.

That evening we went to the fort, drank up Blood's remaining bottle of gin, and dined with him off soup, salmon, mutton, apricots, and a kidney savoury. Afterwards, Little, a functionary known as the 'conductor', and responsible for the troops' stores, and Martin, who came up with the 1904 expedition as telegraphist and has stayed here ever since, came in, the only other Europeans in the place. Martin, a twinkling cockney, fell to reminiscences of his youth. His innate tendency to sin had allowed him success neither as an errand-boy, a race-card seller, nor a bookstall keeper; so that he had been obliged to enlist. 'Oh the music-'alls,' he said sentimentally, 'they used to 'ave some lovely tunes. Did you ever 'ear this one? –

'Lottie Collins 'as lorst 'er drores,
Will you kindly lend 'er yours?'

'Why,' I asked Blood, 'is there a trade agent here at all? It seems a great expense for no apparent reason.'

'I can't imagine,' was the reply. 'He doesn't seem to do anything – nor do we, except meet him at the fourth milestone when he arrives.'

'Obviously the usual process of "peaceful penetration",' snapped G., who had lately assumed a veneer of liberalism. 'We shall soon be ruling the entire country, when the proper "incidents" have been manufactured.'

'We're far from it now,' said Blood. 'We're not at all top dogs here by any means. The Kenchung – that's the Tibetan Trade Agent and the man with the real power here – keeps a very firm hand on things.'

It is in fact somewhat surprising to learn that there are Indian troops in Tibet at all. But it is plain, on second thoughts, that a political representative could not be left absolutely alone in the heart of a potentially hostile country – as Tibet was in 1904 when the agencies were established – and a country lacking the normal means of communication.

Next morning M. and I went again to the fort to send letters and telegrams from the post-office there. Blood, who had been drilling his seventy-five men, was in uniform. He said that they amused themselves with hockey and polo; that the town was forbidden them for fear of venereal disease; and that their winter supply of buried turnips had just gone bad, which was a great blow. During the rest of the morning I sketched the Jong from just over the wall of the rest-house garden, basking in the sun. We were now at 12,000 feet. After lunch, joined by Blood and a stout and intelligent youth in a Tibetan robe and buff Homburg hat, named Pemba, who was educated in Darjeeling and now does most of Martin's work in the Trade Agency, we proceeded across the intervening fields, stubble and plough, to the Jong. The ascent was by means of a precipitous path of loose stones. Above us, the huge convergent perpendiculars produced that unique architectural effect which photographs of Tibetan buildings had always conveyed, and which I had always wanted to see. Creeping along a ledge towards a kind of landing where we halted, shuffled a convict, heavily ironed about the legs, who put out his tongue at us, the extreme gesture of supplication. It appeared that he had been suborned by a woman to destroy her husband; and that having been discovered, both he and she had received a hundred lashes, face downwards, from the heels to the neck, and would receive a hundred more, after which they would probably be condemned to spend their lives in perpetual slavery. The severity of this lashing depends on how far the relations of the prisoner can, or care to, bribe its executioners. At present the convict was being looked after by two little girls.

We were now about 500 feet above the plain. Immediately below appeared a line of more or less substantial houses, piles of yak-dung on their flat roofs, fodder drying in their courtyards, and all round them the busy threshing-floors, from which an unceasing chorus of shouts and songs rang through the air, as the men and women drove their teams of four bullocks, cross between yak and cow, in circular courses through the flying corn. Beyond, the country was dotted with larger farms and country-houses, each with its surround of golden trees. Then the fields stretched away in a series of small, irregular squares, bounded each one by high embanked ditches which are opened in winter to flood them and freeze. Passing to the other side of the battlements, we looked down on to the main street of the town, long and straight, which led to the monastery entrance. Within the walls, houses, temples, and *chortens*, red and white, with brass finials flashing, stretched up the hill to the red wall at the back. The mountains behind, only a mile or two away, reared slopes of gilded purple into the deepening sky. From the walls of the Jong on this side, the cliff fell sheer, casting a deep black shadow of stupendous acreage over the hog's-back and the houses below it.

As we stood looking, the Jongpen came on the scene, a very different type from the deputy castellans at Phari, a man of breeding and comfort, who had preserved his teeth. His hair, instead of hanging in a pigtail, was scraped up into a small sausage on top, knotted in red and adorned at the centre with a gold-and-turquoise brooch of excellent design, a circle of flat segments supported on two bars. This he wore not as Jongpen but as the son of his father, who was an official of the fourth rank. His brother, Pemba informed us, was now Prime Minister. He was dressed in a grey robe of once magnificent brocade, now discoloured and dirty, beneath which he wore canoe-shaped shoes of black velvet embroidered with yellow. A curly moustache descended from his nostrils to frame a perpetual smile. His head was usually thrown back to display a rippling throat. As Jongpen he was said to be much respected, unlike the officials at Phari. His magisterial jurisdiction, unhampered by the cunning of lawyers or the imbecilities of juries, extends from Gyantse to the Tang-La, the pass we had crossed on the first morning out from Phari. He had been here eight years, he said, and had at first found it very windy after the comparative shelter of Lhassa. It was over that cliff there that prisoners such as the convict we had just seen were formerly thrown to their deaths. But capital punishment was now abolished.

He invited us to take some *chang* with him in his house, to which he led the way down a precipitous path with surprising agility for one of his age and deportment. In the rear came his body-servant, a youth with an ill-grown pig-tail, who bandied words with his master and showed little respect for him. Having walked over the roof of his house and peered down his chimneys, we descended by a hole and ladder into a courtyard and thence into a darkish room, where we sat on draped seats about a foot high. The large windows along one side were glazed. The furniture consisted of various chests, the larger being panelled and painted with floral designs of red, orange, and green. From the usual crutch-pillar of carved and painted wood hung two official hats. Against the wall was a pile of hide trunks, and one hat-box, shaped as though to fit a top-hat, of white skin. Over these were fixed a number of swords in worked silver scabbards, and also several umbrellas and a rifle, the latter to give dignity to the Jongpen's progresses. A joss-stick emitted a delicious smell.

Above this latter hung several banners representing Buddha and the Wheel of Life. These paintings, widely used in both ecclesiastical and domestic decoration, like the Orthodox icon, are executed on an oblong of coarse, parchment-like paper, whose length varies from four feet to nine inches, and which is itself mounted on a rectangle of dark and boldly patterned Chinese silk, broadening towards the bottom. This is furnished with a brass-headed roller. The painting, half Indian, half Chinese in character, is extremely delicate and can best be compared with the art of the illuminator. There is a definite iconography for the depiction of the Buddhist pantheon, which produces designs of great beauty. In colour the artists display a sense of conventional harmonies. Gold, as in Greek and Russian icons, is much used for outlining and the indication of auras. Those banners which have been toned with age are usually the more decorative; though the Jongpen possessed one, specially executed for him in Shigatse, which excited our envy. We eventually bought several from other sources, despite our fears that their genuine artistic merits would be obscured by prejudice against the returned Anglo-Indian's trophies.

Chang, a pale-green drink distilled from barley the day before, was dispensed from a blue enamel kettle into little porcelain bowls supported on silver saucers, themselves on stems. After every sip these were immediately refilled. Manners demanded at least three sips. But the taste, sour and refreshing, was not unpleasant, and we felt no difficulties. Over a chest behind the Jongpen peered various servants, and his small son, dressed in the red serge of a monk, who was reluctant to come forward.

On emerging, we observed a number of figures standing on the roof of a house 300 feet below. Blood said that there was a wedding-feast in progress, of which this was the fourth day, and which would continue for another six. Our desire was to attend it. Pemba said we should assuredly be welcome. Remounting our ponies, we descended, a groom going on ahead. I had reached the gateway of the house when a sudden clatter in the rear made me turn: to behold a cavalcade at a smart trot, mules and ponies gaily caparisoned, in whose midst rode a stout figure in purple-and-buff silk, wearing high boots of soft natural-coloured leather, dark glasses, and a small Homburg hat. This was the Kenchung, the Tibetan Trade Agent, monk official of the fourth rank and the preponderant figure in Gyantse, to whom we had brought letters from Laden-La and Macdonald. According to Pemba, while the internal administrative duties fall to the Jongpen, the Kenchung's work is mainly diplomatic, though he has a finger in most pies. Dismounting, he shook hands with us all and invited us to lunch the day after to-morrow.

The wedding-feast was being held by Tuksa, one of the Kenchung's clerks: a rich man; for, in Pemba's opinion, he was more feared by the common people, owing to his contact with them as a subordinate, than the Kenchung himself. Crossing a courtyard, whose stables harboured a row of saddled mules and ponies, we mounted a short double ladder, to be received by our host, an old man with the prominent nose, white moustache, receding chin, and benevolent twinkle of a Victorian general. His grey hair, too short for the process, was scraped back to form an untidy queue, like that of a Hogarth perruque in the tying. He wore a long robe of patterned sapphire silk. Surrounded by a multitude of the curious, he conducted us to the apartment of honour, lately constructed as a testimony to his wealth.

This apartment was without exception the oddest I have ever entered socially. About thirty feet by twenty, its inner portion, denoted by a railed dais and a drop in the ceiling, was approached through a sort of vestibule. This was lighted, at the back, by a long 'studio' window, against which two ghoulish ragged figures, perched on an invisible roof, were pressing their noses. Above the door, which was at the side, and opposite, hung two enormous banners, splashes of scarlet on a light-blue ground. At the approach to the dais the lower ceiling was supported by two crutch-pillars, having brilliantly painted capitals, and stems draped in multi-coloured flounces of different silks.

Beyond the dais the entire end wall was fashioned into a plaster idolry. In tiers of niches, framed in blue, sea-green, and white clouds, on which reposed groups of gazelle and other imperceptible fauna, sat the monsters and philosophers of the Tibetan pantheon. In the centre was a larger niche, containing a huge Buddha, which was draped in a voluminous white scarf and flanked by a pair of tall Chinese vases, red and green on white. At the foot of this deity, opposite the opening in the railing of the dais, the wedding presents were ranged in a pile, bricks of coarse-leaved tea, jars of butter, dried mutton, fine cloths, of the type that tailors call 'Angola', and bales of silk, white and gold, red and purple. To augment these, on returning to the rest-house, we despatched a tin each of ginger-nuts, sardines, and smoked salmon. Meanwhile, seating ourselves on low seats in a corner of the dais, we awaited the advent of *chang*. Our host sat with us, and also an officer of the disbanded Tibetan army, robed in light-blue silk and wearing a khaki hat turned up on one side like a New Zealander's.

A host of spectators crowded behind the railings, from which emerged servants bearing enormous beakers of silver ornamented with brass. These, two feet high and round in body, deserved their name, for from the neck of each protruded a great shovel-like lip. Bowls of gallon capacity, also of silver and brass, were filled from them. From these again, women-servants, armed with silver ladles studded with small turquoises, filled and kept filling our cups of jade or blue-and-white porcelain.

The costumes of the servants were more extraordinary than any pictures of the Celestial Empire have ever told. Each of the women wore the Gyantse head-dress – a stiffened arc of red serge, eighteen inches across and fourteen high, heavily studded with corals and speckled turquoises, and bound, from a centre strut, with ribbons of seed-pearls three inches wide. The blouses and skirts, of an indefinite reddish purple, gave an upholstered, Mrs Noah effect, the former being full-sleeved and the latter partially covered by an apron horizontally striped in green and mauve and finished at the upper corners with triangles of floral embroidery set in gold. Round the waist hung a row of large knobs, possibly of wood, strung on thick cord. At the neck appeared the inevitable charm-box, a silver square studded with turquoises and hung cornerwise. Across the breast stretched, as it were, an order of seed-pearls, to the centre of which was attached a circular plaque beautifully jewelled with differently coloured stones. One wrist was encircled by a most curious ornament, a huge sea-shell, partially cut away and somewhat resembling a nurse's starched cuff. This whole costume, though varying in details, is more or less that of all Tibetan women of all classes on state occasions, with the exception of the head-dress, which is peculiar to Gyantse. That of Lhassa consists of two coral and turquoise horns, from which the hair descends in a black shower on either side. It is curious that these particular ornaments should have become conventional, since the seed-pearls, turquoises, and shell-cuffs all come from India, while some of the coral is even imported from Italy.

The hats of the men-servants were scarcely less astonishing. There were two kinds: one a circular plate, a foot and a half across, balanced on top of a close-fitting cap, which was hidden by a thick red fringe descending from the rim of the plate; the other a buttercup-yellow hot-cross-bun, nine inches in diameter, whose connection with the head was maintained by no visible means; and which, when the head was shaven, as in one case, produced an appearance of fantastic oddity in conjunction with a single blue-and-pearl earring four inches long.

A dessert dish of silver and copper was brought, containing preserved oranges, candy sugar, dried apples, and biscuits from Reading. We nibbled, while the women with their ladles loomed over us like angry nurses persuading babies to their milk. M., learning from some mysterious source that eight was a lucky number, resolved to drink eight cups. I was more diffident. And my apple-cheeked servitor, passably snub and good-looking, complained bitterly to the host of my obduracy. It was an astounding scene: the rows of ladling dolls, beneath their swaying jewelled arcs; the scarlet parasols and yellow buns nodding, as the men poured the beakers into the bowls; the straining crowd below the dais; the reredos of clouds and images; the painted pillars and banners; and the great window framing its ghoulish silhouettes.

Taut, we rose. The host led us through other rooms, smaller but richly furnished: in one, a segregation of women; in another, men at games of dominoes, among whom was the bridegroom, a handsome youth in a high-collared robe of rich brown brocade tied at the waist with a green sash. Already an official at Lhassa, he was now on leave for his marriage. This room contained a cabinet, somewhat in the manner of a Chippendale combination of bureau and bookcase, save that there was no actual bureau. This was wholly covered in wrought brass. In the cornice moved a dragon.

That evening Blood, Martin, and Little dined with us at the rest-house. Unfortunately the *chang* had rendered us inert, and our spirits lagged. The consumption of whisky more than justified G. and M.'s hopes. Martin sang:

'She's only a bird in a gilded caige,
Such a bewtiful sight to see!
You may think that she's 'appy and free from care;
She's not – though she seems to be.

> It's sad when you think of 'er waisted life,
> For youth cannot maite with aige.
> 'Er bewtee was sold for an old man's gold.
> She's – a – bird – in – a – gilded – caige!'

His thoughts then turned to rosy dreams of old age and retirement in a cottage by the sea, as they might, after spending a quarter of a century in Tibet, burying two Tibetan wives, visiting Darjeeling once, and finally winning a substantial sweepstake, whose proceeds were nestling in the bank.

'The south coast I favour,' he mused. 'What's this 'ere Peace'aiven they talk so much about?'

'I think you'd find the south coast rather different from what it was when you left England,' said M., throwing off the lethargy of his eight cups.

'Per-raps I should,' replied Martin slowly, and paused to think. 'But I saiy, Lord Oojah, what about a nice little lodge, where a man could end 'is daiys in peace? I'm serious, mind you – a reformed character and all that.'

Gyantse not so long ago was the scene of doings which reflected sadly on the impeccable reputation of our countrymen. Captain A., now dead, was then in command; and the military treasury, since transferred to the custody of Indian bankers, was his to dispose of. The post-office at the fort was the nucleus of a gambling society, which included the then Jongpen, and whose orgies used to continue for days on end, regardless of meals. Mistresses were freely kept. Upon this happy scene came B., a superior, who proceeded to reforms. A., however, discovered that B. also had his failings, though of a different type, and proceeded to suggest a compromise of *laissez-faire* on both sides, which might have been arrived at had not C., a detached observer, also acquired knowledge of B.'s misdemeanours and officially reported them. B. fled, followed by A., who believed that he was about to murder the then Trade Agent at Yatung, on account of his misfortunes. Finally B. left the service, and A. continued his gambling in peace till, in the natural course of things, he was relieved. The treasury was then found to be 150,000 rupees short. A. was arrested, escaped, and fled down to India in his turn, where he was recaptured and cashiered. His successor was an Indian officer, who being no arithmetician, handed over the treasury and accounts to some of A.'s old *confrères*. Two years passed. The time for the Indian's relief had arrived, when, early one morning, he was discovered in a dying condition. Martin and Little assumed the rôle of detectives. But their surmises are better not repeated.

At a quarter to ten on the following morning Pemba arrived to herald a visit from the Kenchung, to whom we had despatched our letters of recommendation the day before. First, however, there was time to visit the bazaar. We walked across the fields, rounded the base of the Jong, and came to a long narrow street, as much a gutter as a road, from whose walls of sombre grey stucco an occasional head protruded through a tiny window. Behind us now, the Jong assumed a new shape, a fantastic stepped apex like a Rhineland castle, only plainer and untroubled by pepper-box roofs. The booths of the bazaar, which shuts at midday, were contained in a narrow lane, exhibiting beads and mirror-topped boxes from India, the rejected Homburg hats of the whole world, piles of loose turquoises, rows of Gyantse head-dresses, unstiffened and neatly folded, and a peculiar species of scissors whose blades resembled battered table-knives. Tempted by nothing, we returned to the rest-house in a state of exhaustion after walking three miles at this height.

The Kenchung's advent was announced by the naked carcase of a sheep and a dish of eggs. We hurried out to meet him. On entering, he inclined and, stretching out both his arms, presented us with a broad white scarf of closely woven silk. His general dress was the same as yesterday's: short jacket of buff velvet, woven with a bold pattern of bamboos, that vile pattern of lodging-house fire-screens, now redeemed and made beautiful by its context; a skirt of flowered purple; and the boots of natural leather. But his hat, instead of Homburg, was now official: a shallow dome of brilliant yellow silk, rising from a stiff round brim, richly embroidered in bright colours, and surmounted by a large knob of coral. It was an exquisite adornment, tilted sideways from the very top of his head over his bland brown face, with its huge smile and glittering denture. He lay back in a chair, drinking tea.

Did he, we inquired through Pemba, ever telephone to the Dalai Lama? He did, frequently. There was a telephone in his room.

Had he ever visited Pekin? He had: first as a boy of eighteen, when he went to learn Chinese, which he can now speak but not write; again as interpreter to the Dalai Lama, when the latter fled from the British in 1904.

After half an hour he asked permission to take leave, as the custom is, hoping to see us to-morrow.

In the afternoon we received another call, from the two sons of Rajah Tehring. Of the history of this dignitary I shall tell later. Jigmed, the elder, a handsome boy of about nineteen years, spoke English and had his hair short. His brother did not, and sported a pig-tail. Both were dressed in the usual purple robes, fastened by small gold buttons. We delivered Perry's wedding present to Jigmed, and showed him Sir Charles Bell's *People of Tibet*. The frontispiece of this book depicts a family group in which are seated two living Buddhas, small children, and their mothers. 'Why, that's my sister!' he exclaimed, pointing to one of them.

When they had gone I went for a solitary ride, rounding the Jong and striking out into the country through a subsidiary village. My aim was Tsechen, a conical hill spattered with buildings, about five miles away. But I overshot the necessary bridge, and, seeing another village high up in a mountain cleft above my head, turned towards it. The ground was thickly covered with stones the size and shape of biscuit tins, and intersected by deep gullies. The farther I rode, the farther the village receded. The sun was setting, and eventually I was obliged to turn back. The scene confronting me was one of superlative grandeur. In the foreground rose the gentle range on whose other side lay the monastery, and along whose top the red hinder wall was suspended from summit to summit, a chain half a mile long, pinned to the rock by embattled towers. In the farther distance the Jong reared aloft on its pinnacle, a twisted silhouette, save where the falling sun swathed the sides of the receding topmost blocks in sheets of gold. Below stretched the plain, whence the shouts and chants of the threshers still echoed from each trampled floor. And all round stood the purple mountains, with their clefts and valleys bathed in a sharp glinting sapphire. The land swept away, curveted into the foot-hills, fell hesitantly, leapt and fell again to the plain, bounded up like a tidal wave into the nearer mountains, spouted out the Jong, and ran twinkling into the distance, slowed, compressed itself, assumed the darkness, disappeared, and came to light in a farther range, in time to hide the fallen nebula of fire whose last tongues still persisted above the horizon in their appeal to the awakening stars. The red wall darkened to crimson, suspended from peak to peak, a work of giants.

VII

LUNCHING OUT

We awoke to the morning of Thursday, 12 October, with a sense of impending adventure: lunch with the Kenchung. At half-past eleven Pemba arrived, and we all rode out to the foot of the Jong, round it, and up the main street of the town to the monastery entrance. The threshold, flanked by massive portals, revealed another town, more various and polychrome than its civil counterpart, whose temples and dwellings, amounting to some hundreds, lay scattered over a rocky slope. This formation, which rose eventually to something like a precipice, was topped by the chain of pink wall whose rear I had admired on the previous evening. I asked Pemba how a community of five or six hundred monks could find use for such a vast agglomeration of buildings. There were temples, he replied, common to the whole community, which were used at festivals; and there were also, as I understood him, parish temples, each parish consisting of about fifty monks drawn from the same district. Then, in addition, the monks must have somewhere to live. The lower ranks shared their dwellings. Hierarchs and officials, such as the Kenchung, had separate houses, and these again were furnished with stables and servants' quarters.

The scene, though almost deserted of human beings, offered a peculiar animation such as inspires the abstract compositions of modernist painters – save that here it took shape in three dimensions and occupied about twenty acres instead of as many square inches. Nowhere but in lands that have inherited the culture of the Celestial Empire is architecture infused with quite this same radiant activity. The secret of it lies partly in its use of colour on an unparalleled scale, but more fundamentally in its universal convention of the batter, which makes every wall of every building, no matter how small its height, slope inwards in a straight line from the ground-level. Whatever the origin of this convention – whether it be utilitarian, emotional, or merely the legacy of extinct tradition – its ability to produce harmony among buildings and to reinforce the genius of the architectural group is unsurpassed. Architecturally speaking, nothing could have been more haphazard than the medley that confronted us, perched at all levels, jostling together at one place, leaving large unoccupied areas at another. Furthermore, it became evident, on closer inspection, that the buildings were in fact of no great size, while the construction of most, if not actually shoddy, had an air of impermanence which derived, like that of colonial exhibitions, from their coatings of stucco and colour-wash. Yet viewed as a whole, the enormous complex gave an impression not only of movement, but of unity and organic strength. Each crimson temple and pastel dwelling, clear-washed and richly shadowed by the morning sun to distinguish it from the putty-coloured rock of the hill face, thrust its perpendiculars aloft to converge on the long swinging wall that topped the enclosing ridge. Between the pallid rock and the blazing azure sky, with its flotilla of bursting, light-filled clouds, this wall of crushed strawberry, adorned with towers and crenellation of creamy white, formed a line of demarcation in terms of pure colour whose intensity was something strange to architecture as I had hitherto conceived it. Only in two places was the line interrupted: on the right, by a huge stone pylon, grey and serious amidst the surrounding festivity, on which, at sacred occasions, is hung a stupendous painted banner of Buddha, some sixty feet in height; and in the centre, by a smaller building, of flaming golden orange, which leapt into the sky above the wall like the cry of an advancing multitude.

There was still some time before lunch and, accompanied by a band of monks in robes of worn red serge, we set out to explore the individual monuments. Most prominent of these, being situated almost immediately in front of the main entrance, was the chief temple, a severe building of iced-cake pink encircled at the top by a narrow white band, above which ran a deeper band, as it were, of crimson plush, to emphasize its meeting with the sky. Such cornices are a convention of Tibetan sacred architecture, and their richness of texture, as much as their colour, was a puzzle to me until, during our journey back, I came on a temple in the building. Groups of women were at work binding together bunches of some stout, heather-like plant, then cutting off the roots so as to form a neat circular end, and dipping these ends in a clotted crimson dye. When dry, the bunches were placed one on top of the other, with the dyed ends outwards, to make the decoration of the cornice. The effect produced, when seen from below, is that of a rich velvet ribbon, which runs right round each temple, binding the convergent activity of its walls and wings into a coherent design.

Upon the cornice of the chief temple in the Gyantse monastery, above the entrance, were applied two neat golden ciphers, while, as is also usual, a row of tall brass pinnacles of twisted bulbous form flashed from the roof-line above. The entrance was contained in a square arch, which contrasted actively with the pyramidical outlines beside it. This was divided across the middle by a balcony, supported on four crutch-pillars, and itself supporting another four, less in height, which upheld a kind of projecting carved screen immediately below the velvet cornice. Between the lower pillars we now proceeded, to view the interior. This again was supported on crutch-pillars painted red, which cut sharply across the intermittent beams of light that came from small windows. The floor was occupied with rows of padded cushions, which we were careful not to step on, or even to step over, in accordance with the instructions given us by Laden-La. At the back were various shrines and altars, each presided over by a large gold image, whose general arrangement resembled that of any Roman Catholic church. The images were draped in scarves; before them stood vases of artificial flowers and innumerable butter lamps, big and small. Behind the main altars was a sort of ambulatory, lined with further images, whose over-natural dimensions and close juxtaposition filled the stranger with uncomfortable awe. The whole interior was pervaded with the smell of rancid butter − a hideous, overpowering odour, reminiscent of a dairy where one's fears as to the cleanliness of all dairies have at last come true.

Adjoining the temple was a library, where all the books, printed off wooden blocks on long strips of paper and tied between heavy wooden boards, in lieu of binding and cover, were kept in rows of wooden pigeon-holes. In addition there was a museum, and this indeed was one of the strangest apartments I have ever set foot in. Jumbled together in what was ordinarily complete darkness, and covered with a thick substantial dust that one could gather in handfuls and pinch between the fingers, we distinguished such objects as a captured Chinese banner, suits of medieval chain armour, bows and arrows, metal helmets, and stuffed scaly animals resembling armadillos. From this cavern of past and perhaps glorious history we progressed by devious passages and many ladders to other temples, where the statues of celebrated lamas, coloured realistically and robed in their proper vestments, gazed upon us from their ceremonial chairs. Finally we emerged blinking into the sunlight to visit the great *chorten* of the monastery, a babel of polygonal galleries, whose innumerable projecting embrasures, each reproducing in miniature those of the gallery below, and each furnished with its own window, produced an intricate yet apprehensible pattern of shadow and ornament. Atop the five tiers of this huge white ant-heap – for that is what, in general shape, it most resembled – rose a shallow white drum, pierced by four doorways elaborately carved and coloured. This supported a square structure, decorated on the cornice with pairs of eyes, above which glittered the final cone, a fabulous erection of ribbed brass, upholding a fretted double cog-wheel, from twenty to thirty feet in diameter, below its last finial.

It was now one o'clock and time for the anticipated meal. The Kenchung's house was visible up a narrow passageway, whose cobbled slope and high dilapidated walls reminded us of Nuremberg. This gave access to a well-like courtyard, overlooked by three storeys. On the ground floor, sheltered by a cloister on wooden supports, stood the Kenchung's mules and ambling ponies at their feed. The upper storeys were approached by a succession of steep, metal-treaded ladders. Our host received us on the top floor and led us into a long low room divided in the middle by a partition. The windows, looking on to the courtyard, were open, propped inward and upward like those of a skylight. Though glazed on the outside, they still retained the original paper within. Beneath them a square of divans was arranged round a low table covered with American cloth. We sat facing the light, with the Kenchung opposite us. He had divested himself of his buff jacket and now appeared all in purple silk. On his broad brown face and shaven head reposed a pair of gold spectacles. As usual, the unlighted wall of the room was stacked with trunks, which were covered in white skin or black fur, the coverings being separate. In India, he assured us, these trunks would rot and stink.

A cheap kitchen clock hung in one corner. On a chest stood another of a late Empire design, mahogany and ormolu. From his pocket the Kenchung produced a fat silver watch, to whose chain was attached a gold toothpick, later to be freely used. In addition to these, a servant came in bearing an alarm-clock still wrapped in cotton-wool and cardboard. By dint of consulting all four timepieces, our host informed us that we were late. We admitted to five minutes, but he said half an hour. We saw in this stricture no discourtesy, but rather a desire to convince us of a life regulated on business lines.

At first English tea was brought, with sugar, milk, and teaspoons. The Kenchung then asked us if we would care for Tibetan tea instead. We would. This was served to us in bowls of blue-and-white porcelain on silver stands, while he drank his out of a bowl of that very rare jade which is flecked with pale gold. This had a silver lid, finished with a blob of coral. Noticing our admiration of it, he showed us another bowl of whiter jade. But this had been spoilt by a poor carving of trees. The tea itself, made with flour, butter, soda, and salt, might have tasted not unpleasant but for its association with the smell of the temple. I could not touch mine. The others drank two cups each.

At length the first course was brought – a series of small cold dishes containing slices of hard-boiled egg, seaweed, pease gelatine and mutton, cabbage and chile, yak beef, turnip, and other unknown vegetables. Each guest was given a pair of polished bone chopsticks, delicately squared, which had to be manipulated like tongs, the second finger being used as a pivot on which to hinge them. I found myself fairly proficient. But G. and M. were so messy that they were provided with short-handled porcelain spoons in which to catch the drips. After a few minutes my manners were discredited also by my inadvertently swallowing a large piece of chile and being obliged to call hurriedly for a glass of *chang*. Ordinarily, it is not the custom to drink with meals.

These preliminary delicacies were followed by others more pretentious, which were served in larger bowls: sea-slugs mixed with mutton, liver, force-balls, and a kind of flat spaghetti mixed with vegetables.

The latter was accompanied by the most delicious Chinese vinegar, made out of barley and poured from an English lodging-house cruet. A silence fell upon us all, as we jabbed and grabbed and munched and sucked. From outside came the tinkle of mule-bells and the incessant thud-rumble of a strangely melodious drum, denoting a prayer session in the vicinity. The portentous dignity of our host, together with his servants and surroundings, reminded me of similar occasions on Mount Athos – though Tibetan food is preferable to any that is found in Greece – and the reminiscence was strengthened by two white doves in skin-bottomed wicker cages which hung outside the window. There had once, said the Kenchung, been a monkey, but it had bitten visitors. Now only a Saluki puppy prowled about the room, conveniently gobbling up those adamant morsels which from time to time we found it necessary to remove from our mouths when no one was looking, and secrete under the table.

We asked our host if he had a library. He replied that he read a great deal. A book was brought, printed at Shigatse, and consisting of pages eighteen inches by four, with text on both sides and numbered in the margin. The boards containing it, when opened, were held by a ribbon at right angles, so that they formed a sort of reading-desk. The theme was the sanctity of a certain lama who had lived about eight hundred years earlier and whose life had been compiled by his disciples. Once more we were back in the Middle Ages, when the only literature was sacred. I wondered if there were lighter figures among the immortals of the Tibetan Church, such as Susannah or Joseph and Balaam.

When the meal was finished, we asked permission to examine the inner room behind the partition. Here was the telephone, of an antique wooden-box type, on which, our host again assured us, he often spoke to the Dalai Lama. A photograph of a temple at Katmandu, the capital of Nepal, hung diagonally from the beam. In a corner, a prayer-wheel in the shape of a hollow paper cylinder was revolving of its own accord, thanks to the mysterious action of a lamp beneath it, which heated the air in such a way as to produce this uncanny rotation. There were various banners and images. But the pride of the room was a pair of magnificent cloisonné vases, about twenty inches high and a foot in diameter, which had been sent as a present from Lhassa.

By the time we rose it was three o'clock. As we crossed the landing to descend, we noticed that the noise of the drum had come from an adjoining room, where a monk could be observed through an open door reciting his prayers beneath a composite portrait of the Chinese royal family. When we were outside, I asked Pemba if I could go up the hill to the foot of the pink wall, in order to sketch and photograph. It was impossible, he said; there was no path. I therefore waited till he and the others had left, when I made my way up the hill of my own initiative, leaving my groom, who seemed rather worried, to hold my pony near the entrance. I had not gone far when I was joined by a young monk, who stank of butter, but insisted forcibly on carrying my things and helping me over the loose stones. Remembering Laden-La's advice never to remain alone in a monastery, I was glad of his company. While I sketched, he followed every movement of the pencil. Whenever I blew, to remove the shreds of india-rubber, he blew too, asphyxiating me with his rancid breath. But this friendly, almost proprietary, interest in my doings filled the afternoon with soothing and content, as the shadows drew out and I sat on the heights absorbing the remote and gorgeous beauty unfolded at my feet.

On the estate of Tehring, about six miles from Gyantse, there resides a magnate known as Rajah Tehring, whose title is an Indian honour and who was once heir to the throne of Sikkim. At the end of the last century his father, the then Maharajah of that State, had fled to Tibet from the English, and though he himself, as the Maharajah's eldest son, had been invited by the Government of India to return, the Tibetans had prevailed on him to refuse, endowing him with compensatory estates in the neighbourhood both of Gyantse and of Kampa Jong, near Everest. Eventually he had married a Tibetan wife. Among the children she had borne him were the two sons who had already called on us at the rest-house some days earlier. The eldest of these, Kumar Jigmed Namgyal, had been educated in Darjeeling, since the present Maharajah of Sikkim, on his first accession, was childless, and it appeared that Jigmed must succeed him. Since then, however, the Maharajah has had children. Both Jigmed and his brother had recently married daughters of the great house of Tsarong, whose male line was extinguished in a bloody passage by their adopted father, the most remarkable figure, after the Dalai Lama, in modern Tibetan history.

This gentleman, a person of no family – and family counts for much in Tibet – had then assumed the name of Tsarong and had risen to be commander-in-chief of the Tibetan forces. It was he who fought the rearguard action at the Tsang Po which saved the Dalai Lama from the pursuing Chinese in 1910. According to Tibetan custom, his duty towards his 'daughters' had been expressed, on their reaching maturity, in a fashion more intimate than paternal. But as leader of the Westernizing party in the country, he had been at pains to have one of them educated in Darjeeling also, and it was this girl who had married Jigmed. The English had called her Mary, because her real name, which was Tromsa, or something like it, denoted a corresponding divinity in the Tibetan pantheon. It was as Mary that we came to know her. Her sister we never saw, for she was seriously ill. The poor girl died when Jigmed and Mary were away in India, about six weeks after we had left Tibet.

In the bosom of this family, on the day following our lunch with the Kenchung, we had been invited to take lunch once more and spend the afternoon. Blood, thank God, mounted us on his stocky Lhassa ponies, and about eleven o'clock we rode out of the fort in a cavalcade on our way to Tehring. At first we went straight across country – a country of intense cultivation, where a field was never more than fifty yards square and was invariably surrounded on all four sides with irrigation ditches. Since these latter varied considerably in width, and we were going at a fast canter, the ride had an element of the unexpected. Sometimes the pony would jump, sometimes stop dead to step across sedately, and sometimes, at the apparition of a main canal, wade in up to its belly. But there was never a sign of reluctance, and neither stones, banks, nor the hard-baked furrows in the autumn stubble, caused the pace to slacken. By degrees, as we took it in turns to lead the procession, our progress became a race, a literal point-to-point, since its direction was decided by Blood's waving at the horizon from time to time and saying, 'We pass that house next, and afterwards the trees on the left.' At length a row of wooden telegraph-poles no higher than clothes-props came in sight and we joined the Lhassa road. This highway consisted of a number of separate mule-tracks, about a foot wide each, which twisted their various courses over the pebbles and between the boulders.

An imperceptible pass, marked by the usual pair of cairns, brought us to another plain. Being in front at the time, I ventured an inquiry of two pedestrians as to the whereabouts of Tehring. In reply they pointed to a group of trees three miles off. To the north the weather had broken, the hills loomed blue, and threatening clouds had settled on their tops. When we drew level with the trees, a short drive indicated the mansion of the estate, which reminded me of those unpretentious houses occupied by the Hungarian squirearchy. A long, whitewashed façade confronted us, adorned with the usual cornice-band at the top and constructed with the usual batter. Three lines of windows denoted three storeys. Servants were waiting at the top of the drive, who led us round to the other side of the house, where the main entrance was enclosed by a broad courtyard used partly for stabling and partly for the storing of wood and yak-dung. Here Jigmed met us, and we passed through a doorway with richly carved and coloured lintel-brackets on to an earthen floor and up a double ladder. On the landing above, others of the family were assembled: Rajah Tehring, his wife, and his daughter-in-law Mary. The rajah was a small man, with a brown complexion and wispish turned-down moustache, beneath which a twinkling smile lightened his grave countenance. He was dressed in a robe of purple-flowered silk with a high collar, and wore the inevitable single ear-ring. Jigmed wore a robe of maroon silk, beneath which showed an undergarment of amber brocade. This magnificence was marred by a tweed hat, which he now removed. The ranee sported a superlative Gyantse head-dress, whose diameter exceeded anything we had seen. Her charm-box was in proportion. She lowered her eyes to the ground with old-fashioned modesty as she shook hands with us. Mary wore a blouse of thick purple silk and the usual apron of horizontal stripes, which was finished at the hips with triangular panels of gold and silk embroidery. Her hair hung down in thick plaits. She was entitled to wear the Lhassa head-dress, but found it too heavy for all but the most ceremonious occasions.

They ushered us into a low oblong room, whose windows were open. I remarked to Blood that Tibetan rooms never seemed stuffy, as one would have expected in so inhospitable a climate. He replied that they never were, but were consequently very cold in winter. We sat on divans, richly draped, and partook of cakes and dried fruits. English tea was brought, and a new kind of *chang* with a fizz in it. The rajah had his own jade cup of Tibetan tea. Jigmed and Mary fetched two musical instruments – a Tibetan banjo and a Chinese fiddle. They played Tibetan and Nepali tunes, which were quite intelligible to our ears and reminded us of Scottish folk-songs. Then a servant came in and did a shuffling dance.

After lunch, whose thirty or so dishes confirmed our faith in the excellence of Tibetan cooking, the rajah produced three European bottles, whose contents – port, martini, and anisette – warmed our inquisitiveness. Since it was a holy day, he had not eaten meat during the meal. Would he now be obliged, we asked, to attend a religious service? No, this was not necessary; for lamas had been called in to do his duties for him. We could see them, if we wanted. So we trooped across the landing outside to the chapel, where four monks were squatting in yellow cloaks, intoning their prayers – and presumably the rajah's – to the note of a hanging drum, which one of them struck with a long curved stick. From time to time another made passes in the air with bell and thunderbolt, and curious motions with his fingers. But of the significance of these rites Jigmed could not inform us. He excused himself by saying that none of the family ever took any part in religious observances, since they were all conducted by proxy. This was an excellent principle, we thought. Nevertheless, I was later to see Jigmed, at Buddh Gaya, conducting his devotions in person.

Another room on the same landing was occupied by the manufacture of carpets, on big looms, from which depended balls of different coloured wool. A daughter of the house was hanging about to catch a glimpse of us, a pretty girl with a delicate rosy complexion, whose head had been shaved prior to her becoming a nun. Then we went out to see the garden – a patch of coarse grass within a stone wall and sheltered by a plantation of poplars, whose golden leaves showed bright against the threatening sky and fell to the ground in showers before the gusts of an evil wind. Here joined us the Benjamin of the family, an impish creature of four years old, with ears like flails, and a perpetual laugh. His best cap, embroidered with flowers, was fetched that I might photograph him in it. His game was to frighten the servants by peering at them through a forbidding papier-mâché mask.

On the outskirts of the garden was a smaller house, in whose upper storey, approached by an outside stair, lived Jigmed and Mary. Their rooms were in a confusion of packing, as they were starting to-morrow to visit their estate at Kampa Jong, with the intention of proceeding to India and making a pilgrimage to Buddh Gaya. We planned to meet in Calcutta. The house boasted some pieces of European furniture, a portrait of the King-Emperor, and a photograph of Jigmed in a school group. He had been forced, when in Darjeeling, to learn Latin, and now declined the singular of *mensa* to our astonished ears. At length, when all the household had assembled in farewell, some in the court-yard and some on the roof, we cantered off to Gyantse again, in an effort to reach home before the approaching storm could overtake us.

Next morning, by permission of the Kenchung, we had arranged to visit Dongtse, twelve and a half miles away. Blood again mounted us, and we set off at half-past nine, rounded the town, and made for Tsechen, the village on the conical hill that had been the objective of my solitary ride some afternoons ago. Opposite this place the river was crossed by a substantial bridge carried on stone piles. At this point it started to rain, and G. and M. began to question the wisdom of con-tinuing our expedition. On hearing this I dug my heels into my pony and set off at full gallop in the direction of Dongtse, before they could reach an adverse decision. My groom followed, and eventually Blood caught me up with another groom. We then discovered that while we had the plates, knives, and forks, the others were carrying the food. Blood's groom was therefore sent back to effect an exchange, in case they had really decided not to come on.

The road passed at first over unfenced grazing-ground, somewhat resembling an English common, then contracted to a mere footpath hemmed in by cultivated fields. All round the hills looked black, and snow was falling on their tops. Blood pointed out the pass to Shigatse, and I felt that only his presence prevented me from setting my pony in that direction. At one point we passed a huge prayer-wheel worked by a stream and striking a bell every ten seconds. Farther on appeared four monks huddled in a garden beneath hats like red hearth-rugs and chanting their office to the cold wind. A Jong stood up from the horizon, perched on a rock, the centre of a small administrative district. A prayer was written in white stones on a bare hill-side, like the name of an English railway-station in its garden. Eventually the path disappeared altogether. We cantered over a grass slope, through the main street of Dongtse, and up a precipice to the monastery. As we did so, G. and M. appeared in the plain beneath. The rain, for the moment, had stopped.

Before the usual complex of buildings, with their cornices of crimson velvet and flashing brass pinnacles, monks stood waiting to welcome us, robed in serge the colour of dried blood. From below came the inevitable shouts and songs of threshers as they drove the bullocks through the flying corn. In the distance over the plain we could see the Gyantse Jong. The monks conducted us into the temple, where others were seated in rows on the long cushions, each enveloped in a yellow cope. Two tables were set with lidded cups and seats of honour made ready. But the smell of butter was overpowering, and, after showing our appreciation of the honour done us, we begged that the tables might be removed to an adjoining balcony where we could eat our picnic at greater leisure. The cold was fearful, despite the shelter of a yak-hair curtain; but it was preferable to the odour of butter. After lunch we were taken upstairs to see a small room painted with the incarnations of the various abbots of the monastery. The last of those thus com-memorated had been executed by order from Lhassa, for having shel-tered one of the Indian surveyors who traversed Tibet in disguise at the end of the last century.

Sir Charles Bell, in one of his books on Tibet, has illustrated the country-house of the Palha family, which stands at Dongtse. The picture having aroused my interest, I wished to see this house. As always happens on such occasions, my innocent desire roused a chorus of opposition. Pemba asserted that the house did not exist. G. said that, judging by its picture, he would much rather not see it. I then insisted that Pemba should ask the monks where it was. Just below the monastery, was the answer. So eventually we did find it, and very interesting, to me at least, it proved. The courtyard was surrounded on three sides by a double cloister supported on old gnarled timbers, whose upper gallery was entirely filled with row upon row of prayer-wheels resembling enormous empty cotton-reels. The fourth side, which lay close beneath the hill, was occupied by the house, an up-standing construction of five storeys, whose windows and galleries

reminded me of a London inn in the time of Dickens. These features
made little appeal to G., who asks Blenheim or nothing of every house.
I therefore climbed on to the roof of the cloister, out of earshot of his
grumblings, and took photographs.

It rained all the way back. The ponies were out of patience, and there
was no holding them. We felt tired and stiff when we dismounted at
the rest-house just before dark. Poor Pemba could hardly walk. Blood
came to dinner, bringing a bottle of *crème de menthe* to celebrate our
last evening. We talked of the British in India, and he displayed that
tolerance and understanding which is always found among the officers
of Indian regiments and never among the merchant communities of
Calcutta and Bombay. I wished I could have stayed on to keep him
company. We had been very happy in Gyantse. But the weather of the
last two days had shown that the winter was upon us, and we had no
desire for a more uncomfortable passage of the Himalayas than was
necessary.

We awoke to our last morning with feelings of acute depression. It
was Sunday, we remembered, and felt like it, even here. But there was
no time to grieve. For further social duties awaited us. M. and I had
not yet finished breakfast when Pemba, who had been keeping a look-
out, rushed in to say that Rajah Tehring was at the gates. The beds
were not made; we had run out of tea. But by a hint of Providence – or
possibly of Pemba – he sensed our predicament and went off to visit
his second son near-by, with whom he reappeared an hour later. He
wore a purple silk robe, a sleeveless purple velvet jacket over it, and a
hat of the familiar mandarin pattern having an upturned brim of
mole-coloured velvet, through which, at the back, fell a scarlet tassel.
This was his official hat, denoting the rank accorded him in Lhassa.

He drank tea, ate with some difficulty a biscuit covered with butter
and marmalade, and presented us with a very large and honourable
white scarf and a pretty carpet from his own looms. We talked of
Lhassa. He said that owing to his British connection – for his title of
Rajah had been granted him officially by the Indian Government – he
was never entrusted with administrative work. But he had to go every
year to Lhassa to pay his respects to the Dalai Lama, and he enjoyed
himself during these visits. He always stayed with his married
daughter. The food was of the best, there were lots of festivals and

theatricals, and frequently private parties took place which lasted all night. It was evident from this account, and from much else we heard, that the amenities of Tibetan life can only be fully savoured in the capital.

When the Rajah had taken his leave we busied ourselves with packing, before going out to a last lunch-party, for which we were engaged with Tuksa, the host of the wedding feast that had enlivened our first day in the town. The old man and his son met us, not at the door as formerly, but outside the courtyard, thereby doing us great honour. The party was assembled in the room containing the brass cabinet previously described. It consisted of about twenty people, all men, the cream of local society. Beneath the window, occupying the place of honour, was the Kenchung dressed in orange brocade. On his right sat the Jongpen, wearing a jacket of sapphire blue over a robe of greenish yellow. Facing the Kenchung was the postmaster, a pot-bellied, pig-tailed personage in dingy maroon. On the Kenchung's left sat a rich trader, whose top-knot, tied with red, meant that he was ripe for promotion to officialdom. These persons, who formed the main group, were playing a variant of mah-jong which seemed to resemble bridge, though there were sixteen pieces to a suit. Loud shouts greeted the trumping of an opponent, and heaps of Tibetan money, in the form of coarse copper coins and bank-notes imprinted with a woodcut lion, passed between the players. The Jongpen, I noticed, had wrapped his legs in a purple rug. The Kenchung, on the other hand, had discarded a coat of maroon silk woven with gold roundels and lined with red hearth-mat.

The splendour of such garments, which was reflected in greater or less degree by all those present except ourselves, gave the party an air of ceremonious gaiety. Our host was dressed in woollen cloth of the very finest texture, deep green in colour, and tied with a scarlet sash. His son, whose hair was also twisted with red ribbon, wore a robe of buff brocade tied with a yellow sash. Beneath this showed high soft boots of untanned leather, heavily tooled in a darker pattern. The two of them led us up to the principal guests, with whom we shook hands, then placed us at a separate table at the end of the room. The remaining members of the party were ranged at other tables along the wall opposite the window, and were also gambling.

Chang was served immediately on our arrival by the same serving-women, from whom detached herself the same frowning hussy that had stood over me before and was now more determined than ever that I should drink my fill. We slipped away, and nibbled at dried fruits, until a stir in the doorway announced the beginning of the largest meal I have ever been privileged to eat.

The art of eating, as perfected by the Chinese and adopted by the Tibetans, differs radically from the same art as practised in Europe. With us the dimensions and contents of the meal are carefully worked out beforehand; the guest is treated to a finished masterpiece, in whose composition he himself plays little or no part. According to Celestial custom it is the guest who makes the design, out of the materials laid before him. There are no pauses; when one series of bowls is removed, not ten seconds elapse before the next is on the table. There are no drinks either. Consequently eating is incessant and is impelled, apart from pure greed, by the curiosity attaching to so many varieties of food. The chopsticks fly from one to another in endless change, and suddenly, at the end of the meal, some of the earlier courses are repeated, so that one may taste again what was most excellent at the beginning. In the present instance we sat for more than two hours, during which the process of mastication did not cease for one minute. The menu, as far as our joint memory could afterwards recall it, was as follows: monkey-nuts and other nuts, sardines which we ourselves had brought as a present, a chopped vegetable, like celery, with bits of meat, Chinese shrimps, meat balls, meat mixed with walnut that tasted like *marrons glacés*, mutton, curried meat, sweet rice and sultanas, sultanas and candy sugar, doughnuts containing a sweet brown syrup, dough-balls, seaweed too delicious to describe, various other vegetables of hard consistency, bamboo roots, meat with *sauerkraut*, cabbage, mushrooms, small sea-slugs with mushrooms, large sea-slugs without, four kinds of fish tripe, of which one was unpleasantly spongy, shark's stomach, pease gelatine, and liver or kidney. Then followed, to wash it all down, the usual two kinds of tea and glasses of *crème de menthe*.

Throughout this gargantuan repast we were accompanied at our table by the son of the house and also by a person of enormous proportions with a Hindenburg moustache, named Nishup, who was reputed to be the richest man in Gyantse. This reputation he enhanced by wearing on one hand a ruby, and on the other a sapphire, each more than half an inch across. Though light in colour and full of flaws, they gave him a magnificent air. Just as we were about to ask the same question of him, he asked us how much we thought they were worth.

Nishup did not eat much, and G. would fain know why. He said he could not bear to feel his stomach growing. G., whose knowledge of Buddhist lore is no less than his knowledge of everything else, replied that he had always understood the stomach to be the seat of all wisdom. This remark, when translated, sent the whole room into a roar of laughter. Nishup, incorrigibly material, repeated that a big stomach was uncomfortable, and that was enough for him. Pemba, through whom this conversation was conducted, then informed us that, when alone, all Tibetans eat six times as much as they do at parties. We could only be surprised that any of them should be able to move at all.

At three o'clock the women reappeared with *chang*, and we remembered that we had to reach Saugong, fifteen miles away, before dusk. The luggage had gone on. Blood's ponies were to carry us once more on this our first stage of the journey down to India. After sad good-byes to him and Pemba, whose joint sponsorship had enabled us to see far more of Tibetan life than would otherwise have been possible, we set off at a sharp canter. Twilight fell quickly. For the last four miles we went at full gallop. By half-past five, when we reached the rest-house, it was actually dark, and the servants were waiting with lanterns to guide us indoors.

Looking back on Gyantse now, I realize what a precious glimpse that week gave us of a way of life which the world has nowhere else preserved. In European parlance it is a medieval way of life, a stage through which we ourselves have passed long ago, but from which, nevertheless, the roots of our tradition still draw much of their strength. How soon Western materialism will penetrate the barriers so far successfully maintained, no one can tell. From Nepal on the south and China on the west the menace of forcible invasion is ever alive, and has twice since our visit reached such a point of danger that British mediation has been called for. Except by an army trained and munitioned on Western lines, to which the ruling hierarchy is bitterly opposed, it is difficult to see how this menace can be permanently warded off. To a country, moreover, where justice is cruel and secret, disease rife, and independent thought impossible, Western ideas might bring some benefits. But could the benefits outweigh the disadvantages? In the present state of Western civilization, whose spiritual emptiness in relation to Asia is masked by a brutal assumption of moral superiority, it seems to me that they could not. I prefer to hope that the life we saw at Gyantse will endure, and wish Tibet luck in her isolation, until such time as the West itself is reformed and can commend its ideas with greater reason to those who have hitherto escaped them.

VIII

WINTER COMES EARLY

Everyone had prophesied snow for us, and we had left Gyantse expecting to ride into it, since the clouds were lying thick over the Saugong Valley and the hill-tops were already white. As for the passes into India, the Jelep and the Nathu, Pemba had heard rumours of a fall of six feet on them. For the moment, however, we awoke to a cloudless sky and bright sunshine. But the wind was bitter cold, and as a precaution against it we each assumed a green silk mask with worked eye-holes that had been purchased in the bazaar at Gyantse. The precaution was probably unnecessary at this stage of the journey, since it was the coincidence of snow on the ground with wind and sun that was really to be feared. But after the miseries of the journey up we were taking no risks; and we certainly met Tibetans similarly masked. Besides these ghoulish protections, we had also furnished ourselves with whips, which now enabled us to cover the stage between Saugong and Khangma, a distance of fifteen miles, in two and a half hours. Even so, an unreasoning depression, which seems inseparable from travel in Tibet, began to settle on us. After a walk up the Khangma valley, where I watched a toddling infant sending stones from a knitted sling as far as a drive at golf, my head began to feel peculiar again. I therefore retired to bed at a quarter-past two.

A couple of empirin tablets had put me right by the next morning, and I enjoyed a leisurely ride to Samoda. On the way I stopped at the Dekzü monastery, which was in course of reconstruction. It was here that I observed the process of cornice-making by means of dyed twigs. A courteous gentleman with a fine ear-ring appeared on the scene and, though somewhat astonished at my mask and goggles, showed me over the temple. There were no monks about. He alone seemed to be superintending the work in hand. I rode by myself that day, and on reaching the rest-house at Samoda I plucked up my Tibetan to ask for a *shön ya* – in other words, a riding yak. A brute was fetched from a near-by field, on which I perched myself in miraculous discomfort, flinging the yak-hair rein attached to its nostrils from horn to horn in an unsuccessful effort to steer it where I wished to go. Its home, I learned afterwards, was in the opposite direction, on the farther side of a mountain range; and when eventually I let it go in that direction, it set off at a lumbering trot. After a time I tried to turn it, on which it showed resentment by twisting its head and butting my boots. I managed to regain the rest-house in the end, just as the others arrived, who displayed some surprise at seeing me thus gratuitously sampling yet another exigency of Tibetan travel.

From Samoda we had planned a double stage to Dochen, twenty-six miles. Again I rode alone, rising gently through seven miles of rocky valleys, till I emerged on to the Kala plain which stretched another seven miles before me. Across this immense solitude, silent and awesome within its rampart of snow-girdled peaks, was proceeding a herd of seven wild ass, tawny-coloured, with white legs that moved in step like the tights of a chorus in musical comedy. My pony, after its rest in Gyantse, was in fine form and chased the absurd troupe. Then, seeing that the whole plain contained but one single stone, it galloped three miles like an arrow from the bow in order to annoy me by tripping over it. At midday we lunched in the Kala rest-house, and immediately afterwards entered the Kala gorge. As this continued, to bring us out on the shores of Lake Dochen, the whole range of Chomolhari came gradually into view, peak after peak, glassy bright under new snow, in contrast with the leaden waters of the lake, whose sullen, wind-ruffled surface was threatening to freeze as we looked. Flocks of duck were still swimming, in the vain hope of averting this contingency, and two pairs of black-backed crane were pacing anxiously to and fro in the shallows at the margin. I followed one of them. At first the birds marched one after the other in rigid step, separated by a distance of twenty yards. Then, as my pace quickened, theirs quickened also, till suddenly one wheeled about and they continued to march in different directions, still in step, like sentries changing guard.

Being now well over 14,000 feet, we had reached the snow at last, which lay from eight inches to a foot deep, and, being freshly fallen, necessitated our finding the path for ourselves. G. acted as pioneer and led us unerringly to the Dochen rest-house. The sun was setting as we rode. Over the lake the sky became suffused with a luminous greenish blue, a marvel of colour, distant and unearthly, such as one could imagine of inter-planetary space. In front of this the frigid peaks stood out in greater relief than before, with cold, pure blue shadows on their eastern faces and their western bathed in a light of soft yellow. Between each hung clouds in delicate suspense, impalpable as tulle gauze and radiant with the same yellow glow. Below spread the lake, dark, deep, and sinister, though its leaden frown was bluer now. From its edge to the rest-house the virgin snow was interrupted only by a squat cabin and some nearer mounds of yak-dung. Over to the left appeared a lower range, where the snow had not lain, and which now stood out the colour of a faded rose-petal against the green behind. The wind had dropped and silence reigned over the scene, so tense, so inviolable, that it struck the ear like a message from the stars.

With a jangle of bells the mules arrived as dusk merged into darkness. The servants had got it into their heads that we were making for Phari, thirty-six miles away, next day, and were determined to prevent any such thing. The wire was tapped here, and Ah-Chung rushed to the telephone, on which he learned that, though the mail from the north had got through to Phari that day, from Phari to Gautsa in the Chumbi Valley the road was completely blocked. M. was depressed by this news; he suggested summoning 150 yaks to clear the road before our arrival. But a glass or two of hot rum made the prospect of being marooned in Tibet for the winter seem more romantic than tragic. There was still some of Blood's *crème de menthe* left for dinner, and the rest-house contained three volumes of *Punch*. In fact the evening finished in a happier mood than most.

There were no blue skies when we looked out next morning, no mountains even – they had vanished behind an iron curtain of cloud whose downward streaks proclaimed a snowstorm on the other side of the lake. A fearful cold hung in the air. I put on seven thicknesses of clothes. We tried to telephone to Phari again, but by now the line was out of order. Then, as by a miracle, the sun fought its way through and the clouds began to disperse. One by one the satellites of Chomolhari reappeared, gleaming blue and brown and white, till the fantastic cone of their chief was visible and the whole range was reflected in the glacial tranquillity of the lake beneath. To the right, against the sun, flashed a crumpled sheaf of blue crystals, which we took to be Kanchenjunga. In front of us the untraversed plain shone white as a new-laid tablecloth and dazzling even through a pair of smelter's glasses. To the naked eye it was impossible, painful, even for a minute. There had been a wind in the night, so that the snow varied in depth from two feet to two inches. Any mound of eminence was almost bare; some of the lower hills were striped with drifts like huge giraffes. We had not far to go to Tuna, but progress under such conditions was slow. As the sun rose to its full height we could feel the snow-glare burning through our masks. Another herd of wild ass appeared on the horizon; this time there was no chasing them. By the time we reached the rest-house the afternoon was well advanced. Chomolhari was nearer now, and the sunset more spectacular even than that of the previous day.

We left Tuna at eight o'clock in the morning. The snow was thicker, and we had to go on top of it, following a path nine inches wide which had been made by yaks in single file. This had frozen in the night and was hard enough to prevent us sinking through. But the gait of the yak differs widely from that of the pony, so that the feet of the latter cannot, and did not, coincide with the footmarks left by the former. Since the path consisted entirely of these footmarks in all their separate inconvenience, our mounts had to feel their every step, and even then threatened to collapse with legs crossed at one in every four. We thus made an average pace of one and a half miles an hour. On our left Chomolhari grew eternally more imminent, till its furious escarpments seemed to threaten our destruction. At the rest-house below the Tang La I waited for the mules to come up, and fished another sweater from my luggage. The sun had gone in again, and a wind had got up which cut through my seven coverings like a razor.

The ascent to the Tang La is gentler than can be expected of a pass over 15,000 feet above sea-level. But it seemed like an arctic hell as I plodded in the wake of G. and M., two tiny black specks above me in a world of white. The snow grew deeper and deeper. Traffic was coming through from Phari now, and if one left the path the pony would flounder up to its belly and soon become immovable. There was nothing for it but to take a whip to the oncoming beasts and drive them, and their owners with them, out of the road. On in front, M. was unhorsed by two yaks simultaneously. Behind me our caravan was in difficulties, and the mules began to lie down. But I rode oblivious of these incidents, concentrating only on my own progress. A flock of sheep, going the same way as myself, proved almost impassable. When I reached the top, my mask, wet with breathing, froze into a sheet of green silk ice. Dead animals were frequent. A trail of blood led to a mangled donkey, at which a black mastiff was already busy. At last the Phari Jong could be seen on the horizon, a small blue silhouette against the white outline of the Himalayas. I passed through a village, whose natural filth was made more evident by its white mantle stained with blood and urine. The streets of Phari, when I reached them, were equally disgusting. At the rest-house I found that M. had developed a pain in his inside. He dared not take a pill, he said, owing to the long journey on the morrow. To-day we had come twenty-one miles and were as tired as we could be.

Two moths, a clump of Michaelmas daisies, and a pat of yak-dung fell out of the jug with my washing-water. We had planned to be called at six, but did not get off till eight, and even then the mules had not started. As the plain sloped downward to the head of the Chumbi Valley the snow grew steadily deeper. It was only yesterday that the first animals had come through, after a week's blockade. Out of the mist loomed black herds of yak, some of them laden, while from the backs of one or two fluttered pennants mounted on poles – presumably prayer-flags. The marmots had come up through the snow and squatted in hundreds at their circular entrances.

At last the sides of hills were visible and the slope between them became a descent. The Chumbi Valley was beginning. The mountains closed in and the path became once more a twisting narrow ledge, which recalled vivid memories of the journey up and the anxious uncertainty that had attended this stage of it. Giant slopes obliterated the sky, beneath which the human being suffered incredible diminution. It is not my habit to moralize on the smallness of man. But the Himalayas do induce a sense of it. They are out of scale to a degree which evokes something like fear – the sort of feeling, I imagine, that might beset one in the depths of the ocean, however safe the submarine. Then a tree came to comfort us, the first for a week, a friendly little rhododendron bush, three feet high. Conifers followed, gaunt and rugged like a veteran army, whose black, snow-spattered silhouettes maintained their precarious footing up the white towers of rock. Below rushed the river in tremendous volume, making the best of its last freedom before the spring. Already the intervening boulders were fringed all round with icicles, and being covered on top with snow as well, resembled settees upholstered in a ruched white chintz. Vast avalanches had left their dirty smears on the opposing slopes, damming the waters in the bottom and filling our path, if they had crossed it, with mounds of loose cannon balls over which the ponies picked their way with sage deliberation. It was no wonder that the soldier who was carried back to hospital the week before had been unable to get through to Phari.

Rounding a corner, I met a party of monks whose red robes, tall yellow hats, and goggled yellow masks seemed the natural uniform for this outlandish world. The leader of them swung a prayer-wheel as he walked. Farther on I espied two men busy on their knees at the river-bank. A couple of mules stood tethered beside them, and a number of ravens were hopping about. I was wondering what they were up to, when suddenly one of them brandished a bloody limb at me. They were cutting up a body, which I took to be a human one, since it seemed an inconvenient spot for the butchery of an animal, and the dead are always thus disposed of in Tibet. Then Gautsa came in sight, where we met our acquaintances of the journey up, the doctor and McLeod. They told us that the recent snowfall had been one of the heaviest on record.

Here we lunched hurriedly, for it was growing late. Thereafter the trees stood about the path in thick woods, which seemed hospitable after the arid wastes of the plateau. Tibet was already remote; the excursion of the last three weeks had become detached as an experience outside the normal course. The larches were still gold. But for them the autumn colours had been sogged away. Cataclysms of earth and stones had altered the very landscape. In one place a whole clump of trees had come rushing down the mountainside to land upright on the path, so at first, not realizing what had happened and remembering the spot as it had been, I was at a loss to understand why my path should suddenly vanish in a small wood. My pony was less tired than the others, and I rode ahead, for the sun was setting and we still had ten miles to go. As twilight deepened I quickened my pace, cantering helter-skelter down the uneven path, over the boulders and down the beds of streams, past the ruined Chinese barracks, till at half-past five, when it was actually quite dark, I reached the outskirts of Yatung and begged the first man I met to direct me to the rest-house. At first he did not understand. I bellowed the word *dunkang* in every key my voice could devise. Eventually comprehension dawned, and he sent me over the bridge and up the opposite hill, where I found the caretaker waiting on the threshold. To him, by signs, I explained that the others were coming, and persuaded him to send out a lantern to meet them. He rose to the occasion, and when the others did arrive, half an hour later, cooked us an excellent dinner out of his own resources, which consisted of an omelette and some roast yak. Another lantern was despatched to meet the mules, which did not get in till half-past eight, after a march of twelve hours without a stop.

It had been a tiring day, altogether a tiring week. We were glad to spend the next morning in idleness, browsing over the various batches of letters that had been waiting for us here. I was glad to see that, if size of type were any criterion, the *Daily Express* had considered my articles on the flight to India of some value. Later we visited Smith, the Trade Agent, at his official residence on the other side of the valley, the usual Anglo-Himalayan chalet, roofed in red corrugated iron and sporting a tenuous Union Jack. The place was not without amenities. A few roses were still flowering in the garden, and there had been sweet-peas till the snow came. The servants wore purple skirts, in the Chinese fashion, and short scarlet jackets in the English. Smith was just setting off for Gangtok, like ourselves. We promised to catch him up that evening.

A band, whose members wore spangled masks adorned with aigrettes, greeted us on our return to the rest-house. Just as we were leaving, having enjoyed a protracted and soporific lunch, another musician arrived by himself, bearing a magnificent green and gold banjo, which I purchased on the spot for ten rupees. This object my unfortunate groom was obliged to carry for the rest of the journey. But I felt less compunction at thus burdening him than might have been expected, since several of the other servants had bought themselves Lhassa terriers in Gyantse, which they intended to sell in India, and to carry which across the snow-covered plains they had even been able to afford servants of their own.

To reach Gangtok, the capital of Sikkim, and also for the pleasure of taking a different route, we had decided to cross the Himalayas by the Nathu instead of the Jelep La. After a few miles along the Chumbi Valley, we turned up the hills to the right, leaving the telegraph-posts for the first time since our journey had begun. The path climbed steeply and was disconcertingly narrow, winding its way along a terrific semicircular precipice over which a mule had fallen only a few moments before our advent. We could see the poor brute in the bottom, as the vultures came wheeling down like baroque aeroplanes; its ribs were already bare. Then we rode into a cloud, and the forked valley, with its silver thread of river twisting away on its passage to Bhutan, was blotted out. Suddenly a small monastery loomed out of the mist, perched on an isolated ledge. Its roof, but for a gold cupola, was made of flattened kerosene tins painted red. Yet so neatly was this done that the effect was not incongruous. As we passed the entrance, a monk ran out, beckoning to us to stop. But we had no time. The phantom building receded below us. Then, suddenly, a trumpet rang out, one of those twenty-foot instruments of lamaic ritual. Vainly it called, echoing over hidden valleys and rebounding from peak to peak, as though to inform us, in our cloud-swathed blindness, of heights unscaled and recesses unimagined. Another blast, fainter now, caught up the long-drawn phrase; and then a third, hard on the second, so that the echoes crossed and recrossed and the very mist was alive with distant sound. The trumpet rang no more. With infinite reluctance, seeking a last survival in farther and farther ranges, the sound died away. We climbed onward through the trees, knowing, each in his own mind, that Tibet had spoken her farewell.

We were now in the snow again. The going was the worst we had encountered, and the fact that we could not see them in no way mitigated the depths of the precipice below us. Landslides and fallen trees blocked the path at every turn. At the best it was scarcely a yard wide. Occasionally there were bridges, grotesque structures like heaps of tumbled spelicans, through which the ponies' legs might slip and dangle above unfathomable glissades. Cascades of snow fell from the trees, finding their way down our necks and into our boots. A lugubrious moisture, half sleet, half rain, oozed from the impenetrable cloud. The cold was intense. The approach of night added to the gloom of the black and dripping trees. It was with some relief that we reached the tiny rest-house of Champithang, to find Smith installed, with the lamps lit and a wood fire roaring in the grate.

Next morning we made an early start. Smith, a man of generous physique, was mounted on a sleek black mule. My pony, I felt, was gradually turning into a mule with all this mountaineering. Its ears began to lengthen at every obstacle. There had been a fresh fall of snow in the night. But for the moment the sun was shining and the battered, flat-topped silver firs, festooned with long trailers of lichen like tinsel on a Christmas-tree, glittered brightly against the black depths of wooded valleys. At length we passed the tree-line and were faced by a white wall of mountain – the approach to the pass. Simultaneously the clouds descended. A blizzard enveloped us. It became impossible to see more than a few yards. There was nothing to indicate the path. We could only continue upwards and trust that the invisible abysses now lurking in our imagination did not exist.

In the midst of this blind progress my pony lurched forward, tipping me headlong into a drift as high as my chest. M.'s pony, just behind, lurched backward into another, and he slid off over the tail. We dragged the ponies out, remounted, and waited for it to happen again, which it did immediately. There was nothing for it but to walk. Normal kindness would have prompted such a course, it may be thought; but it is none too easy to struggle up a steep slope in the rarefied air of 14,000 feet at the best of times; and when, in addition, one had to contend with snow up to the thighs and sometimes the waist, a vast weight of clothing, a frozen mask which impeded respiration already difficult enough, and complete loss of all direction, there were moments when it seemed as though we might have to postpone our return to India to another day. After every three or four steps it was necessary to stop and rest; on which the ponies would sink in up to the saddle again, and a further effort would be needed to pull them out before bracing oneself for another spurt. At one moment a gleam of hope materialized in the form of some footsteps ahead of us. I followed them as quickly as I could, and the going had just begun to seem a little easier, as though their maker knew where the path was, when I came on him seated behind a rock – a solitary mumbling idiot, whom no gestures of mine could induce to move another step. By this time the slope had become almost perpendicular, and we judged it best to wait for Smith, in case he, by instinct or experience, should know the way. But he did not; neither did his chief Tibetan clerk, whose usual calm was sadly deranged by our predicament. This personage, whose single ear-ring and jacket of piebald fur still lent him an air of authority, hazarded the suggestion that we were within four hundred yards of the top. Whether without further assistance we should ever have completed that four hundred yards is a doubtful point. But, as though by a miracle, assistance came. Smith was for going back, M. was undecided, and I was for making a last try, when out of the blizzard far above us came a shout. Our men answered. The shouts were repeated from above. And by dint of this unison a junction was effected between our servants and the drivers of an equally bewildered caravan from the south. Even the idiot was stirred to activity and took my pony, as we hoisted ourselves up the last rock-face, so steep that little snow could lie on it, and at length stood upright again on the narrow edge of the pass. I was glad of his help, for my groom, laden with the banjo, had got left behind.

Thus we crossed the frontier of Tibet and, stepping into the tracks of the mule-train, descended into India.

The path was now a proper path, decently cobbled and graded. After walking about a mile the snow decreased and we were able to remount. The ride was enlivened by various game – a covey of ptarmigan, another of snow-partridges, said to be rare, and a single deer. A couple of martens were playing on a rock. Also we saw a monal pheasant, most magnificent of the Himalayan birds, which got up at our feet and sailed away into the mist across a bottomless valley, a vision of purple and copper. We reached the rest-house of Changu early in the afternoon, and there parted from Smith, who was due to make another stage before dusk. Our own mules were still tired after the long journey from Phari to Yatung, and we thought it best to spare them as much as possible.

Changu lies by a lake which hangs precariously among the mountain-tops, with a slender dam at one end, whence pours a water-fall. The Maharajah of Sikkim has a boat-house here. I rode out before breakfast, after being nearly overwhelmed by an avalanche of snow from the roof of the rest-house, and discovered the pods of a poppy which I hoped might be a blue one; but it was not. The day, we had decided, should be devoted to botanizing, in the interests of M. Our next stage would take us down from 12,000 to 9,000 feet. It began with conifers, interspersed with innumerable kinds of rhododendron and azalea whose leaves varied in length from a foot to half an inch. Then bamboos intervened, huge feathery clumps of light green, and maples, brilliant yellow and brilliant red. Already, despite the yawning cloud-filled valleys that unfolded at every turn, there was a feeling of luxuri-ance, such as the Chumbi Valley does not possess, an oppressive feeling, as though the moisture were too abundant and the soil too rich for a rational plant life.

I was riding in meditative mood, when up the path came Ward, a soldier friend from Calcutta, with a friend of his behind him. Their comparatively clean appearance made me conscious of our own un-kemptness. They were going up to Changu in the hopes of getting a shot at a monal pheasant, and were interested to hear we had seen one. On reaching Karponang, where the new-built rest-house seemed like a palace, we all shaved, and, like Samson at the loss of his locks, I was filled of a sudden with tragic lassitude. Our journey was nearly over. Next morning M. and I went on ahead. Some of the orchids were in flower, single mauve ones in the clefts of trees, and clusters of small coffee-coloured blooms pendant from the higher branches. From four miles away a square temple roof on a wooded spur proclaimed the imminence of Gangtok. We cantered down the well-made path, and at the entrance to the town found a *chuprassi* awaiting us to lead us to the Residency. He wore a Lepcha uniform, a scarlet coat, a skirt, and a straw top-hat of *Directoire* shape with a peacock's feather in it. In the garden, as we ambled up the drive, Mrs Weir was picking flowers. Colonel Weir was on the doorstep, with Smith behind him. Glasses of beer were handed on a tray, and we found ourselves, after what seemed like an eternity of the unfamiliar, in a normal house.

I cannot speak fondly enough of Colonel and Mrs Weir's hospitality to us. By them, accustomed to travel in Tibet, our little excursion was hardly to be taken as a serious journey. Yet Mrs Weir had anticipated the pleasure we should feel at our return to civilization, and no amenity she could provide was lacking for our comfort and entertainment. That year they had been invited to visit Lhassa and had arrived within about eighty miles of the place when, to their great disappointment, the invitation was cancelled. They were now wondering whether the opportunity would come again. I am glad to say that it did come, not once but twice. Diplomacy moves slowly in the Tibetan capital. Altogether they must have spent more than a year there. Mrs Weir is not only an observer but an artist of considerable attainment. If and when the time comes for them to make public the fruits of their two missions, our knowledge of the least-known city in the world will be considerably increased.

That evening Sir Abdul Karim Ghuznavi, a member of the Governor's Council of Bengal, came to stay, having done eighteen miles by car at an average pace of three miles an hour. On the following morning we all trooped down to the Palace to pay our respects to the Maharajah. The Palace, which had just been newly pointed, resembled a dolls'-house of the seaside villa pattern. The private secretary, dressed in green silk, met us in the drive. The Maharajah, dressed in sky-blue brocade, was waiting on the threshold, a charming little man in smoked spectacles, with a gentle musical voice. His drawing-room, thanks to the taste of Mrs Weir and of Mrs Bailey her predecessor, contained none of those monstrous objects with which Oriental potentates in general seek to create a European *ensemble* for the delectation of their guests. Apart from some carved and gilt tables of local make, the furniture and atmosphere might have belonged to some pleasant English country-house. The Maharajah complained of his wireless set, which could only get Calcutta. He had ordered a bigger. He also complained of the difficulty he experienced in leaving his front gate, owing to an adverse spirit which lived in a tree beside it. We gave him a message of regard from Rajah Tehring, at which – or was it our imagination? – he seemed rather displeased. At length he took us out to see the temple on the point of the spur. In front of it lay an open space which had been levelled for the erection of a new palace. I had a side-conversation with the private secretary, who promised to procure me a couple of dancer's masks. Sir Abdul Karim played the heavy politician, exhorting the Maharajah to develop his mineral resources.

In the afternoon the royal party came to tea, headed by the Rimpoché, a twinkling monk wearing a yellow hat like a pagoda, whose holiness was such that the servants fell on their knees at his white clogs. The Maharanee came also. They arrived on richly caparisoned ponies. Despite their affability, it was a difficult meal. Dinner I found still more difficult. For my stomach, which had been uttering certain warnings for the past day or two, now refused to assimilate any more food whatsoever, and I was obliged to rush from the room. The following morning, after I had been dosed with castor oil, we took leave of the Weirs, whom we were later to see again both in Calcutta and London, and rode down to Pakyang. And on the day after, which was 2 November, reached Rungpo, where a car was waiting for us. Here we lunched among sweet-smelling shrubs, bathed in the river, and said good-bye to the servants, than whom none could have been more dutiful and efficient. A year or two later I saw Ah-Chung's photograph in *The Times*. He had been acting as cook to the Kamet Expedition.

A good road took us to Siliguri. Once more the Bengal plain spread out before us. There were three hours to wait for the train. We ordered a bottle of burgundy in the station restaurant. This, on being opened, emitted a light orange liquid. We sent for the manager. It was burgundy for all he knew; but there was no need for us to pay for it if *we* thought differently. We then ordered claret, port, and kümmel instead. After a comfortable night in the train we reached Calcutta for breakfast. It was a luxurious meal. Central Asia had become a dream.

IX

A TIBETAN PILGRIMAGE

Jigmed and Mary, who had left Tehring the day we went to Dongtse, had a difficult journey to India. They had intended to cross into Sikkim direct from Kampa Jong. But the pass of their choice, which is over 17,000 feet high, was completely blocked by the same snowfall as had so hindered ourselves. And after a very unpleasant night in the crudest of shelters they were forced to turn back, eventually rejoining the trade route at Tuna. At Kalimpong they spent a few days with their old friend Mr Macdonald, and thence came down to Calcutta, where with some difficulty I found them, occupying a balcony at the top of that Chinese caravanserai which had previously supplied us with ceremonial scarves. The ostensible reason for their trip was a pilgrimage to Buddh Gaya. But for the moment they were employed in tasting the pleasure of a Western city. In this I could be of some help; after which, perhaps, I might ask them to allow me to come on the pilgrimage too.

The following night, therefore, we dined at Firpo's, where the entry of a Tibetan couple in full regalia caused a stir of surprise and – as far as I was concerned – of disapproval. To consort with Indians was bad enough; for these outlandish folk, celestially brocaded, there could be no excuse. I gave them champagne, whose flavour, to my mortification, reminded them of *chang*. Thus primed, we went to the theatre. It was a gala performance, the first night of *Journey's End*. The Governor was in his box and everyone else in the stalls. I was interested to see this play; but its significance, in my mind, was disproportionately exaggerated by the company of two people who knew no more of the war than we do of famines in China. The dialogue proved unintelligible to them, and they were further mystified by the bursting shells. Yet by some abstruse instinct they appreciated the humour of the cockney cook. On the whole the evening was a success.

The next thing was to get them to lunch at Government House. This I accomplished, after taking them to write their names in the book, through the offices of a friendly ADC. 'I think,' said the ADC to the Military Secretary, 'it is politically important to have them.' 'I think,' said the Military Secretary to the Governor, 'it is politically important to have them.' So had they were, and enjoyed it. They also lunched with me at the flat I had been lent, and complimented me on the banjo I had bought at Yatung. It was of an old Lhassa type, they said, very uncommon, and the price I had paid was small, even by Tibetan standards.

Besides pleasure, they had certain business to transact. Two servants from Lhassa had been sent down with them, one of whom could not stop laughing, owing to the fact, apparently, that he had once been a rich man and had gambled away his inheritance. These were to be sent by ship to China in order to buy silks and brocades requisite for the strictly prescribed Tibetan uniforms and dresses of ladies of rank. Owing to the anarchy of the interior the overland trade routes were closed and this was the only means of obtaining such stuffs. Then, when the passages of the servants had been arranged, there were purchases to be made. Already Jigmed had bought a typewriter. Now he was contemplating a gramophone. One evening, however, we all met at the station, Jigmed and his servant, Mary and her maid, myself and my servant, and took the train to Gaya.

Mary had visited Gaya before, in company with her 'father', the commander-in-chief. On our emerging from the train at a quarter to seven in the morning an old station official shuffled up, of whom, to his great astonishment, she asked, 'Haven't you got a goat with long ears?' He then recalled the visit of the commander-in-chief in 1925, and the little girl who had accompanied him and had played with the goat. Meanwhile, another Tibetan had appeared – a lama, also on pilgrimage – and attached himself to us. We heaped ourselves into two cars. During the drive Jigmed and Mary, who had thought that India was always hot and had brought no overcoats, shivered in the foggy dawn. The Tibetan servants, unused to this form of locomotion, were sick over their chauffeur. On reaching Buddh Gaya we found a new but very small dak bungalow awaiting us, to which we were the first visitors. Outside it the *chowkidar* had made a little formal garden, whose rows of neatly bedded flowers he showed us with pride.

Two or three hundred yards away, from a depression which represents the level of the spot two thousand years ago, rose the tower of the great Mahabodhi temple, a square cone, slightly truncated and surmounted by a pinnacle which brings its total height to 170 feet. To the base of this immense structure, whose shape resembles that of only one other temple in India, we proceeded after a short breakfast, threading our way among flowering trees and groves of ancient stone monuments – stupas, pillars, Buddhas, and Bodhisattvas – till we came to the main entrance. I accompanied the pilgrims inside – and then, as they pressed their foreheads to the knees of a Buddha, stopped short. My intrusion, of a sudden, seemed vulgar and inquisitive, the more so since Jigmed, having been at school in Darjeeling, had evidently acquired that self-conscious embarrassment in religious matters which is inseparable from English education. So I left them and, wandering off among the precincts of the temple, consoled myself that, even if Buddhism were not of my inheritance, I could still do homage to its founder as the philosopher he was, instead of as the god he has been made.

A wisdom whose conception of space and time was forecast of our own, and whose canon of individual self-reliance is as high a compliment as any ever paid by man to man, must always command respect, even among the ignorant. But it was a warmer, an historical emotion that held me now, which celebrated not the wisdom itself, but the event of its coming, on this hallowed site. For it was here that Buddha, arrived at last on the centre of the Universe, seated himself beneath the pipal-tree and received the Illumination that illumined the earth. In the hard still light of the Indian morning, when the sun enforces peace and nothing moves or sounds but the wafted scent of a flower or the call of some quick melodious bell, I sought the *genius loci*. During sixteen centuries, between the reign of King Asoka in the third century BC and the Mohammedan conquest of the thirteenth century AD, the Mahabodhi temple was the focus of unremitting devotions, whence the genius of the place has descended, through a period of ruin and desuetude, to benefit from English guardianship and welcome pilgrims in motor-cars. Jigmed and Mary had their ritual. To me, the interloper, remained the figment of human aspirations which had centred on this spot, and to which Jigmed and Mary now were adding.

An earlier temple than that which now exists was built by Asoka, or soon after his time; stone railings belonging to it have survived, adorned with bosses at the intersection of laterals with uprights, in the style of other early Buddhist monuments. These were eventually rearranged to enclose the present and larger structure, whose date cannot be later than the sixth century AD and may well be earlier. Fa-Hian, the Chinese pilgrim who visited the place in the first decade of the fifth century, saw a temple of sorts, but gives no description of it. Huien-Thsang, who arrived in the thirties of the seventh, is more explicit; his dimensions correspond exactly with those of the building as it still stands. The tower, he said, was made of bluish bricks faced with plaster. Each niche in each tier of the design contained a gilded image of Buddha.

In the eleventh century the Burmese did repairs. Thereafter the temple fell into a state of increasing ruin, until in 1880 a thorough restoration was undertaken at the instance of the Government of Bengal. Almost the whole of the outer surface of the tower was renewed, though with strict regard for the existing pattern of niches and mouldings; the pinnacle was repaired; and the four corner pavilions, of which no trace remained, were reconstructed from the somewhat uncertain authority of a model found near by. Altogether two lakhs of rupees (£15,000) were expended. The English have left their mark, as they do, in a peculiar fond manner, when engaged in archaeological reparation; I doubt if the temple, in all its long life, has ever worn such a tidy, solid air as it does to-day. Yet the genius of the place, instead of being expelled, has been rejuvenated. The Mahabodhi temple is once more a living shrine, and the prayers of its pilgrims, from all parts of Buddhist Asia, bring poetry more vivid than the picturesque futility of negligence and decay.

The pipal-tree, whose shade induced so momentous a consequence, still exists by courtesy, though its position has altered and it is probably fifteenth or twentieth in descent from its original ancestor. An actual child of the latter has survived elsewhere, at Anaradjpura in Ceylon, where I saw it, now but a fragment of arboreal senility. This was planted about 240 BC, and its guardianship at the hands of Buddhist monks has suffered no recorded interruption. The trees of Buddh Gaya, on the other hand, have endured much violence. The original was cut down by Asoka of all people, when he was still an unbeliever. Next day, having sprung miraculously to life, his queen cut it down again, and the roots had to be revived with perfumed milk. So tells Huien-Thsang. When he saw the tree its height was no more than forty or fifty feet. For in the year 600 the Rajah Sasangka had cut it down again, and had further dug up the roots and burnt them. Twenty years later came the Rajah Purnavarma, who revived the roots once more with the milk of a thousand cows. The next mention of the tree is by Doctor Buchanan in 1811, who described it as in full vigour and not exceeding one hundred years in age. When, in 1876, this tree had decayed and was blown down, there were seedlings ready to replace it. A few years later, remains of a pipal-tree were found which could not have been less than twelve hundred years old, owing to a buttress which had stood that time on top of them. These were in the proper place, the vicinity of the Vajrasan throne, the diamond meridian, centre of the Universe, a sandstone seat which still survives and which marks the actual point of the great Illumination.

As I looked now, the shiny dark green leaves of the tree were hung with the prayer-flags of many different races; while from the dark shade below glowed the tiny flames of countless little lamps. I sat myself beneath a fig-tree and gazed up at the tower through the glinting, steely fronds of a palm. Through the courtyard moved the custodians of the temple, Hindu monks – for there are no Buddhists in India now – dressed in long robes of pale strawberry faintly tinged with orange. Occasionally a brighter stuff flashed past, rich golden yellow, the vesture of a monk from Burma or Ceylon, occupant of the elaborate hostel of red brick and white marble which subscribers in those two countries have caused to be erected in the neighbourhood. At length Jigmed and Mary emerged from their initial rites, and we walked back together to the rest-house for lunch.

Mary, having made the pilgrimage before, was the leader in their various observances; and she now announced that this afternoon we must visit a certain cave where Buddha had lodged prior to his Illumination. As part of the pilgrimage it was a very essential visit, and they would be interrogated in Lhassa as to whether it had been performed. To reach the cave we should borrow an elephant: so she remarked in a casual voice, as though about to ask the loan of a neighbour's bicycle. An elephant? I said. She replied, yes, an elephant. They had been on one before, and that was how you did visit the cave. Meanwhile two babus, as though in answer to the need for an elephant, had conjured themselves on to the verandah. An elephant? they said; of course we must have an elephant. Ponies could be provided; but an elephant was indispensable. It should be arranged. After lunch, therefore, we all trooped down the village street, to the portals of the Hindu monastery, where the elephant was to await us.

After crossing a large court filled with evidences of monastic husbandry and surrounded by whitewashed buildings of irregular height and shape, we were conducted on to the topmost roof, where sat the *mahut* or abbot of the sect, crosslegged beneath a rush canopy. He wore a pale strawberry shirt and gold spectacles. His head was bald. His features, in shape and immobility, resembled those of an American Indian. He puffed without cease at the tube of a hubble-bubble. Three chairs were brought for us, and we seated ourselves opposite him. He continued to puff. Being unable to address him myself, I begged Jigmed and Mary to break the silence with their few words of Hindustani. They refused. Still he puffed, vouchsafing neither glance nor word. After ten minutes my self-control began to ebb. I rose. The others rose. We all three bowed, hoping thus to convey our gratitude for the loan of the elephant. He inclined his head a quarter of an inch. So we took our leave.

Downstairs in the court the brute was in readiness, kneeling down with a ladder against its ribs. In place of the expected howdah was a red mat, corded under the belly. The elephant is not an animal which persons of normal stature can bestride. We seated ourselves sideways, Mary clinging to the *mahout* between the ears, Jigmed clinging to Mary, myself clinging to Jigmed, and Mary's maid clinging to me. Then the elephant rose, straightening first its forelegs, when we all but slid off over its tail, and then its hind-legs, when only the *mahout* saved us from being precipitated over its forehead. A pause having enabled us to resettle, the word was given to proceed. On which the animal hurried up a flight of steps, through a gateway, and down another flight into the open country. At each motion the grip of Mary's maid on my waist had grown tighter and tighter. The steps were too much for her. The voluminous creature flung her arms round my neck with an expression of alarm that boded the continuance of such intimacy for the rest of the journey. The weight I could have borne; but not the smell – the effluvium of rancid butter that issued from her parted lips. Firmly I disengaged myself. She lurched backwards, saved herself by a miracle from the precipice of the animal's hindquarters, and broke into a volume of protest. On this Jigmed and Mary decided not to go at all. To leave her behind did not occur to them. Then, after further discussion, they decided to try again. Meanwhile the elephant had stopped and knelt down. Seeing that ponies had been provided as well, I took the opportunity of exchanging mounts. The elephant rose, Jigmed comforted his henchwoman, and we set off once more for the cave.

After crossing several fields we came to a broad river, whose surface refreshed my feet as we forded our way among the evil-horned water buffalo that inhabited it. There was no colour, no distance to the landscape. Only a line of hills gave feature to the horizon, marking our objective. A sandy waste, covered with tall pampas grasses such as shelter tigers in pictures, brought us to another river. The banks were steep, but the elephant negotiated them without ado, floundering in the soft sand to the distress of its passengers. My pony was of a frisky disposition. When it cantered, the elephant did likewise. All through the hot afternoon we rode, through the insipid blue-green plain with its eternal park-like trees, till at length the ridge was above us, and we dismounted at a spot where some ancient arrangement of stones gave evidence of human activity. Hence led a steep path, overhung with bushes and admitting only one person at a time, which brought us eventually to a tall mimosa-tree. Beneath this appeared the entrance to the cave, a small hole guarded by a grill. Jigmed and Mary took off their shoes before entering. I peeped in, and seeing the place to be empty, remained outside under the tree.

Of the cave's tradition, of the antiquity of this lesser pilgrimage, I was completely ignorant; and so remained until several years afterward, when the account of Huien-Thsang, thirteen centuries old, following on that of Fa-Hian, two centuries older, recalled me from the prosaic surroundings of an English garden to my seat under the mimosa-tree, while my two Tibetan friends were engulfed in the bowels of that lonely hill and the elephant waited below.

As he [Buddha] went to the north-east he saw this mountain that it was secluded and dark, whereupon he desired to seek enlightenment thereon. Ascending the north-east slope and coming to the top, the earth shook and the mountain quaked, whilst the mountain Deva in terror spake thus to Bodhisattva: 'This mountain is not the fortunate spot for attaining supreme wisdom. If here you stop and engage in "*Samadhi* of the diamond", the earth will quake and gape and the mountain be overthrown upon you.'

Then Bodhisattva descended, and half-way down the south-west slope he halted. There, backed by the crag and facing a torrent, is a great stone chamber. Here he sat down cross-legged. Again the earth quaked and the mountain quaked. Then a Deva of the pure abode cried out in space, 'This is not the place for a Tathagata to perfect supreme wisdom. From this south-west fourteen or fifteen li, not far from the place of penance, there is a Pi-po-lo tree under which is a "diamond throne". All the past Buddhas seated on this throne have obtained true enlightenment, and so will those yet to come. Pray, then, proceed to that spot.'

Then Bodhisattva rising up, the dragon dwelling in the cave said, 'This cave is pure and excellent. Here you may accomplish the holy aim. Would that of your exceeding love you would not leave me.'

Then Bodhisattva, having discovered that this was not the place for accomplishing his aim, to appease the dragon, he left him his shadow and departed. The Devas going before, led the way, and accompanied him to the Bodhi-tree.

Fa-Hian, two centuries earlier, had actually seen the shadow. In length it was 'somewhat about three feet'. Perhaps Jigmed and Mary saw it too. I would have asked them had I known of it. Such shadows do remain. There is one like it in Ceylon, though I could not see it, even when pointed out to me. I climbed up Adam's Peak and saw the footmark instead. But these relics are not historical. Whereas the topography of the Gaya district is as authentic as that of Jerusalem. Many of its more revered associations, particularly in the neighbourhood of the temple, eluded me. I have given some attention to the cave, as few Europeans have been there and fewer still in such company as was mine.

On descending the hill again the Tibetans admitted that even they found physical effort at sea-level considerably easier than at 12,000 feet. As we reached the elephant, Mary pointed to the antique stones, which she said were the remnant of a burning ghat where Tibetan visitors, on completing their pilgrimage, were wont to sacrifice a part of their hair. Neither she nor Jigmed, however, showed any sign of complying with this custom. Already the sun was low on the horizon. During the long ride back it sank behind the inevitable line of trees, leaving the spike of the temple tower silhouetted against a line of red fire. On reaching the river I dismounted to paddle, while waiting for the elephant to come up with me. The water buffalo had gone. There was a shiver in the air and the mists were rising. By the time we returned to the village, darkness was complete.

The village street was lit, and the elephant, discerning as it thought the end of its journey, turned in towards the gateway of the monastery. Its *mahout* intended otherwise, for the rest-house was still some distance and the passengers had no wish to walk. Raising the gaff-like weapon which *mahouts* carry, he struck the animal's forehead to divert it. The result proved unexpected. For the elephant, frankly, was incensed at such treatment. Pirouetting like a ballet-dancer on two of its immense feet, it swung back into the street and broke into an infuriated gallop. Round the corner came a cart. The two collided with a crash. But what was the fate of the cart I never saw, for by this time I too was galloping, determined not to miss the fun. On up the hill sped the enormous brute, with its passengers bumping about on their mat like tennis-balls in a basket. At the rest-house compound it swerved like a dirt-track rider, dashed up to the verandah, and came to a sudden halt. The *chowkidar*, hearing the noise, emerged from the door with a lantern. Simultaneously the elephant, in a last spasm of revenge, proceeded to commit an act of nature. An appalling cataclysm hit the ground. Seconds grew into a minute; there was no abatement. Suddenly, above the noise, rose a cry of rage and despair. It was the *chowkidar*. His garden – I looked: it had *gone*. Uprooted by the inexorable spate, each precious flower was floating away into the night. When the flood subsided, in place of those loving beds there remained but a confused depression. Then the elephant, satisfied at last, gathered itself together, discharged its human burden, and walked sedately off. The *chowkidar* was left speechless at the catastrophe, invoking curses of heaven with uplifted arms.

The next day we spent quietly. Seated beneath a fig-tree, I drew the temple. When the drawing was finished, Jigmed said he thought it almost as good as a photograph. Most of the day they were busy in the temple. But the labours of pilgrimage had been lightened for them by the opportune presence of the lama we had picked up at the station, who prepared and lit no less than a thousand lamps for them.

I grew to admire Mary. She assumed responsibility for our comfort. In all her movements, no matter how commonplace their purpose, there were grace, breeding, and authority. Her whole person was the outcome of a confident tradition. At meals she talked of life in Lhassa in tones of effortless esteem, such as a duke's daughter might use in talking of London.

Her adopted father, she said, was now a *shapeh*, one of the four great ministers who are next in importance to the Dalai Lama himself in the administration of the country. As such he wears, on state occasions, a robe which is woven so stiff with gold that it stands up by itself, and which needs two servants to bend it round him. This alone costs £750, while the winter hat of the uniform, made of black fox fur, costs as much again. Lately, however, he had obtained a similar fur from America at a more reasonable price. He had, in fact, instituted a system of barter with certain Americans. In return for curios they were to send him chiefly flower seeds. He maintains large flower and vegetable gardens in Lhassa, the former containing snapdragons and sweet-williams.

In the old days he had been commander-in-chief, had accompanied the Dalai Lama to China in 1904 and had saved his life, as already recorded, in 1910. As a good soldier he had become imbued with Western ideas, and had eventually raised the Tibetan army to a decent level of efficiency. But during his tour of India in 1925 the Dalai Lama had listened to other councils, and when the commander-in-chief reached Gyantse on his way back to Lhassa, he learned that his officers had been degraded and his work undone. The office of commander-in-chief was abolished, and he became a *shapeh* instead. Not that he minded; it meant less work, and he liked being at home and enjoying himself. Perhaps he is unpopular with the monks. But the common people adore him for his benevolence.

Her eldest brother, Mary added, was not so promising. In the last two years he had gambled away £1,000, had pawned his wife's jewels in the process, and had even misappropriated State funds, for which he had been dismissed the Government service. The hope of the family was her younger brother, who was very serious and was now in a Government school being trained for the administration. The Dalai Lama approved of him and sometimes even sent for him.

When Jigmed and she returned to Tibet, they would stay in Gyantse for a month and then go up to Lhassa with the whole family for the New Year games. Each of the *shapehs* on this occasion has to provide an entertainment, and her father's is always the best. The Dalai Lama gives away the prizes. There would be many evening parties, to attend which electric torches were necessary, since the streets are unlighted. Jigmed said they entertained a great deal at Tehring also. In the summer, for large parties, they erect a marquee in the garden. He and Mary were planning to build themselves a house in the English style. I thought of the English style as they knew it, and my face betrayed regret. It was useless to try and explain. They could not understand.

And then said Mary: 'I love Tibet. If only it had trains or motors, I think it would be the nicest country in the world.'

'But,' I answered, 'the monks don't like that sort of thing.'

'No,' she sighed. 'Some people don't seem to want to be civilized.'

I tried to sympathize with that sigh. The hardships of travel in Tibet can hardly be expected to appeal to those whose lifelong fate they are. But I could not. For once trains or motors have been introduced, the Tibet that Mary loves will be Tibet no longer.

That evening, after Jigmed and Mary have paid their last visit to the temple and have come back from it with scented garlands round their necks, we all three walk down the road together. The mist is rising. We stop by a well, to watch the oxen treading out their immemorial circuit and the water coming up in a chain of buckets. I ask them if they will ever come to England. They ask me if I shall ever return to Tibet. We ask each other if we shall ever meet again. Perhaps we shall, even if we shall have grown old before the time comes. For I always, as though by some hidden law, go back to places. Then Jigmed gives me two rings, for my two sisters, one mounting a ruby, the other a turquoise, in rich Lhassa gold-work. And so we retrace the road to the rest-house, where the cars wait to take us to the station. I think once more of the blue sky and clear air of the plateau, of the wind and sun, of the sweeping ranges, and the chant of ploughman and thresher. Once more I see Tibet immune from Western ideas, and once more I wonder how long that immunity will last. I look at Jigmed and Mary. They have met Western ideas. Yet their poise, especially in Mary's case, has not suffered. Beyond them, the future is concealed. Beyond me – what is the future of my own country? The dusk thickens. The luggage is packed, the servants are on the threshold. At Gaya station we buy a box of fancy chocolates before the train comes in.

FOR THE BEST IN PAPERBACKS, LOOK FOR THE

In every corner of the world, on every subject under the sun, Penguin represents quality and variety – the very best in publishing today.

For complete information about books available from Penguin – including Puffins, Penguin Classics and Arkana – and how to order them, write to us at the appropriate address below. Please note that for copyright reasons the selection of books varies from country to country.

In the United Kingdom: Please write to *Dept JC, Penguin Books Ltd, FREEPOST, West Drayton, Middlesex, UB7 0BR.*

If you have any difficulty in obtaining a title, please send your order with the correct money, plus ten per cent for postage and packaging, to *PO Box No 11, West Drayton, Middlesex*

In the United States: Please write to *Dept BA, Penguin, 299 Murray Hill Parkway, East Rutherford, New Jersey 07073*

In Canada: Please write to *Penguin Books Canada Ltd, 2801 John Street, Markham, Ontario L3R 1B4*

In Australia: Please write to the *Marketing Department, Penguin Books Australia Ltd, P.O. Box 257, Ringwood, Victoria 3134*

In New Zealand: Please write to the *Marketing Department, Penguin Books (NZ) Ltd, Private Bag, Takapuna, Auckland 9*

In India: Please write to *Penguin Overseas Ltd, 706 Eros Apartments, 56 Nehru Place, New Delhi, 110019*

In the Netherlands: Please write to *Penguin Books Netherlands B.V., Postbus 3507, NL–1001 AH, Amsterdam*

In West Germany: Please write to *Penguin Books Ltd, Friedrichstrasse 10–12, D–6000 Frankfurt/Main 1*

In Spain: Please write to *Alhambra Longman S.A., Fernandez de la Hoz 9, E–28010 Madrid*

In Italy: Please write to *Penguin Italia s.r.l., Via Como 4, I-20096 Pioltello (Milano)*

In France: Please write to *Penguin France S.A., 17 rue Lejeune, F-31000 Toulouse*

In Japan: Please write to *Longman Penguin Japan Co Ltd, Yamaguchi Building, 2–12–9 Kanda Jimbocho, Chiyoda-Ku, Tokyo 101*

The Road to Oxiana

'What *Ulysses* is to the novel between the wars and what *The Waste Land* is to poetry, *The Road to Oxiana* is to the travel book' – Paul Fussell

At once poetic, scholarly and acidly humorous, Robert Byron's account of his pilgrimage through Persia and Afghanistan in the 1930s, in search of the origins of Islamic architecture, is a masterpiece of the genre. Bringing to life characters and landscapes with vivid authenticity, *The Road to Oxiana* is a passionate ode to the pursuit of adventure, and an evocative portrait of heroic, visionary traveller.

'He was an improviser of genius, a natural player-by-ear. Into *Oxiana* went scholarly essays, aphorisms, farcical playlets, wonderfully exact notations of moments of time caught and frozen in the particularity of place, along with documents like visa forms and newspaper cuttings . . . It is a brillaintly-wrought expression of a thoroughly modern sensibility, a portrait of an accidental man adrift between frontiers' – Jonathan Raban in *The New York Times Book Review*

'Extremely diverting . . . rich, though sometimes acidulous, entertainment' – *The Times*